ELIZABETH OAKES SMITH

Selected Writings

VOLUME I

EMERGENCE AND FAME,

1831–1849

ELIZABETH OAKES SMITH:
Selected Writings

Editor TIMOTHY H. SCHERMAN

Volume I
Emergence and Fame, 1831–1847 (2023)

Volume II
Feminist Journalism and Public Activism 1850-1854 (2023)

Volume III
The Western Captive, Old New York, and Later Fiction: 1842-1870 (2024)

ELIZABETH OAKES SMITH

Selected Writings

VOLUME I

Emergence and Fame,
1831–1849

Timothy H. Scherman, Editor

MERCER UNIVERSITY PRESS
Macon, Georgia

MUP/ H1034

© 2023 by Mercer University Press
Published by Mercer University Press
1501 Mercer University Drive
Macon, Georgia 31207
All rights reserved

27 26 25 24 23   5 4 3 2 1

Books published by Mercer University Press are printed on acid-free paper
that meets the requirements of the American National Standard for
Information Sciences—Permanence of Paper for Printed Library Materials.

Printed and bound in CANADA.

This book is set in Caslon.

Cover/jacket design by Burt&Burt.

ISBN   978-0-88146-885-4
Cataloging-in-Publication Data is available from the Library of Congress

CONTENTS

Editor's Note (An Invitation)	vii
Chronology	xiii
General Introduction	xix
Introduction to Volume I: Emergence and Fame	xxviii
LETTERS	1
A. Correspondence of Elizabeth Oakes Smith and Seba Smith, 1833	3
B. Correspondence of Elizabeth Oakes Smith to Seba Smith, 1836–1837	35
POETRY	51
"The Sinless Child"	53
FICTION	123
"The Black Fortune-Teller"	125
"How to Tell a Story"	135
"The Witch of Endor"	144
"Coming to Get Married"	154
"The Defeated Life"	170
"Beauty, Vanity and Marble Mantels"	204
MEMOIR	219
A Pilgrimage to Katahdin	221
Bibliography	257
Index	263

MERCER UNIVERSITY PRESS

Endowed by

TOM WATSON BROWN
and
THE WATSON-BROWN FOUNDATION, INC.

EDITOR'S NOTE
(AN INVITATION)

It might sound strange to begin by saying I've been working to recover the life and work of Elizabeth Oakes Smith for more than thirty years, and yet I still can't tell you within a mile where she was born in Maine in 1806 or even how many brothers and sisters she grew up with. I don't know exactly where she lived, or how she supported herself after 1869, or who brought her body back from North Carolina to be buried on Long Island in 1893—especially if, as the newspapers reported, she was laid to rest "without a single mourner present." It's not that I'm bad at this, or particularly lazy, I don't think. I have found all kinds of clues that would help us clarify these mysteries at some point in my search, but the clues haven't yet firmed to anything I would dare call "facts," and there's just a lot of work left to do here. I've kept at it for reasons that are obvious to anyone doing this sort of research. As slow as it is, the process is at least, in part, its own reward. Watching clues multiply in the same direction, triangulating evidence, discovering details that fit (or challenge) one's original idea—every step in the process generates a physical, chemical response in the brain, and it's addictive. Of course, if the dopamine rush of discovery waxes and wanes over the long haul, something larger must be at stake, and to me, it's simple justice. There aren't many projects that can hold one's attention for more than thirty years, but the sense that a person's work—or the complexity and truth of that work—has been unjustly forgotten and ignored has been motivation enough for me. In our economy we speak of corporations "too big to fail." In literary history we ought to refer to figures "too big to ignore." Elizabeth Oakes Smith's figure is far too big to ignore.

When I talk with friends or strangers about Oakes Smith, the question of why she has been ignored or forgotten comes up a lot. I have my theories, no one of which satisfies me, so I will not land on one here. I will only say that a sign that a writer might need further investigation is the tone of her culture's response to her and her work. I have taught dozens of nineteenth-century women writers in my classes over the years, and none of them, in their own time or after, has generated anything close to the visceral reaction elicited by Oakes Smith. In the 1840s, Oakes Smith was hailed as one of the most elegant and gifted writers in the literary marketplace, showered with effusive love letters and tributes mistaking her for her characters or the personae of her poetry. Just a decade later, in the 1850s, the conservative media mercilessly attacked her appearances when she entered debates over woman's rights and even blamed her for broad social unrest. In part, the plain nastiness of these attacks should remind us how unpopular the first wave of the woman's rights movement actually was, but in Oakes Smith's case, bitter resentment for her at times sarcastic criticism of patriarchy, capitalist greed, and political corruption lasted well into the twentieth century, with some academics and journalists in places that had forgotten her completely bringing her name *back* into circulation just to curse it all over again—especially, it seems, with regard to her supposed monstrous treatment of her mild-mannered husband, Seba Smith.

Certainly there is no "getting to the bottom of it." But given the lack of corroborating evidence for much of what was written about Oakes Smith during her life (especially her autobiography), very early on in my search I turned to material culture—not only the kind in library archives but the kind still left in places where she lived and the places she wrote about. At times, these searches have led to dead ends—for example, when I spent the better part of the day in the New York Public Library looking for a map to identify the location of Hope Chapel, the New York venue where she first lectured, only to discover it had made way for a thirty-story 1970s high-rise on Broadway. But around the corner from that spot, the home she bought for $11,000 at 46 Stuyvesant Street still stands in a designated historic district, as does her home for some years in the 1840s at 86 Clinton Street in Brooklyn. The "Old Meeting House below the ledge" in North Yarmouth was torn down when Oakes Smith was a child, but the weathervane that once marked it remains, as do graveyards both at the Ledge and in Portland proper where

VOLUME I: EDITOR'S NOTE

her people are buried. Scripts from her plays and the lectures she delivered in the 1850s and '60s are kept in the archives at the University of Virginia, in many cases eaten away by acid where her perspiring fingers turned the pages. And even if hikers have rubbed some lichen from the stones on the way to Katahdin's five peaks, get within ten miles of the mountain and you realize the place hasn't changed much at all since Oakes Smith climbed it in 1849. (Walk into the woods with a guide and you might see a circle of stones marking a well dug for the animals on Hunt's Farm). None of this evidence speaks for itself. All of it must be interpreted. But material objects—especially anything in stone—have a way of staying put in a way words and ideas do not. They have given me and the people I meet in these places something solid, something undeniably shared in common, with which to begin a conversation about this fascinating figure. If all my reading and all these traipses looking for Liz haven't brought me any closer to knowing her or her work, they've given me the confidence it takes to tell a story about them, and to guess with some authority about the details.

In the final thirty-three years of her life, Oakes Smith wrote parts of an autobiography or memoir eventually titled "A Human Life."[1] Parts of it—mostly reminiscences of famous persons she knew—were published in various journals, but it was never published as a complete work. The more I read in it and about it, the more fictional it seems to me and the more obvious it becomes that such a work could never be finished. It was, finally, not a record of her life but an argument. Its purpose was to represent her as a full

---

[1] "A Human Life: Being the Autobiography of Elizabeth Oakes Smith," Series 2: Writings, Elizabeth Oakes Smith Papers, Manuscripts and Archives Division, New York Public Library. The description provided for the autobiography by the NYPL manuscript archivist warns scholars away from reading it as a factual account: "[Oakes] Smith did not conceive of her autobiography as a straightforward narrative retelling of her life, and researchers seeking such factual information will be disappointed." The most helpful introduction and analysis of Oakes Smith's autobiography is still Leigh Kirkland's dissertation, "A Human Life: Being the Autobiography of Elizabeth Oakes Smith: A critical edition and introduction," Georgia State University, 1994.

and independent human being—or, more specifically, to prove that she had not been, like so many women of her time, forced to "live her life in fragments." What I've spent these thirty years doing is to add to this last work what has been lost or forgotten or missing, not to justify her claim that she had achieved wholeness, but to continue her argument: to honor her struggle on behalf of women of her time and ours, and to join it. I hope these volumes inspire others to do the same.

Many others have begun this work before and after me, and to them I owe much of what has gone into these volumes. Noted scholars of American literature and culture Cathy Davidson, Susan Belasco, Cameron Nickels, Judy Bean, and Rebecca Jaroff provided the earliest support of this work and its circulation at academic conferences in the 1990s, and since then, a host of other fine scholars have informed, enriched, and challenged my understanding of Oakes Smith's work, among them Angela Ray, Holly Kent, Mary Louise Kete, Yopie Prins, Cynthia Patterson, Irene Di Maio, Eliza Richards, Caroline Woidat, Lesley Ginsberg, Adam Tuchinsky, Tiffany Wayne, Jane Rose, Dorri Beam, Jon White, and Elissa Zellinger.

Other academic colleagues have inspired this work in other ways—Cindy Damon-Bach, Ashley Reed, Melissa Homestead and the Catharine Sedgwick Society, Jennifer Tuttle, Helen Deese, Robert Dale Parker, and Sandra Tomc—and I remain indebted to many outside the ivied walls, among them the late Charles Pitts and Nona Lockhart, Buck Logan, William Coleman, Loren Christie (brilliant locator of images!), and Bob Lewis. Among Oaksmith descendants who have shared with me not only family history but also some of Oakes Smith's copies of her work, I owe many thanks to Louise Barker, Elizabeth Oaksmith, and, most of all, Mary Oaksmith Nichols, who provided me detailed work on the family genealogy and who currently serves as treasurer of the Oakes Smith Society. My colleagues Donald Hoffman, Tim Libretti, Ryan Poll, Bradley Greenburg, Kristen Over, and Olivia Cronk have provided the kind of kick in the pants any writer needs for a project of this scope.

VOLUME I: EDITOR'S NOTE

Of course, ideas and academic debates that make up an author's recovery are all grounded in the material world, in manuscripts, documents, and even landscapes—access to which is made possible by some of the most important yet often unheralded workers in our field. For their work to maintain the largest collection of Oakes Smith manuscripts, I owe thanks, originally, to the late Laura Monti, and more recently to David Whitesell, Heather Rise, Brandon Butler, and the rest of the staff at the Albert and Shirley Small Special Collections Library at the University of Virginia; to Kelly Wooten and Heather McGowan at Duke University; to Peter Rawson at Trinity College; to Kimberly Reynolds at the Boston Public Library; to Maurice Klapwald at the New York Public Library; and to Dan Hinchen at the Massachusetts Historical Society. Nick Noyes, emeritus librarian, along with Bill Barry, Tiffany Link, and Jamie Kingman Rice at the Brown Special Collections Library at the Maine Historical Society have greatly aided us in recovering details in Oakes Smith's early life in Maine. Amy Aldredge, former curator at the Yarmouth History Center, let us in on the material history at the base of Oakes Smith's "The Defeated Life," and the Gorman Foundation afforded me a venue to ramble on for well over an hour in their annual lecture series there about what that material history might reveal. Of those attending that lecture, I owe Bob Bishop for all the material facts we have about Oakes Smith's school days and David Little for the idea to put together this series as a down payment on the full biography.

Still others have informed my study of Oakes Smith's life and work in their knowledge of physical landscapes. For my experience of tracing Oakes Smith's footsteps on Mt. Katahdin, I owe John Neff, historian of the mountain; Susan Adams and Connie Barnes, whose knowledge of the place and its flora brought Oakes Smith's travel narrative to life; and John Ginn, my videographer and editor of the film about my traipse in Oakes Smith's wake there. Rhonda Brophy, curator at the Patten Lumberman's Museum, provided a clearer view of Hunt Farm, where Oakes Smith's trek began in earnest. I am indebted to the late William Diebold for a reminder of how much of Oakes Smith's work is set in the Ramapo Valley on

xi

the border of New York and New Jersey. On my traipse there, Susan Kurzmann and Cathy Hajo at Ramapo College of New Jersey and local historians Tom Dunn, Edward Lenik, and Marianne Leese guided my explorations and enabled me to hear the voices of those silenced and forgotten there nearly two centuries after Oakes Smith did.

I am equally if not more indebted to the work and inspiration of the students who have joined me in this recovery project over the past thirty years—Melissa Radja, Cherri Gottesleben, Ellen Shepard, Alisa Kumykova, Abigail Harris-Culver, Kyle Rogers, Rebecca Wiltberger Higgins, Carly Joy Gielarowski, Christine Dunford, Vanessa Macias, and Mary Clemmensen. Mark Behringer, Rebecca Gawo, and Sylwia Jurkowski were particularly helpful in their research, proofreading, and indexing of these volumes.

In the "tree falls in the forest" category, it is crucial to acknowledge that this project would not have seen the light of day without the initiative of my editor, Marc Jolley, and the staff at Mercer University Press, along with the kind support of Amy Bramen Armiento and the Poe Studies Association, who directed them to my work and thus to the work of all those I've mentioned above. Making Oakes Smith's work available in this new form can only broaden the ongoing collective effort.

Finally, none of this or any of my research would be possible without the support of my family, and particularly that of my wife, best friend, and partner for life, Pam Davidson, who has given more to the cause of literary and cultural history, over the past thirty-two years, than any corporate attorney I know.

CHRONOLOGY

1806–1823

Elizabeth Oakes (Prince) Smith, born August 12, 1806, near North Yarmouth, Maine, to Sophia (Blanchard) and David Cushing Prince, a merchant seaman. Father dies at sea, March 26, 1809, and family lives alternately with her maternal and paternal grandparents until December, when mother marries Captain Lemuel Sawyer and family moves to Cape Elizabeth, then Portland. As a result of moves around Portland or her mother and stepfather's choice, attends a series of schools—Amelia Folsom's School at Chadwick House, Misses Mayo's School, Rachael Neal's School, Mr. Loring's School on Back Street, and finally "graduates" from Penelope and Eliza Martin's School on King Street.[1] At age twelve may have taught in Sunday school for black children. Plans to become a teacher, but mother demurs. Marries, instead, on March 6, 1823, Seba Smith, editor of a Portland weekly, *The Eastern Argus*.

1824–1838

Manages Smith household (among them, a house at the north end of Tukey's Bridge, North Deering), which includes both the family and apprentices and printers of Seba Smith's journals, who board. Bears six sons: Benjamin (1824), Rolvin (1825–1832), Appleton (1828–1887), Sidney (1830–1869), Alvin (1832–1902), and Edward (1836–1865). Contributes poems, sketches, stories to journals edited by her husband, the *Daily Courier* and *Family Reader*, either anonymously or using the signature "E," and acts as editor in 1833 when her husband travels to Boston to supervise the publication of *The Life and Writings of Major Jack Downing*. In her unpublished autobiography, claims during this period to have read and

---

[1] D. C. Colesworthy, *School Is Out* (Boston: Barry and Colesworthy, 1876): 490–91. Colesworthy indicates Oakes Smith attended Loring's School, where he attended, toward the end of her formal education and only for "a few days," suggesting that for a time Oakes Smith may have attended a school for boys.

studied the works of Shakespeare, Milton, Blackstone, Mill, and others after the rest of the family had retired to bed. Husband loses his fortune speculating in the volatile market for land preceding the Panic of 1837, attempts to recover his losses by backing his brother-in-law's invention designed to clean Sea Grass Cotton. Oakes Smith writes and later publishes *Riches Without Wings* (1838), a conduct novel targeting children and other victims of the Panic. Fall of 1838, travels with her husband to Charleston, South Carolina, where the invention proves unsaleable and where she is exposed for the first time to the reality of slavery.

1839–1845

Arrives in New York, January 1839, boarding with cousins on her father's side, Dr. Cyrus and Maria Child Weeks. Publishes stories in *Godey's Lady's Book*, *Snowden's Ladies' Companion*, and other journals, using the signature "Mrs. Seba Smith" or a pseudonym, "Ernest Helfenstein." First wide literary notice with "The Sinless Child," published serially in *The Southern Literary Messenger* in January and February of 1842. Summer of 1842, moves with her family to Brooklyn. First edition of her poems, *The Sinless Child and Other Poems*, published by John Keese in July 1843, with introductions by Keese, John Neal, and H. T. Tuckerman. Continues writing poetry and fiction for other popular magazines and giftbooks throughout the decade. Her second novel, *The Western Captive*, appears as two supplements (nos 25–28) in Park Benjamin's *The New World* in 1842. Contributes short stories, poems, and probably editorial to *The Rover*, a journal edited by her husband from 1843 to 1845. *The Complete Poetical Writings of Elizabeth Oakes Smith*, edited by Rufus Griswold, appears 1845.

1846–1849

With publishers Saxton and Kelt, produces three volumes of children's stories (*The True Child*, *The Moss Cup*, and *The Dandelion*), all subtitled "stories not for good children, or bad children, but real children." Edits Saxton and Kelt's annual *The Mayflower* for 1847 and 1848. In late 1847, invited to contribute a "romance of the

CHRONOLOGY

revolution" to Alice Neal's *Saturday Museum*, which is published as *The Remapo* [*sic*] *Pass: A Story of the Revolution* in January 1848, later revised for Beadle's dime novel series as *The Bald Eagle* (1867). Putnam publishes her third novel in book form, *The Salamander* (later reprinted as *Mary and Hugo*), with illustrations by F. O. Darley. Acknowledges the death of her pseudonym "Helfenstein" in the preface to *The Salamander* yet continues to publish occasionally under the name in later years as "by the late Ernest Helfenstein." In this period also begins writing plays; *Old New York, or Democracy in 1689*, perhaps her first, is advertised to producers by fellow member of the New York literati William Cullen Bryant. Negotiations in 1853 for Anna Cora Mowatt to star as Elizabeth in the play end with Mowatt's illness that year. *The Roman Tribute, or, Attila the Hun*, published in book form in 1849, is produced at the Arch Street Theatre in Philadelphia in November 1850 with Charlotte Barnes Conner in the lead female role. On a summer trip home to Maine in August 1849, joins her friend Nancy Mosman, along with James M. Haines and Mosman's husband, climbing Mt. Katahdin and reaching Pamola, its lowest peak. Her account of the feat is printed in local papers and reported in New York.

1850–1852

Attends Woman's Rights Convention in October 1850 in Worcester, Massachusetts, and begins a series of ten articles for Horace Greeley's New York *Tribune* entitled "Woman and Her Needs" (November 1850 to June 1851), published in pamphlet form by Fowler and Wells in late 1851. Amid first attacks from conservative editors, begins lecturing in New York in June 1851, and by fall has several engagements in New England. Lecture tours in spring and summer 1852 bring her west to Buffalo, Cincinnati, St. Louis, and Chicago. Continues writing: publishes *Hints on Dress and Beauty* and *Shadowland; or, The Seer*, and projects a woman's journal, *The Egeria*, soliciting $500 in support and fifty subscribers. At Woman's Rights Convention at Syracuse in September 1852, her nomination as president of the convention is rejected by Susan B. Anthony when Oakes Smith and convention organizer Paulina

Wright Davis arrive in dresses exposing neck and arms, but plans for *The Egeria*, with Oakes Smith appearing as editor, are widely circulated at the convention. Writes another play in a classical backdrop entitled *Destiny: A Tragedy*.

1853–1859

Plans for Oakes Smith's involvement in *The Egeria* suddenly curtailed in December 1852; Paulina Wright Davis retitles the journal *The Elucidator* and then *The Una*, which appears in February 1853, to which Oakes Smith contributes. Continues lecture tours through New England, Pennsylvania, New York, and Ohio and attends yearly woman's rights conventions. In New York, helps edit *The Weekly Budget* with her husband (1853 to 1854). Publishes two new novels with Derby and Jackson in 1854: *Bertha and Lily; or the Parsonage at Beech Glen*, under her own name, and *The Newsboy*, anonymously. Spring of 1855 moves back to New York City with family. Contributes articles to New York *Tribune* on marriage and divorce, capital punishment for women. In 1856 becomes coeditor, again with her husband, of *Emerson's United States Magazine*, reprinting earlier stories and poems, including a slightly edited reprint, *The Intercepted Messenger of Ramapo Pass*. Writes voluminous unsigned editorial matter. In November 1858, family buys the magazine, which continues as *The Great Republic Monthly*, published by Oaksmith and Co. for eleven months. In 1859, the couple purchases a large home and property in Patchogue, Long Island, names it "The Willows."

1860–1868

Lives a more retired life in Patchogue. Lectures occasionally on woman's rights, temperance, and other reforms. Addresses Union troops at a small pageant near her home in October 1861, contributes cloaks and mittens to the soldiers. Son Appleton is captured and indicted for equipping a slave ship, December 1861. With Lincoln's suspension of habeas corpus, he is jailed but soon escapes or is mysteriously released. Visiting friends in New York, Oakes Smith is caught in a draft riot in July 1863 and later records the experience

CHRONOLOGY

in her diary. Son Edward dies of yellow fever in Cuba, August 31, 1865. Visits Appleton, exiled in England, returns to find Appleton's estranged wife has left the Willows deserted. Begins publishing "Autobiographic Notes" in *Beadle's Monthly*, continues to seek aid from Gerrit Smith, Thurlow Weed, and other political figures to have Appleton pardoned. Seba Smith dies July 29, 1868.

1869–1879

Publishes her last novel, *The Two Wives*, appearing serially in *The Herald of Health* from January to November 1870. Sells the Willows, rents and lives with her son Alvin's family in nearby Blue Point, Long Island. Son Sidney dies in a shipwreck on the way to Cuba in 1869. In 1874, sails for Beaufort, North Carolina, where Appleton has settled, loses almost all her possessions in a shipwreck. Continues to publish poetry and editorial in both popular and religious journals, mostly *Baldwin's Monthly*, *Potter's Monthly*, and *The Phrenological Journal*. Serves as pastor of the Independent Church in Canastota, New York, for much of the year in 1877 and continues to attend conventions on temperance and woman's suffrage. In January 1879, delivers "Biology and Woman's Rights" at Woman's Suffrage Convention in Washington, DC. Internal evidence suggests that two unpublished novel manuscripts—one untitled, on the place of women in Massachusetts in the early eighteenth century, the other entitled "The Queen of Tramps, By One of Them"—were written in the late 1870s or early '80s.

1880–1893

Spends summers renting in Blue Point, Long Island, and winters in Beaufort. Writes much of her autobiography, "A Human Life," between 1881 and 1885. Lectures on "Emerson and His Circle." Finds herself forgotten by most, and many friends now dead. Burns large quantities of correspondence. One chapter of "The Queen of Tramps" is published in *Baldwin's Monthly* in 1888, with a complete manuscript of the novel left in her papers at her death. Son Appleton dies in New York City in 1887. Although editors at *The Home Journal* advertise her autobiography as near completion,

ELIZABETH OAKES SMITH

it is never published. Writes in her journal that she is ashamed to see so much of this writing reflect not her life but "the promise of her childhood." Dies after a short illness in Beaufort, North Carolina, November 15, 1893, buried in Patchogue, New York.

GENERAL INTRODUCTION

In a career spanning seven decades of the nineteenth century, Elizabeth Oakes Smith was a poet, a fiction writer, a wife and mother, a novelist, an essayist, a journalist, a lecturer, a playwright, and a memoirist (in roughly that order), writing thousands of pages which in either published or manuscript form stand today as a record of a nineteenth-century woman's expression probably unparalleled in extent. Working as a contributor and editor for her husband's Portland, Maine, newspapers even as a young mother of four in the 1830s, she quickly emerged as a literary celebrity when the family moved to New York, gaining a reputation that made her name one of the most recognizable and welcome in journals and newspapers of the 1840s. Mid-century, she outed herself as a supporter of the first organized woman's rights movement, and in an attempt to lend to it the power of her reputation, actually lost the good will of many editors and friends. Controversy continued to sell her name, however, to the point that P. T. Barnum stole it for use in an advertisement for one of his Baby Shows in 1855. By the 1880s, she was still remembered fondly as a "household name" by Elizabeth Cady Stanton in *History of Woman Suffrage,* while others associated the name "Oaksmith" (the name her children adopted in adulthood) with the scandal following her son's indictment for equipping a slave ship in 1859. By the twentieth century, relatively few remembered her once ubiquitous name at all, even in academic circles.

In literary-historical terms, much of Oakes Smith's work is part of an entire tradition of nineteenth-century women's writing temporarily devalued and discarded by the modernists who succeeded it. But while the lives and writings of women with whom she worked, and some whom she inspired—Catharine Maria Sedgwick, Margaret Fuller, Harriet Beecher Stowe, Fanny Fern, E.D.E.N Southworth, Charlotte Perkins Gilman—have been recovered over the past four decades in biographies and new editions, Oakes Smith's own recovery has been late in coming. This three-volume collection is meant to provide new texts and contexts to expand the view of those already familiar with Oakes Smith, but it also stands as an invitation to new readers to engage with her work and to discover texts and details within them to add to our conversations on this emerging historically significant figure and to the literary and political culture of the nineteenth-century US.

Oakes Smith was given a brief but relatively dismissive treatment in Nina Baym's *Woman's Fiction: A Guide to Novels by and about Women in America, 1820–1870*, a book which provided a major impetus to the recovery of many American women writers of Oakes Smith's time, but as the first two volumes of this series should make clear, Oakes Smith's novels hardly serve as a full introduction to her life work in any case. Since the 1970s, feminist historians, journalists, and literary critics have increasingly engaged with other genres and aspects of Oakes Smith's life and career—in some cases countering Baym's early appraisal by acknowledging her as a "towering figure of nineteenth-century literature and politics" in her time,[1] and citing her work as a model of particular modes and styles of women's writing.[2] The publication of a critical edition of Oakes Smith's 1842 novel *The Western Captive* in 2015 and her appearance in two recent anthologies of US literature[3] seem to mark an institutional break, with publishers once again including her name as one worth bringing before students and the broader public. But if relatively recent critical and historical forays into Oakes Smith's life and work have made her work more familiar and newly valuable to some readers—

---

[1] See Adam Tuchinsky, "'Woman and Her Needs:' Elizabeth Oakes Smith and the Divorce Question," *Journal of Women's History* 28/1 (Spring 2016): 40.

[2] See for example, Cheryl Walker's description of Oakes Smith's work in "A Composite Biography" of the nineteenth-century female poet in *The Nightingale's Burden: Women Poets and American Culture before 1900* (Bloomington: Indiana University Press, 1982).

[3] In 2010, the *Bedford Anthology of American Literature* began to include examples of Oakes Smith's poetry and excerpts from *Woman and Her Needs* (1851). Broadview's *Anthology of American Literature* (2022) includes Oakes Smith's poem "The Drowned Mariner" in its electronic supplement.

GENERAL INTRODUCTION

essays and chapters, for example, on her carrying forward the feminist work of Margaret Fuller,[4] or on her eyewitness account of the New York Draft Riots of 1863,[5] or the transcendentalist philosophy behind her most well-known narrative poem[6]—most readers lack a sense of the full breadth, scope, and complexity of her career. The volumes making up *Elizabeth Oakes Smith: Selected Writings* are meant to remedy this need for a more capacious view, even if the quantity of manuscript and scrapbook material that remains untouched in only two of the major archives in which her papers are held[7] reminds us of how provisional any view of her life and work must be at the moment—a map sketched in the midst of exploration.

Until recently, the primary obstacle to a more complete view of Oakes Smith was *access*. Like Edgar Allan Poe, who complained to a colleague in 1844 that his work was generally too scattered in various journals to receive a fair and full assessment, Oakes Smith, too, was "essentially a Magazinist,"[8] publishing far more in journals and

---

[4] Tiffany Wayne, "A Woman's Life and Work: Self-Culture, Vocation, and the Female Intellectual," *Woman Thinking* (Lexington Books, 2005) 79–106.

[5] Joy Wiltenberg, "Excerpts from the Diary of Elizabeth Oakes Smith," *Signs: Journal of Women in Culture and Society* (1984) 9/3: 534–48.

[6] Mary Louise Kete, "Gender Valences of Transcendentalism: The Pursuit of Idealism in Elizabeth Oakes Smith's 'The Sinless Child,'" *Separate Spheres No More*, ed. Monika Elbert (Tuscaloosa: University of Alabama Press, 2000).

[7] Oakes Smith papers at the New York Public Library and at the Alderman Library at the University of Virginia alone account for eight feet of shelf space.

[8] In a rambling draft of a letter to Professor Charles Anthon in October 1844, Poe admits that since he had spent his career thus far as "essentially a Magazinist," and he is thus liable to be "grossly misconceived & misjudged by men of whose good opinion he would be proud...but who [have seen] perhaps, only a paper here & there, by accident,—often only one of his mere extravaganzas, written...to supply a particular demand." Publishing fugitive pieces in a variety of periodicals, Poe continues, "He loses, too...whatever merit may be his due on the score of *versatility*—a point which can only be estimated by [the] collection of his various articles in volume form and altogether." *The*

xxi

newspapers than she ever published in book or even pamphlet form, and thus until the emergence of searchable digital archives in the early 2000s, the opportunity of a broader view of Oakes Smith's career was limited to that cadre of scholars with both time and access to major research libraries and rare book collections scattered across the country. In fact, as this series aims to show, if one scholar grabbed a #2 pencil in 1990 and read through Oakes Smith's physical papers at the New York Public Library or at the Alderman Library at the University of Virginia, and another spent hours today reading her magazine work through electronic databases such as hathitrust.org or newspapers.com, both would still miss a host of important texts key to understanding the full arc of her career.[9]

An additional challenge to Oakes Smith's recovery has been a stubbornly enduring tradition—especially outside academic circles, but within them as well—of separating literature from its material ground—specifically economic—assuming or finessing away the complex intervention of literary agents, publishers, printers, and the readers they marketed to in our interpretation of any public writing. Without taking the numerous intermediary "producers" of literature into account, we can easily misread what we find on the page as the transparent "expression" of the artist instead of the result of a complex negotiation between the writer and the marketplace. The more one reads of her life and work, the more it becomes clear that for Oakes Smith, writing was in the first instance wage labor. Even if for many years she could count on her husband as a partner in that labor, evidence we have in her personal correspondence and reviews

---

Letters of Edgar Allan Poe, 2 vols, ed. John Ward Ostrom (New York: Gordian Press, 1966) 470. I am indebted to Jeffrey Savoye for locating this relevant passage.

[9] Portions of Oakes Smith's papers are owned by dozens of libraries across the country, while some of the journals in which she published her earliest work are only available in fragile paper in Portland archives. Key manuscript correspondence from a variety of not-yet-digitized collections is made available in all three volumes of *Selected Writings* for the first time, as is Oakes Smith's manuscript lecture "The Dignity of Labor" and her "Prospectus" for the feminist journal *The Egeria* in Volume II.

GENERAL INTRODUCTION

of her work from the time of her emergence as a professional writer to the end of her life indicate that she never enjoyed the economic independence that allowed her to discount what readers were willing to buy.[10] Moreover, as we consider the meaning of her writing in terms of its particular content, we need to recall that Oakes Smith put property ownership and the benefits it afforded at the top of her list of a woman's needs in her time. In this view, one of the most basic facts we might glean from any of the texts a woman produced over the course of her career is that she was paid for them. Despite the continued imbalance of power between those who worked at writing and those who controlled the access to publication during her lifetime, a woman writer's potential to earn a living outside of the support of a father or husband was a revolutionary advance in her social, economic, and political opportunities.[11] Beginning from these considerations, *Elizabeth Oakes Smith: Selected Writings* attempts to see Oakes Smith's work specifically as the labor of one whose gender effectively closed avenues of equally gainful employment.[12]

---

[10] In *The Profession of Authorship in the United States*, William Charvat argued that Henry Wadsworth Longfellow was the first writer in the US to make a living solely by writing. While more research is needed to verify the financial situation of Oakes Smith and her husband at the time of their arrival in New York in the late 1830s, they might have been the first married couple to support themselves in this way—without the support of inheritance or income from other sources.

[11] In her article "Cheap Poe and Other Bargains: Unpaid Work and Energy in Early Nineteenth-Century US Publishing," (*ELH* 86/1 [Spring 2019]: 189–222), Sandra Tomc details the ways both men and women were taken advantage of by publishers in this period. For a more expansive treatment of nineteenth-century women writers and their relation to the marketplace, see Melissa Homestead, *American Women Authors and Literary Property, 1822–1869* (New York: Cambridge University Press, 2005).

[12] On woman's opportunities for gainful employment, see *Selected Writings*, Volume II, for Oakes Smith's treatise, *Woman and Her Needs* and "The Dignity of Labor." Her editorial for the New York *Tribune* dated January 15, 1853, illustrates the problem succinctly: "At least one-half of the women of the country are driven to their own resources for a livelihood. Hundreds are engaged in teaching at a miserable pittance. The proportion supposed to be

ELIZABETH OAKES SMITH

Writing for money leaves a mark, but especially in light of Oakes Smith's clear determination to break gender barriers and revise the thinking habits of her society, we cannot reduce her work to what Herman Melville derisively referred to as "sawing wood," or simply feeding readers what they wanted. As even friendly critics pointed out, only rarely did Oakes Smith have the time or opportunity to revise her published writing, but we should consider that at least the greater part of the unevenness or even contradictions found in her work may have resulted less from haste or a lack of skill than from her need, as a professional, to fit whatever designs she had on her readers' minds within popular and thus saleable themes, styles, and political positions of the mid-nineteenth century, even when they seem at variance with the personal or political preferences she revealed in diaries or correspondence. Thus, if on one hand Oakes Smith's priority of "selling" might give us something of a steady compass by which to measure the popular styles, themes, and forms of the burgeoning literary market of the mid-nineteenth century, on the other, taking this context into account alerts us to the need to acknowledge the strategies she employed to adapt the many times unpopular or unpalatable or challenging or radical ideas she intended to convey to readers into palatable forms of writing and speech.

Thus, whether or not readers are always consciously aware of it (and there is plenty of evidence some editors knew this in her time), Oakes Smith's writing, speaking, and even her physical self-presentation were more complex than they may first appear. Layered with nested narratives and multiple perspectives, many of her works begin with situations, styles, or tones easy for readers to recognize and accept, only to question or overturn common assumptions as they progress ("The Defeated Life" or "The Dignity of Labor"). In other instances, she presents what readers are already familiar with and simply adds a new interpretation or emphasis ("The Witch of

---

adequate remuneration for teaching compared with other expenses in a family, may be little intrinsically reached by comparing the items of expense in the letter of Mr. Folsom, Minister to the Hague, where a plain Yankee official pays $400 for wine, and $225 per year to a governess."

Endor"). On the occasions her writing was unapologetically radical, either her audience was prepared for it (for example, in the context of a woman's rights convention) or her publishers would sell her name under a false guise—as when Park Benjamin circulated a completely inaccurate synopsis of her novel *The Western Captive* as a celebration of the "great" men and battles in the late Indian Wars in order to attract readers who might have balked at the novel's clear critique of both patriarchal strictures on white women and US Indian policy. Needless to say, it would be easy to dismiss Oakes Smith as a somewhat innocuous writer merely following the trends of her time if one read a story or novel only partially or listened to only part of her lecture; but setting out with hopes that she might be read or heard completely by many, her complex strategies were calculated to capture both income and the attention of a greater audience, frustrating those who would reduce her work to its radical edge in order to dismiss it. Perhaps the best example is, again, material: according to newspaper reports of her 1851 lecture "Dress: Its Social and Aesthetic Relations," she wore an elegant full-length dress to the stage as she defended the Bloomer costume, and while some captious editors attacked her for sartorial hypocrisy, many more were intrigued enough—or perhaps confused enough—to hear her out.

Organization and Selection

The three volumes making up *Elizabeth Oakes Smith: Selected Writings* are framed to introduce readers to gradually increasing levels of historical and textual detail. Beginning with this most general frame, each volume offers an additional introduction geared to its specific contents, providing biographical and historical contexts for the works that follow, while each selection in the series is itself introduced by a headnote offering more specific background, along with suggestions for the work's relation to others in Oakes Smith's writings, relations to the writing of her contemporaries, and suggestions for further reading. In some cases, allusions will be made in one volume to writings found in others, but overall, the attempt has been made in each to select texts representing a particular

ELIZABETH OAKES SMITH

development in Oakes Smith's writing. This is most evident in volumes one and two, which present two distinct phases of her career in biographical order, her emergence as a public figure in Volume I (1831–1849), and her turn to public activism in Volume II (1850–1854). Volume III is designed to introduce readers to some of Oakes Smith's longer works, presenting excerpts from several novels written across the arc of her career, along with one of her full-length plays. To make these volumes as accessible as possible to students and other readers outside of the academy, allusions to professional literary-critical developments and terminology have been limited mostly to footnotes.

Editorial Methodology

Copy-Texts: For texts of which only one version was published during Oakes Smith's lifetime (e.g., "The Defeated Life"), texts in this volume are prepared from the original journal publication, retaining archaic spellings where they do not impede the modern reader's understanding while silently correcting typographical errors. For texts republished in Oakes Smith's lifetime, the *latest* edition has been preferred, based on the well-documented and oft-cited fact in private correspondence and public reviews that Oakes Smith had little time for (not to say interest in) the stylistic precision enabled by careful revision. When such an opportunity presented itself (as with her poem "The Sinless Child" in its republication in 1843 and 1845, and her series of articles entitled "Woman and Her Needs," republished in pamphlet form in 1851), the revisions she made are consistently significant. Analysis of Oakes Smith's emendations, variations, and changes among editions are left to future scholars, but changes to revised texts are annotated to the extent possible within the format of the series and the current state of Oakes Smith's recovery.

Manuscripts: The *Elizabeth Oakes Smith: Selected Writings* presents several manuscripts (lectures and correspondence) previously unavailable in any form outside of archival collections at research libraries or held in private collections. All have been transcribed

GENERAL INTRODUCTION

meticulously, with empty brackets [ ] indicating words still undecipherable. Dates, salutations, and signatures have been regularized, with deletions in the original marked with a strikethrough effect [~~strikethrough~~] and interpolations retained in superscript. Marginal notes and graphic symbols (for example, the nineteenth-century emoji that ends Oakes Smith's letter of November 11, 1833) are explained in annotations.

Accidentals: As noted above, obvious typographical errors in published texts have been silently corrected. Variable spellings in printed texts have been regularized for consistency. Editions of manuscripts in all three volumes have retained orthography common in Oakes Smith's day ("today" spelled *to day*, "something" spelled *some thing*).

INTRODUCTION TO VOLUME I

Emergence and Fame

The first volume of this collection includes selections ranging from one of Oakes Smith's earliest stories, "The Black Fortune-Teller," published in her husband's Portland weekly, the *Family Reader*, in 1831, to what might have been her first truly autobiographical work, a travel narrative recording her ascent of Mt. Katahdin, published in the *Portland Daily Advertiser* in the fall of 1849. Yet even coincidentally beginning and ending in the city of her childhood, the bulk of this volume more properly represents the decades of her emergence and rise to fame as one of the most well-known and sought-after public figures in New York City, which by 1835 had become the center of the US publishing industry.

Details of Oakes Smith's domestic or personal life in this period have not yet been brought into focus. She left no early diaries or journals (in her late autobiography she records burning them, in fact), and much of her manuscript correspondence before 1849 that has been preserved in manuscript archives principally involves business dealings. For whatever reason, however, she saved at least some of her personal correspondence with her husband, who was absent from home for a month in late 1833 and then periodically traveling in the year leading up to the Panic of 1837. What remains of these two early series of letters are so few in number that all twenty-five are reproduced here, providing readers at least a glimpse of Oakes Smith's day-to-day life as a young married woman living just outside the city of Portland, Maine. It is important to note that by the time of their first correspondence, the couple had been married for more than ten years.

Recovering the identities of family relations, friends, neighbors, and business associates alluded to in these letters will give us a clearer picture of her social life and even her early exposure to political issues, but even without such details, the contents and the tone of this correspondence provide us a more complex view of her

INTRODUCTION: VOLUME I

marriage than that recorded in her manuscript autobiography, written mostly in the 1880s, where her marriage is reduced to the curtailment of her independence and a forced relation with a bookish and passionless man incompetent in business matters. Nonetheless, the facts we do know of Oakes Smith's first ten years of marriage might reasonably lead readers to identify the writer with the most tragic female characters in her work. Indeed, no imagined handicap for "different expectations" of a distant century could justify the shock of being married off at sixteen to a man nearly twice her age in 1823, and the fact that she became pregnant that summer and bore a child who lived just barely a month had to have multiplied the pain in ways Oakes Smith could never publicly express. When her husband sold his share of the *Eastern Argus* and in 1830 founded the *Portland Courier* and *Family Reader*, six printers and apprentices were added to the family board, which by then included three sons: Rolvin, born in 1825; Appleton, born in 1828; and Sidney, born in 1830. Impossibly, it seems, not only did Oakes Smith take on the additional domestic work required to run a cottage industry with (as we witness in her letters of 1833) babes in arms—she also began contributing poetry and editorial to her husband's journals when space required it. "The Black Fortune-Teller," reprinted here, is one of half a dozen stories and at least a dozen poems identified as her work in *The Family Reader* for the years 1831 and 1832 alone, alongside more than a dozen editorial pieces, including an advice column entitled "Hints to Parents." Add to these conditions Seba Smith's loss of most of his fortune in land speculation in the days leading up to the Crash of 1837, and we have at least a general idea of the challenges Oakes Smith faced before her professional writing career began.[1]

---

[1] As detailed in the headnote to the second series of letters reprinted here from this period, Smith had been convinced to invest in a parcel of public land around the frontier settlement of Monson, Maine, designated as "No. 8" on contemporary maps of that division of the new state. In the massive loan foreclosures that swept the nation in the Panic, Smith lost nearly all his fortune and spent what was left backing a failed invention to clean Sea Grass Cotton in Charleston, South Carolina.

ELIZABETH OAKES SMITH

Faced with broadly shared personal trauma and social expectations that led to what she called the "disappearance" of most women of her place and time in the marriage relation, Oakes Smith's emergence as a literary professional constituted a unique self-assertion and resistance. As the early letters show, Oakes Smith was already more than her husband's moral support at this point in their relationship—both with her editorial work in his absence and as the author of poetry and sketches she had begun to publish in John Neal's *New England Galaxy* and elsewhere. Before leaving for Charleston, South Carolina, with her family, it seems she had completed her novel *Riches Without Wings*, a conduct novel (or "Sunday School book," as she called it) that sold well and established for her a reputation that, with the encouragement of personal friends and colleagues of her husband, gained her invitations to publish in larger circulation journals in New York and Philadelphia. In a scrapbook, she saved a short note from Louis A. Godey, whose *Lady's Book*, founded in 1837, would become the highest circulation magazine of the 1840s:

> I offer you your own terms for a Story for the Lady's Book. Refer you to my friend Samuel Colman,[2] Esq. of your City.
>
> Very Resp Yr Obedt,
>
> L. A. Godey
>
> Mrs. Seba Smith   Phila July 11 1839

If Oakes Smith was still learning the politics and economics of a "trade" that was becoming a full-blown industry in the United States in the 1830s, by the time the family settled in New York in 1839, she was well beyond the "apprentice" stage, ready to earn a

---

[2] Colman had been Seba Smith's publisher in the early 1830s, but the company of Lilly, Wait, Colman and Holden, with offices in both Portland and Boston, dissolved soon after.

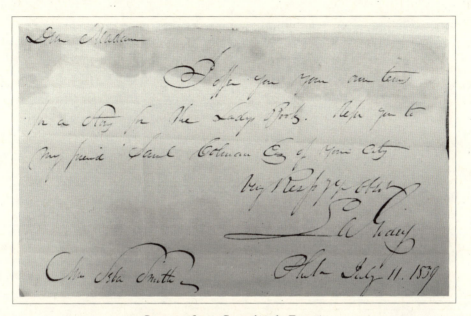

Section from Scrapbook, Box 4.
Papers of Elizabeth Oakes Prince Smith, Accession #38-707.

Courtesy Albert and Shirley Small Special Collections Library, University of Virginia

INTRODUCTION: VOLUME I

living with her husband as a reliable contributor to *Snowden's Ladies' Companion*, *Godey's Lady's Book*, and other literary periodicals and popular giftbooks. She published fiction, historical sketches, and poetry along with her first stories featuring Native American culture, a subject she would repeatedly turn to in future decades. According to fellow Maine writer Charles Fenno Hoffman, her first "Indian" novel, *The Western Captive* (1842)[3] was already complete when she arrived in New York, and she would write several others works sympathetic to indigenous people in later decades,[4] leaving a nearly complete manuscript novel in her files at her death involving Wabanaki/French relations around the time of Father Rale's War in the early eighteenth century. This continuing interest explains Oakes Smith's brief but close relationship, in her early New York years, with Jane Johnston Schoolcraft (Bamewawagezhikaquay) as well as her collaborations with Schoolcraft's husband on translations of Native American poetry, even after his wife's death from tuberculosis in May of 1842.

It was Hoffman who brought Oakes Smith's work to the attention of editor, agent, and anthologist Rufus Griswold,[5] who, at least

---

[3] Eventually distributed as one of the first paperback novels, *The Western Captive* was originally published and sold on the New York streets as an "extra" edition (nos. 22–25) of Park Benjamin's *The New World* newspaper in October 1842. In her autobiography, she records having been paid $100 for the copyright.

[4] Caroline Woidat's Broadview edition of *The Western Captive* (2015) includes several of these stories as appendices, though many others Oakes Smith wrote remain uncollected. A typescript of her unpublished novel featuring relations between the Norridgewock and the community of settlers near Castine, Maine, likely written in the 1870s, is available on the Oakes Smith website. Oakes Smith's other two novels featuring Native American culture, *The Bald Eagle* (1867) and *The Sagamore of Saco* (1868), were published in Erastus Beadle's Dime Novel series. Both had their origins in stories she published in the 1840s.

[5] Griswold (1815–1857) is best known for his *Memoir* of Edgar Allan Poe, printed just after Poe's death in 1849—a work of sensational misrepresentation that created not only many inaccurate impressions of Poe that endure to the present day, but also, arguably, an outsized literary figure produced

in his own mind, succeeded in "escorting" Oakes Smith into prominence as a literary celebrity in New York City and as far as magazine circulation could reach in the quickly expanding nation.[6] The more details emerge from Oakes Smith's early professional writing, in fact, the more obvious becomes her use of Griswold's growing literary power even as she (along with a long list of other writers of the day) was used by him. In their early correspondence, Oakes Smith performed the part of the unassuming female "poetess" Griswold would cater to for decades, all too pleased for him to "arrange" for her publications with George Graham[7] and others, eager to "serve" him with a variety of genres—not only poetry but also fiction, historical sketches, and the novel she had on hand, leaving compensation to his "better judgement":

Tuesday eve

I received, dear Sir, your very kind letter yesterday. I am truly grateful to you for your kind efforts in my behalf, but must really confess that you have a poor subject for your magnanimity. Mr Graham is undoubtedly a practical man, and sees, as I do myself, that my talents are not of a popular order[.] My writings are not things to take with the mass. Indeed, I have felt some compunctions at presenting my claims at all, feeling, as I do, that my success has depended mainly upon the partiality of my personal friends. This is a delightful conviction to me, for to such only do I wish to possess abilities.

---

in more than a century of international debate over those misrepresentations. Griswold's negative relation to Poe has unfortunately distracted scholars from his larger role in the circulation of work by women writers of the period and the formation of modern practices of book promotion. "Spin" strategies he employed in the 1830s and '40s are often assumed to have originated much later, in the twentieth century and beyond.

[6] Any digital search for her name in the1840s will locate thousands of advertisements of her work in newspapers circulating in every state in the nation save Florida, as far west Iowa.

[7] Griswold was briefly editor of *Graham's Magazine* from April 1842 to October 1843.

INTRODUCTION: VOLUME I

I enclose you a short poem, which I trust may please you. I do not profess to be a judge in these matters.

As to prose I have a Romance, upon an American subject[8] which I should be glad to offer you. It consists of about 250 pages in Mss Portions which I have read to some friends, have been highly approved. We are scarcely in a situation to look after a publisher in the shape of a volume, and I should like to test it in a Magazine. Shall I send you on a few chapters for the August No?[9]

Just how much Oakes Smith was performing here is hard to determine (along with how many other instances of this practice we would find in Griswold's correspondence with other writers), but the bare facts—that Oakes Smith had been married to a professional newspaper editor for eighteen years; had spelled him in that position at intervals; had published her poems, stories, and sketches in a variety of journals in Portland, Boston, New York, Richmond, and elsewhere; had published a popular novel four years earlier; and, indeed, had a written invitation from the publisher of *Godey's* to *name her price*—all seem to indicate that she was not a woman hoping to be "escorted," but a canny professional strategically positioning herself with respect to a figure known for making reputations in the literary marketplace of the 1840s.

Less than a year later, after her first collection of poems appeared in June of 1843, another letter to Griswold reveals the markedly different tone of a writer now widely sought-after, who no longer needs to perform for power—indeed, the tone of a woman

---

[8] Very likely the MS of *The Western Captive* (see note 3 above). Griswold's serving as Oakes Smith's agent here blurs with Oakes Smith's allusion to benefiting from "personal friends." Benjamin had known and worked with Griswold since their early newspaper venture, *The Evening Tattler*, in 1839, and Hoffman knew and worked with both men as well.

[9] Elizabeth Oakes Smith to Rufus Griswold, "Tuesday Eve," undated, Gratz American Poets Collection, Case 7, Box 9, Historical Society of Pennsylvania. Internal references date the letter soon after Griswold began as editor of *Graham's* in April 1842.

xxxiii

already beginning to show her impatience with power relations in the American literary marketplace:

> I enclose a story for the Magazine, for which you tell Mr. Graham he must pay in advance, for it is one of the best I ever wrote, one of the very best, and he needn't think I will take a sixpence for it[;] he must send me a good round price, and thus show he is a man of sense, and appreciation.[10]

Thus, while "The Black Fortune-Teller" should be viewed as truly early work, the five other pieces of fiction in this volume demonstrate Oakes Smith's attempts at more complex approaches to her readers. Still posing, on one level, for conservative readers and editors looking for approved representations of women's limited moral role in literary culture, all of them contain attempts to revise her readers' expectations and understanding. Moreover, across these selections, one can discern some of the major themes to which she would return for the remainder of her career—the power of the "unseen" or spiritual realm to determine human destiny; transcendental thinking as a response to a rising materialism; the value and quality of the natural world; and, above all, a resistance to the compromised position of women and other disenfranchised persons in US society—socially, economically, politically, legally, and psychologically.

In the course of the 1840s decade, Oakes Smith became not only a literary professional, but one whose name magazine publishers wanted to advertise nationally in their lists of regular contributors. What distinguishes this period from the rest of her career, however, is Oakes Smith's position in relation to the publishing industry (even when the industry was represented by her husband) and, as her reputation grew, her decision to remain behind the public reputation constructed in her name by that industry and the social order that supported it. Reviewers such as George Ripley and

---

[10] Elizabeth Oakes Smith to Rufus Griswold, undated, Gratz American Poets Collection, Case 7, Box 9, Historical Society of Pennsylvania. Internal evidence dates the letter close to the publication of Keese's edition of her poems in June 1843.

INTRODUCTION: VOLUME I

Edgar Allan Poe periodically complained of inaccuracies in her prosody as well as her overblown or archaic diction, but the critical consensus (even from these latter critics) celebrated her works most commonly for characteristics expected in work by women writers: "delicacy of conception," "simple grace of language," and "exaltation of sentiment." "However brilliant" her "rare endowments of mind," as he called them, Henry Tuckerman made it clear those endowments, especially in women writers, depended "for their value upon the moral qualities with which they are united."[11] Passing silently over the social and political protest of *The Western Captive*, Tuckerman offered only passive praise for the work's "graphic depictions of scenery" and "graceful simplicity of style." That "she has often written from the spur of necessity," for Tuckerman, was a fact to be politely excused. Words used by the reliably iconoclastic John Neal to describe Oakes Smith in his portrait for the *Family Companion* in 1839—"unswerving and self-dependent"—were not considered appropriate for women writers, and thus were neither repeated nor approved, at least publicly, by others in the 1840s.

It is intriguing to wonder if the literary authorities of Oakes Smith's time appreciated, even if they did not agree with, the protofeminist subtexts of her fiction—her revision of the term "witch" in her telling of the biblical story of Saul's last days, for example, or her sympathy, in a popular giftbook tale, with a woman who finds her calling passing as a male minister. What did they make of the imprisoned wife's desperate plea to "take that man from my presence...let me die, without those hateful eyes upon my face!" ("The Defeated Life"), or, indeed, the young woman's description of a married existence: "to sit all day in the house, and do useless work, and read words that mean nothing"(*The Western Captive*)? In 1892, when William Dean Howells and other editors of major periodicals rejected "The Yellow Wall-paper," Charlotte Perkins Gilman's story of a woman's domestic imprisonment and descent into madness, they might have claimed it was "too good"—and too terrible—

---

[11] Henry Tuckerman, "Elizabeth Oakes Smith," *Graham's Magazine* 22 (April 1843): 54.

xxxv

ELIZABETH OAKES SMITH

to print, but as one critic has argued, that did not mean they did not understand its feminist point.[12] In fact, it was certainly the story's frank depiction of a woman's suffering that left genteel editors handling it like a hot potato, with only *New England Magazine* brave enough to risk publishing it. In this light it is not surprising that, roughly fifty years earlier, Oakes Smith's critics were loath to highlight the more radical subtexts of her fiction—not only to maintain their positions as guardians of "polite" literature produced by an industry looking for the broadest market, but also because what we might call the vocabulary of feminist literature, along with its readership, was only then coming into being.

In a letter to Griswold in June of 1843, Hoffman predicted Oakes Smith would "take a stand out of hooting distance of any other of our writing women—that is if her constitution be strong enough for the necessary mechanical labor of triumphant authorship."[13] It is perhaps rare to see the "mechanical labor" of writing described so bluntly as Hoffman does, even in praise, but he seems to have simply meant her ability to keep pace with the demand for her writing rather than her ability to withstand criticism. For by continuing to emphasize the traditionally female qualities of her work, editors had ensured the radical undercurrents of her work would remain *sub rosa*. If she could continue to supply the market with the image of womanly patience, purity, and grace, her editors and the publishing industry would take care of the demand. Thus Oakes Smith's entries in new anthologies of women's writing published at the end of the decade—by Griswold, Caroline May,

---

[12] Although some have disagreed with the tone of her work, Julie Bates Dock's Charlotte Perkins Gilman's 'The Yellow Wall-paper:' and the History of Its Publication and Reception—A Critical Edition and Documentary Casebook provides the most detailed material analysis of the rejection and publication of Gilman's famous story. In a letter to Gilman dated October 7, 1919, nearly thirty years after passing on it, Howells asked to publish "The Yellow Wallpaper" in an anthology to be called "Little American Masterpieces of Fiction."

[13] Charles Fenno Hoffman to Rufus Griswold, June 12, 1843, Rufus W. Griswold Papers, Boston Public Library.

INTRODUCTION: VOLUME I

Thomas Buchanan Read, and even conservative editor Sarah J. Hale—gathered scores of stanzas by Oakes Smith that would become nearly unrecognizable as her work by the 1850s, when she joined the woman's movement in earnest and sacrificed the editorial screens that during the 1840s had allowed her to enjoy, as she wrote in her autobiography, "the delights of authorship, without its penalties."[14]

What this recollection seems to elide, however, is not only the "mechanical labor" Hoffman alluded to in writing, editing, and correspondence, but the exhausting effort required to balance her publishers' demands for popular forms and themes with her own more progressive ideas. We will have a better idea of Oakes Smith's cumulative effort when a full bibliography of her work is completed, but as the decade went on, editors increasingly took advantage of her professional ability. In one instance, a magazine editor who had failed to secure an appropriate entry for "best Revolutionary romance"—despite their prize offer of $150—guaranteed Oakes Smith the prize money if she could produce a novella-length work to fit the editor's specifications in two weeks. In the midst of other projects, she completed the task,[15] and, in a pattern typical of her need to make the most of her work, reprinted the same work with various revisions twice over in the next twenty years. Nor did the torrid pace of her writing go unnoticed by other writers. In May of 1849, Connecticut poet Lydia Sigourney, a notoriously prolific writer herself, marveled at Oakes Smith's productivity, asking,

---

[14] "A Human Life," 539.

[15] *The Remapo* [*sic*] *Pass: A Story of the Revolution* appeared in Alice Neal's *Saturday Gazette and Lady's Literary Museum* on the date announced for the prize-winning work, January 29, 1848. It was subsequently published under Oakes Smith's own editorship, serialized as *The Intercepted Messenger of Ramapo Pass* in *Emerson's United States Magazine* (August 1856). After a more significant revision, detailed in Volume III of *Selected Writings*, the novel was expanded to its final form, *The Bald Eagle: Last of the Ramapaughs* (New York: Beadle and Adams, 1867).

xxxvii

frankly, "How many hours out of twenty-four, do you write? And when are your thinking times?"[16]

Periodically, Oakes Smith would take to her room with headaches that persisted for days, protesting to Griswold in one letter that her constant effort was seriously affecting her health and that she would have to "ruralize" to recover.[17] For her, this meant returns, mostly in the summer months, to the state of Maine to visit friends and family. Beginning in 1845 or earlier, her excursions included hikes into the wilderness north and west of Bangor, with trips to Moosehead Lake, Mount Kineo, and, in 1849, her rugged climb of Mt. Katahdin, the highest point in the state of Maine and today the remote end of the Appalachian Trail. By this time, her fame had reached the sort of celebrity status we associate with Hollywood stars today, and reports of her journey were circulated in newspapers up and down the Eastern Seaboard, including *Scientific American*, founded a few years earlier in 1845.[18] Reading of Oakes Smith's adventure for the first time in a newspaper, her friend Elizabeth Bogart[19] at first chided her for leaving the city without a word, but then joked that "the Editors, my dear friend, will not leave you to pursue unnoted, either the 'even' or uneven tenor of you ways."[20] Of all the events her manuscript autobiography leaves out, this is doubtless the most baffling, marking as it does the most significant turning point in her career. True, by this time Oakes Smith had already begun

---

[16] Lydia Sigourney to Elizabeth Oakes Smith, Papers of Elizabeth Oakes Prince Smith, Accession #38–707, Special Collections, University of Virginia Library, Charlottesville, VA.

[17] Elizabeth Oakes Smith to Rufus Griswold, undated, American Poets, Case 7, Box 9, Historical Society of Pennsylvania.

[18] *Scientific American* (September 15, 1849): 410.

[19] Elizabeth Bogart (1794–1879), who never married, was left with an income to ensure her financial independence. She was a frequent contributor to New York periodicals, chiefly the New York *Mirror*, under the pen name "Estelle."

[20] Elizabeth Bogart to Elizabeth Oakes Smith, August 22, 1849, Elizabeth Oakes Smith Papers, Box 2, Papers of Elizabeth Oakes Prince Smith, Accession #38–707, Special Collections, University of Virginia Library, Charlottesville, VA.

experimenting with a new genre as a playwright, presaging her use of her body and voice in more direct ways with her audience in order to short-circuit the interference of editors "pursuing" her for their own purposes. But if one is looking for evidence that Oakes Smith's full personhood was something quite different from what readers had seen in print until 1849, and obviously something completely forgotten in her later record of the period, we find it in the elated tone of the woman narrating her experience climbing a wild mountain stream toward Katahdin's Avalanche, and an unmistakable declaration to a friend on her return: "Nothing of what I have felt, nothing of my real self, my whole self, has appeared in my writings.... [I]f this state, so deep, so earnest, and clear should continue, I feel as if some poem or tragedy beyond what I have done hitherto must grow out of it."[21]

---

[21] Elizabeth Oakes Smith to Lydia Sigourney, October 3, 1849, MSRetro 071, Lydia Howard Sigourney Papers, Watkinson Manuscripts Repository, Trinity College.

LETTERS

A. Correspondence of Elizabeth Oakes Smith and Seba Smith, 1833

By the fall of 1833, Elizabeth Oakes Smith and her husband had shared both the joy of a growing family and the tragedy of the death of children (Oakes Smith's firstborn, Benjamin, died soon after his birth in 1824; their second son, Rolvin, had died just the year before, at the age of six). At this stage, there is some evidence that their marriage entailed not merely a traditional domestic arrangement but an intellectual, professional, and even physical partnership, despite the relative disparity in their ages (cited prominently in Oakes Smith's later writing) and the "arranged" nature of their marriage. Much of this evidence comes from a three-week correspondence between October 29 and November 18, 1833, when Seba Smith traveled from Portland to Boston to see his first book, *The Life and Times of Jack Downing*, through the press in Boston, leaving the couple apart for the first time in more than ten years. Though not all the local references made in this series of letters have been traced, these early writings allow readers a glimpse of the challenges in Oakes Smith's daily life—of a woman who was, by this time, both the mother of Seba Smith's children and the editor of his newspaper in his absence; both his emotional support and already a fellow contributor to their economic subsistence; both a woman familiar with the arts of child-rearing and the appropriate arrangement of a kitchen and one familiar with the construction of an effective sentence and the best methods of dealing with the men who took umbrage at her position of editorial authority.

Surprising to those who might view Oakes Smith's criticism of the marriage institution throughout her career as straight autobiography, these letters reveal a relationship of mutual respect and support. Moreover, the tone and content of these letters differ so markedly from that found in representations of marriage not only in Oakes Smith's autobiography but much earlier, in her popular fiction, they should give scholars serious pause: considering her later, more general reflections on her marriage in the autobiography, does the rare evidence of a continuous, daily written conversation between Oakes Smith and her husband over a period of several weeks weigh differently in our own reconstruction of her life? Letter writing, one might argue, is always a "performance," and not merely some open window into a personal relationship, but reading these letters, what we see is less a suffering child-bride beneath the thumb of an unworthy cradle-robber than a woman who takes on the role of both mother and partner in her husband's business enterprises, and a husband who respects his wife's judgment and creativity and uses his editorial position to offer her a place to exercise both.

The first letter of this series, written on October 29, 1833, from a man settling uncomfortably into a Boston hotel room to his wife home in Portland,[1] sets the tone for the whole, reminding us that these are the words of a married couple whose relationship after ten years is more or less unrecognizable in "The Defeated Life" or any of Oakes Smith's fiction or autobiographic writing.

---

[1] The MSS in both Sections A and B of *Elizabeth Oakes Smith: Selected Writings, Volume I* are held in Box 2, Papers of Elizabeth Oakes Prince Smith, Accession #38–707, Special Collections, University of Virginia Library, Charlottesville, VA.

Boston, Bromfield House, Tuesday evening[1]
half past ten o'clock, Oct. 29 1833

Cold and tired as I am, I cannot retire to rest without holding a few minutes converse with my dear wife and children. Dear Elizabeth, you can better imagine my feelings than I can describe them, therefore I shall not attempt it. For ten years that we have been permitted to walk hand in hand on the rough journey of life, we have never before been separated as long as twelve hours at any one time; and nothing but what seemed to be a strong necessity would have induced it now. I had for some years set my heart upon the idea of never being separated for twelve hours while we should live. It is what the world would call weakness, but for that I care not; you know I never felt much deference for the world, or its fashions.

But so it is—I <u>must</u> come to Boston[2] and you <u>could not</u> come to Boston; therefore we are a hundred miles apart. I feel as though it were a thousand. The goose-quill has risen in value with me tonight a hundred per cent. I fly to it with feelings that I have not been accustomed to. But where there is the strongest interest and the strongest affection, <u>facts</u> are more welcome than sentiment, therefore I will hasten to them.

---

[1] Envelope addressed to "Mrs. E. O. Smith, Portland Me," "By the politeness of Mr. Dana." From this point on, Seba Smith addressed his letters to "The Editor of the Courier, Portland Me."

[2] Smith's "Jack Downing" letters were already being pirated and copied in 1833, but in late October, it became clear to his publisher that at least one imposter was bringing together a volume for sale. After several letters negotiating terms for Smith's book, on October 23, Lilly and Wait wrote Smith an urgent request (with a note under the address "Please Deliver Immediately") not to delay his trip: "We have this day been informed by an artist of this city that he has been applied to by a house in Phila Littell and Holden to make 8 or 10 illustrations for a vol which 'they' are preparing and which <u>they</u> say are the <u>genuine Letters of Major Jack Downing</u> now in Washington—We shall write something L&H this day of the real facts and shall announce it also in the papers....It will be advisable to get the Book out <u>at once</u>" (Lilly and Wait to Seba Smith, Elizabeth Oakes Smith Papers, Box 1, Albert and Shirley Small Special Collections Library, UVa). Appendix V of Wyman's *Two Pioneers* provides a list of six rival editions not prepared by Smith or his printer Charles Davis (Wyman, 237).

I should have sent a letter to you to day had I not been mistaken as to the time at which the mail closes here for the eastward, which is twelve o'clock at noon.

We had a beautiful night, and a fine run from Portland,[3] though I got but a poor night's rest. We reached the wharf here at a quarter past nine this morning. My first call was at a barber's, where I got a smooth chin, and then made my way by guess into the heart of the city. Not having been here for a dozen years before, every thing appeared as strange, ~~as though~~ except the State House and a few prominent objects,[4] as though I had never seen the place. I soon found the Journal office and called on Mr. Thatcher,[5] who was laboring at his vocation with newspaper and scissors in hand, much as I do when at home. After a few minutes conversation I went to Lilly and Waite's store. Find them wide awake about the Major's book, and ready to dash on upon it. They carried me to Johnston[6] to converse with him about some plates. He is going to undertake it, and appears to enter into the subject with much spirit. Lilly and Waite

---

[3] In 1823, the trip to Boston was considerably shortened by the arrival of steamships. Earlier in 1833, two new steamships, the Chancellor Livingston and the Commodore McDonough, began competing for passenger and freight business between Portland and Boston. The distance Smith cites in his letter is not an exaggeration or approximation; from Portland to Boston by sea is 100 miles.

[4] Bromfield House, where Smith was staying, stood only a few hundred yards from the State House on Beacon Street off of Boston Common. The most "prominent object" in Boston was probably the Park Street Church steeple, which could be seen from a distance. Smith could walk just past the church through the old Granary Burial Ground to the State House.

[5] Benjamin Bussey Thatcher, a fellow alumnus of Bowdoin College who grew up some miles east of Smith's home in Maine, was at this time editor of the *Boston Mercantile Journal*. An abolitionist then dedicated to colonization, he published one of the early biographies of African American poet Phillis Wheatley (~1753–1784) along with several works on Native American cultures.

[6] David Claypoole Johnston, born in Philadelphia in 1798, studied engraving but made his first career in Boston as an actor. He returned to engraving and lithography and became well known for caricatures and humorous drawings published in a series entitled *Scraps*. Johnston is credited for inventing our national image of Uncle Sam, which clearly resembles the early caricature drawing of Smith's Major Jack Downing.

LETTERS

think the Philadelphia edition will not go on, though they will hasten this as fast a[s] convenient for fear it may.

I dined with Mr. Coleman[7] today, found Mrs. Coleman and family well, and living very prettily. Grenville and Frederick Mellen[8] and two or three others are boarding with'em.

This afternoon I had another conversation with Mr. Johnston, who seems to be a very sociable pleasant man. Read over the memoir to him; fancied he was not so much pleased with it as with the letters. Feel fearful myself that it will prove to be a failure, though I recollect that some parts of it pleased you, and that encourages me again.

They want some of the copy to commence with tomorrow morning, and I have been preparing some this evening for that purpose. But I have not a comfortable situation, and must try to better it tomorrow if I can. I am stowed away in very much such a character as we were once ushered into at Augusta. It is a little square box in the upper story with one small window and <u>no fire</u>. I tried for a better room with a fire, but they were all taken up. If it were only warm I should feel as contented as Goldsmith[9] in his garret. For I have a comfortable bed, a little table, a looking glass, a couple of chairs, a washstand, and a pitcher of water. But having set here four or five hours without a fire I have become rather chilly. It is now nearly midnight, and for the last half hour the bells have been

---

[7] Likely his cousin Samuel Coleman, who joined Lilly and Wait's publishing house in 1832.

[8] Sons of Prentiss Mellen, former senator from Massachusetts and then chief justice of the Maine Supreme Judicial court. Born in Biddeford 1799, by 1823, Grenville Mellen had married and moved to Oakes Smith's home of North Yarmouth and formed part of a circle of Portland writers who published work in *The Portland Magazine*, edited by Oakes Smith's sometime rival Ann S. Stephens. He left for Boston after the death of his wife and child in 1828. Like Oakes Smith, he eventually made his way to New York, where his prolific writings were considered by Poe and his contemporaries as "hyper-fanciful."

[9] Oliver Goldsmith, eighteenth-century Irish novelist best known as the author of *The Vicar of Wakefield*. The reference to his "garret" refers to Goldsmith's lack of social or monetary success despite his literary talent and connections to well-known figures such as Boswell and Johnson.

7

ringing for fire; but as they have ceased I conclude the fire is out without much damage.

I feel very anxious about you all at home; you must write me every day, and write me all you can think of. I meant to have talked some with the little boys tonight, but have filled up my paper. When you kiss them and put them to bed I know you will talk to them of me, and you must tell them to remember their promise that they would be good children while I was gone.

I hope and trust that you and the little ones are long before this hour enjoying a quiet and refreshing night's rest; and praying that you all may be the peculiar care of a kind Providence. I bid you good night, and drop into bed.

Wednesday morning, 11 o'clock. Had a good night's rest after I got warm. Nothing special to add this morning. Intend to send a package by the boat tonight for the paper. Your affectionate Husband,

S. S.

Boston Wednesday evening Oct. 30. 1833
My dear wife,

Another day has passed, the nine o'clock bell has rung, and that my last hour's labor for the day may be the pleasantest, I again turn my pen in the direction where my thoughts have wandered much and often during the day. I am yet at the Bromfield House, and have managed to be much more comfortable this evening than I was the last, though I am not exactly satisfied in my situation yet. I happened to find this evening a snug little drawing room adjoining the dining room, which contained a roaring anthracite fire, and a brilliant gas light, and which I found a comfortable ^{place} for writing, having it entirely to myself a part of the evening, and at other times but two or three being present. I put about twenty pages into the hands of the printers today, and have been preparing some more this evening to ~~put into~~ give them in the morning. I have a great many misgivings yet. I fear the thing will be pronounced very flat after all. The novelty of a few plates however may be the means of getting off one edition if not more. Mr. Johnston had another letter from Littell and Holden, Phil. today making him great offers if he will prepare some illustrations for their edition. He however will not meddle with it, and whether they will go on without his assistance remains doubtful. I have found no leisure yet to move about town or make any visits.

After wishing you and the little boys an affectionate good night and commending you again to that kind Providence whose watchful care is over all, I shall lay this by and close it tomorrow. In the morning I shall expect to find a letter from you at the Post Office, and hope to ^{get one} every morning while I remain here.

Thursday Morning 11 o'clock. I called at the Post Office[10] about an hour ^{ago} and inquired for a letter, not doubting I should find one, but judge of my disappointment when the Clerk told me there was none. I turned away and went into Mr. Topliff's Reading Room in the same building, and spent an hour in looking over the papers.[11] Not satisfied, however, I went back to the Post Office and demanded a second look, when lo! out came the letter.[12] I read it with great joy. Tell Appleton[13] I am very glad to hear that he was good during the first day after I left, and tell Sidney I hope he wont let the "brush" or anything else keep him from being <u>dood</u>[14] till I get home. Tell them also that although I cant come right home, I shall make haste as fast as I can. I ~~told~~ am glad to ^{perceive} you managed

---

[10] Post Office Square was only a few blocks east of Bromfield House, down Milk Street.

[11] The Old State House was rededicated in September 1830. The post office was on the first floor, next to Topliff's Reading Room, "which provided domestic and international newspapers for local merchants," and the Merchants' Exchange. ("The Old State House," Boston Landmarks Commission, 1994).

[12] Only Seba Smith's half of the correspondence has been preserved until Oakes Smith's letter of November 11, but as Seba's letter of November 5 (6 and 7) indicates, Oakes Smith's letters were more numerous.

[13] After the death of their second son, Rolvin, in 1832, three children were at home: Appleton, eight; Sidney, four; and Alvin, two.

[14] Smith frequently writes out his young children's pronunciation.

prudently with regard to Mr. Davis'[15] editorship. If he has a pride about it, it is best not to offend it but endeavor to guide it in the most useful manner. I expect him to send the letters [to] you unless any are particularly directed to him, and also send up what money he does not find it necessary to use.

I should like to have you mention to me from time to time whether you receive any money and how much, for should you have any to spare, I may find it necessary to send to you to pay some before my return. I shall perhaps have to stay here more than a week yet, if you get along well at home. Dont be afraid of writing me long letters; it takes me but a short time to read them. The more minute you are, the better. Tell me how you get along every hour of the day; how you make out for fuel and food, not forgetting <u>milk</u>, who calls, and where you go, &c. &c.

The papers generally in this quarter have noticed my article concerning the Major's Life and Letters rather favourably.

I am expecting the first proof sheet now every minute, and as the mail is about to close, I must run with this to the Post Office.

Yours, with how much affection, I am sure I need not ~~say to~~ describe to <u>you</u>.

S. S.

Boston Thursday evening Oct. 31. 1833[16]

Again, my dear companion through the world's wide wilderness, I take up my pen at ten o'clock in the evening to bid you good night if nothing more. Having passed another day without seeing or

---

[15] Charles Davis was listed as printer of the *Courier and Family Reader* until October 1833 and considered himself in charge of the *Courier* while Smith was in Boston. He is referred to by the fictional Jack Downing in the preface to Smith's collected Jack Downing letters of 1833 as "Mr. printer." This Davis is easily confused with Charles Augustus Davis, the New York merchant who imitated the Jack Downing letters for the *New York Advertiser*.

[16] Addressed "to Editor of the Courier, Portland Me." Postmarked "Boston Oct 31."

speaking to you, upon whom I have looked and with whom I have conversed every day for ten years, I feel that I cannot let a day pass, now that we are separated, without saying <u>something</u> on paper. It is not necessary for us to declare our affection and talk of love, like young lovers who have never wintered and summered together, and have faced together not a few of the wintry storms of life. We are no strangers to each other's feelings; and therefore a simple statement of our health, condition, movements, and prospects is more acceptable than whole pages of fine sentiments and warm professions.[17]

I have read one proof sheet today of the Major's book. It looks tolerably well on paper, but I cant get over the notion that to most readers it will appear flat. The public expectation is considerably raised with regard to the book, and this I am afraid will operate against it. Yesterday Mr. Coleman sent the title page to the Mercantile Journal as an advertisement, and by a mistake of the printers they added at the bottom "just published by Lilly, Waite and Company." The paper had not been out scarcely an hour before the book was called for, and has been called for several times today. So they bite quick.

Mr. Johnston has commenced to day on the Major's portrait. There will be several other illustrations, but the scenes are not yet decided upon.

I must bid you good night, and add something in the morning. Tell the little boys I do not go to bed in my little lonely cold chamber, away up in the fourth story, without thinking of them and loving them a great deal.

Tuesday morning. 11 o'clock. I received a second letter from you, my dear wife, this morning, and rejoiced to find you were still well and getting along comfortably. What you did about the note was very well, though I should not have cared much about it if it had lain in the Bank till I returned. I did not know that there was any

---

[17] Although this note may address what Oakes Smith had written in her first letter received by her husband that morning, as their correspondence continues, it becomes more clear that Seba is addressing his own emotions—all the more notable given the truth of his reminder: they have been married more than ten years.

such note in the Bank, or I should have made provision for it. Nor can I think now of any person who held a note against me for the sum you mention, $37. However probably it is a true one. Should ^you receive a notice of any more notes becoming due, I think you may venture to let them lay till you can write to me the particulars and receive an answer.

Give little Alvin one good shaking in remembrance of me.

Wholly and affectionately Yours,

S. S.

Tare off the other page and send to the Office.

Boston Friday evening, Nov. 1. 1833.

Half past ten o'clock. To you my dear Elizabeth, my last thoughts for the day must again be given in compliance with my plainest duty and greatest pleasure. I have passed through a scene this evening which I must hasten to communicate to you; a scene in which I figured somewhat more conspicuously than I could have desired. I have been to a Boston [ ]. A party of two or three hundred gentlemen met at the house of a Mr. Hastings to pay their respects to Mr. Clay,[18] who is yet here in the City. I incidentally received an invitation and went. The rooms were crowded and there was much sociability and pleasantry. Mr. Clay had to shake hands and bow almost as fast as President Jackson did when he was in Philadelphia and New York. It so happened I met two or three persons there who knew me; and they at once began to introduce me to their acquaintances as Major Downing. The name soon spread, and several came up and were introduced to me. At last mine host took me by the arm and turned to Mr. Clay and presented me as Major Downing.

---

[18] Henry Clay (1777–1852), Kentucky congressman and presidential candidate from the Democratic Republican Party (1824) and the Whig Party (1832, 1840, 1844, and 1848), had recently lost the election of 1832 to Andrew Jackson and returned to the US Senate. Though Charles Augustus Davis's appropriation of Smith's "Major Jack Downing" character in New York newspapers was more obviously critical of Jackson, Smith's need for publicity to sell his book and his own political allegiances made Clay's notice gratifying.

LETTERS

I assure you I felt rather awkward; but Mr. Clay very cordially held out his hand, and with more deliberation and emphasis than I had seen him address any one before, remarked that he should be very happy to be introduced not only to Major Downing, but to the whole family, Cousin Nabby not excepted. He added that he understood there were some counterfeit Majors in the field; but, said he, I believe they are <u>vetoed</u>.[19] After that there were nearly as many eyes turned on me as on Mr. Clay himself, and I was of necessity introduced to a large number, among whom was the venerable Matthew Carey of Philadelphia,[20] a short, fleshy, black-eyed, cheerful old gentleman, distinguished for his benevolence and many sensible writings. Mr. Gorham,[21] Representative to Congress, asked to be introduced to me, and was very sociable. On the whole, as the Major would say, I think I've got myself into a pretty considerable of a sort of a scrape.[22]

It is past eleven o'clock, and praying for the blessing of Heaven to rest on you and the little boys, I bid you good night and retire to rest.

Saturday. The Steam boat is about to start and I have not time to another word.

---

[19] For "counterfeit Majors," see note 15 above, and 36 below.

[20] Irish-born publisher, printer, and political writer Mathew Carey (1760–1839) immigrated to the US in 1784, establishing the first major publishing house in Philadelphia. By 1833, he had long retired from publishing, but he would have been recognized as an early proponent of protectionist policies on banking and tariffs that pitted him against Jackson and the Democratic Party.

[21] Benjamin Gorham (1775–1855) had served both in the Massachusetts State House and in Congress as a representative from Massachusetts. He had been elected as an "Anti-Jacksonian" in the election of 1832.

[22] Smith alludes to the dissonance created by the voice of his satiric portrait of Major Jack Downing, with which he had been identified and in whose name he was actually introduced at the political gathering. Standing among Jackson's opponents, he had to rely on their understanding of the difference between what his character had said, as it were, "straight," and his own political convictions.

Boston Saturday evening 11 o'clock Oct 2. 1833[23]

My dear wife, I commence a few lines to you again to night, late as it is, because it is the pleasantest substitute I can find for the conversation I have been accustomed to enjoy. I received your letter which came by steam boat to day just as we were sitting down to dinner. I took it to the table with me, and read part of the time while others were eating. It served well for desert. You should not put "Bromfield House" on the letters unless sent by private conveyance for if they are so marked they are put into the Bromfield box at the Post Office. I sent you a few lines today by George L. Drinkwater by steamboat. Don't laugh too much at my interview with Mr. Clay.

I met Leonard[24] this evening for the first time since I have been here, for I have been so constantly engaged I could not get time to hunt him up. There was another fire this evening and in going about half a mile to see where it was I met Leonard in the street. His health is rather poor, cough continues bad, though he has been taking some medicine within a few days that he thinks helps him. He talks of taking an emetic tomorrow morning and a sweat. I shall go and see him tomorrow. The book does not get along very fast yet, though they say they shall drive it more rapidly next week. Johnston has made a drawing for the Major's portrait, and put it into the hands of the engraver. It is a queer phiz.[25] I cannot tell by seeing it on the block how I shall like it. It represents the Major sitting at a table writing letters, with one finger up by the side of his nose to help him think. He has two or three letters written, one addressed to Uncle Josh, another to Cousin Nabby &c. His military dress and sword hang up by him. He is rather a slick headed knowing looking chap, but I cannot tell whether I shall feel satisfied with it till I see an impression from the engraving.

"Health peace and competence" be with you and the little ones. I am weary and sleepy and must bid you good night.

---

[23] Postmark and internal evidence indicates that Smith seems to have forgotten to change months in his first two letters written in November.

[24] Seba Smith's younger brother, born August 25, 1812.

[25] Facial expression.

Sabbath morning Oct 3. Eight o'clock. I intended, my dear Elizabeth, that you should receive a line from me every day during my stay here. But should you receive one tomorrow you must consider it counterfeit, as I have not deposited any in the office today. I had not time to add much to the letter this morning before meeting time, and besides I wanted to receive one from you before closing mine; but I could not get yours till five o'clock this evening, as the Post Office is not open on the Sabbath till that hour. I have received it however and read it not only "twice" but three times. Before answering it, I will tell you how I have spent the day. I did not rise very early, say about seven o'clock, having set up rather late every night since I have been here. By the time I had shaved, dressed, and eaten my breakfast, and conversed a little while with Philip Greeley who boards here and who returned yesterday from Virginia, the bells rung for meeting. I sallied forth and wandered away to the southern part of the City to Hollis Street Church, for the purpose of hearing Mr. Pierpont;[26] but was disappointed, he having gone to Buffalo, N.Y. I believe to preach a dedication sermon. I heard a tolerable sermon however from Mr. Gilman of Charleston, South Carolina.[27] After dinner I took a walk towards the northern part of the City, and when the bells rung, dropt into the first Church I came to. It proved to be the First Baptist Church, of which Mr. Hague is Pastor. I heard an ordinary discourse from a young man who appeared

---

[26] John Pierpont was pastor at Boston's Hollis Street Church from 1819 to 1845. Oakes Smith and her husband would have known him through John Neal, who was Pierpont's lifelong colleague, friend, and defender. An activist for temperance and abolition, Pierpont wrote sermons and poems often cited at anti-slavery meetings in Boston and elsewhere beginning in the 1830s. Oakes Smith would later use lines from his most famous poem, "Passing Away," as one of her chapter epigrams in "The Defeated Life."

[27] Samuel Gilman (1791–1858) was a Unitarian minister born in Exeter, New Hampshire. Completing his degree at Harvard in 1811, he married Caroline Gilman, future founding editor of *The Rosebud*, a juvenile magazine where Elizabeth Oakes Smith would publish work in the 1840s. In 1819, the couple moved to Charleston, where Gilman was ordained as minister of the Unitarian Church. http://www.charlestonuu.org/WhoWeAre/History/The SamuelandCarolineGilmanYouNeverKnew/tabid/201/Default.aspx.

to be a stranger. After meeting I wandered round till I found Fleet Street, and called at Mr. Wilson's. Mrs. Wilson appeared very glad to see me; asked when I came into the City, and on my telling her I had been here ever since Tuesday morning, she said I was "naughty." Celia also came in directly from meeting and I could not get away until after tea. Mr. W. was out piloting in a vessel. Mrs. Wilson urged me very hard to come there and spend the rest of the time I should remain in Boston; room, fine, light paper and ink, and any thing I wanted should be at my service if I would only come. ~~About seven o'clock I went again to see Leonard.~~ Between meetings at noon I went again to see Leonard. He was at Doctor Elias Smith's where he staid last night and today. He had first been taking an emetic, which operated powerfully, and which is one of Dr. Smith's famous remedies for a cough. He thought some of taking a sweat too but gave it up. I advised him if his lungs continued some to put a blister upon them. I went again about seven o'clock this evening to see him, when he told me he felt considerable better; should go out again tomorrow, and should call up and see me. He says he wrote to Manly[28] three or four days ago.

My climate is wonderfully meliorated today. The barkeeper at noon began to grow uncommonly polite. He said some of their rooms were cleared now, and if I would like it he would have my baggage brought down into a lower chamber where I could have a fire by myself, as he saw I had considerable writing to do. I told him [ ] would be an accommodation, and he accordingly showed me a snug little chamber on the first floor, and asked if I would have a fire. I told he might have one made in the evening. Accordingly when I came in at eight o'clock and went to my little chamber I found it almost as hot as an oven, and bright with a glowing grate of anthracite coal. I was obliged to take a seat clear back by the window where I have found a very comfortable time in writing you this scrawl. I suspect you will not get so long a one again for some days.

You must not sit up quite so late at night. If old jackets need mending you must call on Mrs. Higgins or somebody else. I fear you

---

[28] Seba and Leonard Smith's youngest brother.

expose yourself too much, by your being visited with the tooth ache. The reason I did not send the package by Steam boat as mentioned was that I got down to the wharf a little too late; the boat was gone, and I sent letters by next mail. I hope you have not applied to Capt Dow about the three hundred dollar note. It has not been discounted at the Bank, but I suppose has been put in there for collection by the assigned of Shirley and Hyde. It will do no harm for it to lay till I return. I think it was not Mr. Fox whom you saw at the office, for I don't recollect that ever I saw him use tobacco. The article in the N.Y Mirror I have not seen, but shall try to look it up. I think the Courier looks pretty well as yet. That was an interesting article from N. P. Willis, with an appropriate heading. Who prepared it, you or Dr. Mighels? N. B. Where is the [Law]? My anthracite has got pretty low, and so have my eyelids. I shall read a chapter in the bible, with which each room in the house appears to be furnished, and retire pretty soon to bed. I met my friend Mr. Greenleaf[29] here to day a few minutes, who looked as good as ever. He invited me very politely to come out to Cambridge and see him. If I can get time I shall go.

Dear Appleton: I hope you continue to be a good boy and do all you can to help your mother, so that she need not have to work so hard. And I hope you are very kind to your little brother and don't do any thing to make you or them unhappy. I shall tell you about a great many things when I come home.

Monday, half past 2 o'clock. I have been engaged most of the day in reading proof and preparing copy. Have not time to send any thing to day for the paper. Leonard has been up and spent an hour with me this forenoon; says he feels some better.

I received another from you by mail today.

---

[29] Born in Newburyport, Massachusetts, in 1783, Simon Greenleaf was admitted to the Bar in Cumberland County, Maine, in 1801 and moved to Portland in 1808. On April 23, 1833, he had been named Royall Professor at Harvard Law School.

Dear Sidney, father thinks of you every night and every morning, and wants you to try to be as dood as ever you tan so that when he comes home he can love you twenty bushels.

Dear little Alvin, father wants to give him a shaking that would make him giggle right out.

Boston Tuesday Nov. 5. 1833

My dear Elizabeth, I have time [to] write but a few lines to day, but judging your feelings by my own, I conclude even a single line to say that I am well would be acceptable, and therefore will scribble what I can before the boat goes. I am in hopes in a day or two to be able to send something more for the paper. As yet it takes nearly all my time to prepare my copy and read proofs. They have put nearly half the book in type, and will go on with the rest pretty rapidly. I think they will have to wait a few days for engravings.

Grenville Mellen has been proposing two or three days past to prepare some humorous and satirical poetry to intersperse along through the Major's book, and receive some compensation for it according to the sales. He thinks he can introduce some that will hit pretty well. What do you think? Had I better accept his offer? Or send the Major to sea in his own tub?

Leonard has been in twice to day. His lungs are rather sore. I went into the factory yesterday where he has been at work, and I tell him he must quit it or he will never get well. The machinery keeps a thick dust flying through the building that would destroy any body's lungs in a few years. I think he will not work in it anymore. If he does not find other business he will probably return when I do to Portland.

What Bill was that you speak of, for which Capt Sawyer[30] was sued? Have Capt Larrabee and Ann[31] gone home. Is he going to sea this fall? Have you got any wood yet? If you get out of flour, send to Mr. Winship's for a barrel of his best. I got your Sabbath day letter this morning, which as usual gave me much pleasure.

---

[30] Possibly Lemuel Sawyer, Oakes Smith's stepfather.
[31] Seba Smith's sister married Captain Larrabee in 1832.

LETTERS

Tell the children if they will learn to read a good deal before I come home I will try to fetch them something new to read. I am expecting some proof to be brought in every minute, but I believe I shall run out long enough to carry this.

Now as ever affectionately,
S S.

Wednesday 4 o'clock P.M. I was mistaken yesterday with regard to the boat's going, and you have consequently had to do without ~~another~~ a letter another day. Yours of Monday I received this morning. I do not yet find any leisure. Am sorry I cannot send more for the paper, though as yet I perceive it gets along very well. I find it much more work for me to prepare the copy and read the proofs for the book than I expected. Johnston has made another drawing representing the Major at Philadelphia shaking hands for the President. I think it a pretty good one.

Boston Wednesday evening Nov 5 1833[32]

Again at ten o'clock in the evening, my more than friend, I take you my pen to commence a letter by bidding you goodnight. When through with the labors of the day, and about to retire to rest, my thoughts recur to my home, my dear wife and children, with intense interest. It seems to me that this ardent undying affection which glows and burns in our bosoms the more strongly the more we are separated, is a convincing argument of our immortality. It is true the lower orders of animals discover affection, particularly for their offspring; but it is an affection which can live through but a short separation, while ours endures lively and warm for ages. Do you not feel if you and I were to live fifty, or even a hundred years, and not see each other during the whole of the time, that our affection would remain as vivid to the last as it is now? I think much and often of

---

[32] Smith wrote this letter over several days. It was eventually postmarked "Boston, Nov 8."

our dear little Rolvin;[33] I cannot write that name now without a tear, though it is a year and a half since he left us. Can it be that such ardent love is planted in our bosoms never to be gratified?

But I am weary, and feel need of rest, and must commend you and the dear little ones you have with you, once more to the beneficent author of all beings, praying that he may be unto us all that we need, now and forever.

Thursday evening November 6. I intended, my dear wife, to close this letter this morning and mailed it so that you could receive tomorrow morning; but I could not get time, and you will have to go without another day, which I very much regret, if it affords you as much pleasure to receive a letter as it does me.

I am glad you are able to manage so well with the little Courier as you do. I don't see but it holds its character so far very well. It seems to be necessary for me to stop here some days yet. It takes me nearly all the time to prepare the copy, read the proofs, and write a few lines now and then home. I shall probably give all the copy out by Saturday, and the printing may be done by the middle of next week. Then they may have to wait a few days ^{for} engravings and binding, so that it will hardly be ready for delivery before week after next. There is considerable call for the book at Lilly & Wait's store. I was in there this evening when a gentleman came in and subscribed and paid for four copies to send to Charleston, S.C. Every body as far as I can learn, but myself and Mr. Holden,[34] seems to think there will be a "considerable bunch" of them sold. Mr. Edward Everett[35] called to see me to day in behalf of the writer who writes under the

---

[33] The couple's son Rolvin had died in March 1832 at the age of six, from a scalding accident.

[34] Holden was one four partners at the bookstore and publishing firm of Lilly, Wait, Colman and Holden, located at what was 121 Washington Street in Boston and 6 Exchange Street in Portland.

[35] Edward Everett is best known as the featured speaker at the dedication of the Gettysburg battlefield memorial in 1863, speaking for more than two hours before Abraham Lincoln delivered his famous two-minute address. At this point in his career, Everett was a member of Congress and a National Republican, an adherent of Henry Clay, and staunch opponent of Jackson.

signature of Major Downing in the N.Y. Daily Advertiser.[36] Mr. Everett says the writer is a friend of his, and wrote to him to see if I would consent to introduce some of his letters into my volume. He wants no pay or profits, but is only desirous that some of his letters should appear. I think I shall introduce two or three of them. Indeed I had about made up my mind to take one or two of them before I left home. I shall however preserve a distinction between them and the others. I am afraid you wont like the Major's portrait very well. He has a shrewd knowing eye, but his face has a little too much of the caricature about it. Johnston's drawing of the shaking-hands scene in Philadelphia I think a pretty good one. He is to work now upon the scene where they jawed all night in the chamber at Concord before turning about for Washington. Johnston can hardly touch any thing without running into caricature. I have to watch him, and sometimes get him to alter. They will not wait for more than five or six cuts, but will have some additional ones prepared for a second edition. It is half past eleven o'clock and I must again bid you good night.

Friday Morning, Nov 7. I have just received yours of Wednesday my dear E and will add a line or two in answer. I am gratified that the Courier is so well sustained. But I fear you have too much to do, and dread every letter I receive, lest it may bring me word that you are sick. Be sure and call in such help as you need for sewing and helping to take care of the children.

I had written thus far when J [Merrell?] came to my room and brought me yours of Thursday. Rejoice to hear you are still well and getting along comfortably. You beat me in writing letters, out and out. Dont know how you can get through with all you have to do and write so much.

---

[36] Charles Augustus Davis, a wealthy merchant in New York, imitated Smith's work with the letters of "J. Downing, Major." Seba Smith's work parodied Jackson's adherents, but Charles Davis's unauthorized version of "Downing" Letters were more purposely offensive. For context of the Downing letters, see John H. Schroeder, "Major Jack Downing and American Expansion: Seba Smith's Political Satire, 1847–56," *The New England Quarterly* 50/2 (June 1977): 214–33.

ELIZABETH OAKES SMITH

I owe Mr. Gale twenty one or two dollars in borrowed money. He told me when I came away he did not know but he should have a use for it in about a fortnight. Perhaps he wont care anything about it till I return. If however you should have enough by the middle of next week, that you could spare as well as not, it would be well to pay it.

It is nearly time for the mail to close, and I have a proof to read before dinner. So my dear, good by for to day.

Affectionately yours, as ever,

S. S.

Boston, Saturday 3 P.M. Nov. 9. 1833

My dear Elizabeth, I have time to day but barely to say how do you do, but even that, I know will be acceptable to you, if it does but tell you how I do. Having two letters from you yesterday, I got none today, and it makes rather a long day of it. What makes it worse is, the Post Office will not be open tomorrow till 5 o'clock P.M. so that your next letter will be here a whole day before I can get it. It is rather provoking but I don't know how to help it.

Tell Maria her uncle called to see me a few minutes the other evening; appeared gentlemanly and polite. I shall call on him if I have time before I leave.

I have given out nearly all the copy for the book, but shall not get through with the proof sheets probably till about the middle of next week.

I have been about the City but very little yet, and seen but very little; but am in hopes to have more opportunity next week. I am very anxious to get home however and shall start as soon as the Major can spare me.

The communication in the Courier, "The Maniac," it strikes me I have seen it before but am not sure. Your notice of the Medical lecture did very well.

I inclose a "picter" of the Major; rather an imperfect copy; it will probably appear better on good paper. I would not show it

LETTERS

much. We are not exactly satisfied with it, and don't know but we may have it altered. Tell me what you think of it.

With due and undying affection,
Yours,
S. S.

On looking back I see I have not mentioned the children. Tell them again I love them and want them to be very good and very happy.

Boston Sunday evening Nov. 10. 1833.

My dear Elizabeth, it is half past ten o'clock and I feel weary and sleepy, but I cannot retire to rest without again resorting to the best substitute in my power for communing a few minutes with you. I got your Friday's letter at six this afternoon. I feel more and more desirous to get home. Sometimes my anxiety about you and the children is so great I feel as though I must start immediately and hasten home as fast as possible. But when I reflect again that there is a kind and watchful Providence in whose hand you are, my anxiety is in some measure relieved. Your tooth ache gives me uneasiness; I fear you expose yourself too much. Appleton, too, splits wood. Do caution him not to use the axe when Sidney is near. I am writing this at Mr. Wilson's. They urged me so hard to come and spend some time with them, that I came last evening and spent the night, and went to meeting with them this forenoon. At noon I went to Mr. Coleman's by invitation and dined.[37] I have not been there before since the first day I came into the City, tho invited almost every day. I could not find time to go there or any where else. However I hope I shall not be quite so much engaged for the few days that I shall remain here. This afternoon I went to hear a very eloquent and interesting discourse from Mr. Taylor at the 2nd Bethel Church, and this evening I have been to a political caucus at Faneuil Hall. As I intend to say something of both for the paper I will not now attempt

---

[37] See note 7 above.

to describe either. Heaven bless you and the dear children. Good night.

Monday 2 P.M. I received your Saturday's letter, my dear E, this morning. My feelings at your affright and escape you can better judge than I describe. It is [a] melancholy thought, that there are so many brute tigers and wolves who bear the semblance of our species. I am glad to hear you say it will induce you to be careful. I sent my last letter by Philip Greeley by Steamboat, which I hope you received yesterday morning.

I have more copy to prepare this afternoon, and must bid you bye for today.

Affectionately Yours
S. S.

Monday Portland November 11th 1833[38]

I know, my dear husband, you feel disappointed at not receiving any letter from me yesterday and I almost fear to tell you the reason, but I know affection is lynx-eyed, and if I do not tell you, you will imagine something more serious than it actually was. The terror to which I somewhat exposed myself, occasioned one of those turns of sickness, which I have before had, consequent upon any shock of the nerves, and yesterday, your mother who very kindly staid to take care of me, advised me to send for a physician, as I was in much distress from unequal incubations. He came and gave me powders &c. and to day I am nearly in my usual health, below, and writing to my earthly protection, friend, and husband. Now don't hurry home, and feel anxious about me, for I assure you I shall run no risque again, and indeed had I acted like the general run of good wives I should have said nothing about it, but I cannot endure insincerity from whatever motive. Now if you come home any sooner

---

[38] The envelope, seen here, and the panic Seba described in his letter of November 14 indicate that he did not receive this letter in Boston. Oakes Smith's original address "Seba Smith Boston, Mass" is struck out, with "Portland Maine" substituted in a different hand, as if the Boston postmaster was not aware of Smith's visit or otherwise misdirected it.

Monday Portland Nov 11th 1833

I know, my dear husband, you felt disappointed at not receiving any letter from me
yesterday — I almost fear to tell you the reason, but I know affection is lynx-eyed, and
if I do not tell you, you will imagine something more serious than it actually was. The
terror to which I somewhat imprudently exposed
myself, occasioned one of those turns of sickness, which I have before had, consequent upon any shock of the nerves, and yesterday, your mother who very kindly staid to take care of me, advised
me to send for a physician, as I was in much
distress from unequal circulations. He came
and gave me powders &c and to day I am nearly in my usual health, below, and writing
to my earthly protector, friend, and husband.
Now dont hurry home, and feel anxious
about me, for I assure you I shall run
no risque again, and indeed had I acted
like the general run of good wives I should
have said nothing about it, but I cannot
endure insincerity from whatever motive.
Now if you come home any sooner for this,
my dear, I shall feel sorry I have told you.
The portrait of the Major I dont like, I
have not shown it to any one lest it
might cause disappointment. The look is
not honest. Jack is showed but is he not
honest? The eye is a little too much turned
the person too lean and the countenance too
sheepish; tell Johnstone there is no necessity to make him so mortal homely. I
would have a man about the age of the first
sleigh, with a figure more rounded an eye less
oblique, the nose will do, but the chin retreats too much. The hands & regimentals are

---

Elizabeth Oakes Smith to Seba Smith, November 11, 1833, page 1.
Papers of Elizabeth Oakes Prince Smith, Accession #38-707.

Courtesy Albert and Shirley Small Special Collections Library, University of Virginia

A pictographic closing—Section from Elizabeth Oakes Smith to Seba Smith, November 11, 1833. Papers of Elizabeth Oakes Prince Smith, Accession #38-707.

Courtesy Albert and Shirley Small Special Collections Library, University of Virginia

for this, my dear I shall feel sorry I have told you. The portrait of
the Major I don't like. I have not shown it to any one lest it might
cause disappointment. The look is not honest. Jack is shrewd but is
he not honest? The eye is a little too much turned, the person too
lean, and the countenance too sheepish; tell Johnstone there is no
necessity to make him so mortal homely. I would have a man about
the age of the first design, with a figure more rounded, an eye less
oblique, the nose will do, but the chin retreats too much. The hands
and regimentals are very good, so is the neck, Table, &c. The Major
enjoys a laugh, therefore he ought not to be so thin. Don't let this
one go in without revision, for I am afraid it will give others the
same sensations of disappointment. Your mother, saw it when I
opened the letter. I expressed no opinion till I had heard hers. She
did not think it looked like the Major, thought he was a better looking man. I wish the lines were nicer—to make a better finished engraving. Perhaps I have said too much. I know I am a poor judge in
such matters, but I know what suits me, and that is all. The children
are very well, and pretty good. They once in a while have run a part
of the Major's motto, which I think they have caught from hearing
us read it over. Alvin begins to call, dad da, most earnestly. He is all
spirit. Manly has just come in. He don't like the Major. Thinks his
hair looks too much like a Methodist minister. A man of the promp-
titude which characterizes the Major might have a more determined
look. Manly wants me to remind you of the letter Y. again. They
need it very much at the office. Mr. D. paid me ten dollars to day. I
have paid Mr. Gale, and have $12 left. Have you no more orders?
Mrs. Carry called in this afternoon. She says J. Neal[39] is publishing
a series of letters in the N. York Inquirer. In one which he sent to
his sister addressed to the care of Mr. G. Warren, and which Mrs.
W had the reading of, he says Major Downing is the subject of

---

[39] John Neal (1793–1876), born into a Quaker family in Portland, was a
businessman, lawyer, and man of letters. Iconoclastic, irascible, and prolific, but
scattered in his pursuits, he published in several genres, practiced law, and trained
himself and others in boxing and gymnastics at an athletic club he began in Portland in the 1820s. An ardent abolitionist, he abandoned his own athletic club when
members balked at an African American's participation.

conversation in all the steam boats Stages and Taverns along the road. And no one will believe, that the Major, and his pretty wife live ᵃ way down east in the State of Maine. Now I hope you wont suspect me of vanity for writing the above. You know I am free of it. However, if the paragraph should give you that impression, I will not try to reason you out of it. Do go all about the City and see and learn all you can to tell me when you come. I want to see you, but I want you to make the most of your visit. The 'Maniac' was written by Dr. M. I ventured to alter a few words that were repeated several times and to substitute other words and in one instance to change the phraseology where it was objectionable, and fear I may have offended him as he has not called at the office but once since, however it will be an easy matter to conciliate him. Speaking of Dr.'s I ought to say I called upon our old physician Dr. C. yesterday. I hope the length of this letter will convince you of my restored health to day. The Steam Boat bell rings, and I can only say kiss   this place because I have kissed it for you.

E. O. S

Boston Wednesday Nov. 13. 1833[40]

My dear wife, Two mails have now arrived from Portland without bringing me a letter, which gives me no little uneasiness. A thousand causes present themselves to my disturbed imagination, and some of them not a little painful. The only way I can satisfy myself that all is well with you and well with the children, is that you omitted to deposit a letter in the Post Office on Sunday, and on Monday, sent one by the Steam boat Macdonough, which I understand put back to Portland, and has not arrived here yet. I passed an anxious day yesterday, and my anxiety would be increased to day were it not in some little degree relieved by the by seeing the Courier of Monday morning. Still if you had been sick, the Courier would not have mentioned it. Your cure for the tooth ache was very well told. I did not design to have the Major's Proclamation go into the Courier

---

[40] Addressed to "Editor of the Courier, Portland Me." Postmarked "Boston Nov 13."

LETTERS

yet, and particularly some part of Mr. Thatcher's remarks which were a little out of taste. However it is not of much consequence.

The publishers sold five hundred copies of the Major's book day before yesterday to a bookseller in Baltimore, though it is not yet through the press.

But I cannot write more till I hear from you. Trusting in Providence that you are all well, I am, as ever, yours affectionately

S. S.

A load of a thousand tons weight was this afternoon removed from my heart my dear Elizabeth, by receiving once more a letter from you by the Macdonough. The boat arrived here about two o'clock this afternoon. I had almost made up my mind to take the stage which started an hour before; but had been down upon the wharves looking for the boat so long, that I had hardly time to get ready. I could do nothing all day till I got your letter, and hardly anything yesterday, my anxiety was so intense. Your Saturday's letter I received Monday morning. Tuesday morning I went to the office as usual and asked for a letter. The man shook his head and said there was none. I turned away disappointed; felt uneasy; It was the first day I had failed to receive one since I had been here.[41] It might be my dear wife was too much fatigued to write, or it might be the letter was deposited in the office a little too late, or it might by some means have been miscarried. In the afternoon, the Chancellor[42] arrived a [*sic*] took a long walk to the boat in hopes to obtain a letter, but found none. Learnt that the Macdonough had come out and gone back. Built my hopes on the thought that the letter was on board of her. Went to the Post Office again on Wednesday morning; was told there was no letter. My anxiety increased. But still rested upon the hope that you had written by the Macdonough and

---

[41] Seba Smith's statement shows how small a portion of Oakes Smith's letters to her husband during this first separation have survived, since the first letter we have from her in this correspondence is dated eleven days into Smith's journey.

[42] Along with the McDonough, one of the two steamship packets running between Portland and Boston.

therefore had not sent by mail. I went to the Post Office again this morning, not allowing myself to doubt if you were all alive and well, that I should receive a letter. When I asked for a letter and the man answered no, my hear sunk within me. I asked him if he was sure, but he had so many others to wait upon that he gave me no answer. I turned away with the conviction that sickness or accident had visited those for whom alone it is life [ ] to live. I had proof to read, but read it but poorly. I took a long walk to the wharf twice to see if the boat had arrived. Pondered much upon taking the stage and riding all night. My imagination was boiling over with sickness and accident and death in every shape and variety. Just as we had done dinner, for which I found but little appetite, they told me the boat had arrived. I hastened to the wharf, with that mixture of hope and dread which Pope ascribes to our feelings with regard to a future state—"That while he dreads it, makes him hope it too—" I met Mr. Brooks[43] on the wharf; asked him if he had seen or heard anything of you for two or three days past. He had seen you in the bookstore, but could not tell whether it was this week or last; said there was a letter on board for me. I hastened, got it, read, and the lead fell from my heart as one escapes from a heavy incubus when waking from a troubled dream. But still you <u>had</u> been sick and recovered. I trust my gratitude rose to Heaven for its mercies. You allude to your sickness by saying "the two days you were sick you could select little for the paper." Had you written me a letter informing me of your sickness which I have not received, or did you write as you sometimes talk, thinking I knew by intuition what was passing in your mind?

But you will think I am spending too much time on this subject; so I will break off, and renew it when I get home. I sent a letter on Saturday by Philip Greeley enclosing a portrait of the Major. You do not mention it, and I am afraid you have not received it.

I gave out the Title page and Contents to the printers last night, and thought I had done, except reading a few pages of proof, but

---

[43] Possibly Erastus Brooks, a newspaper editor and later a New York politician.

was at the office this afternoon, and the printer told me there were still a couple of blank pages, so I sat down in the office and wrote a Preface, just to fill them up. I shall see the proof of that in the morning. The book is all in type and nearly all printed, but the engravings are a little behind hand. They probably wont be able to bind any before the middle of next week. They have concluded to go right about a second edition, somewhat larger than the first. A New York paper says an edition of the New York letters is in preparation to be published there.[44] But the publishers here are making considerable effort to get possession of the market. I feel very desirous of staying to see the engravings completed for the first edition, for I find they need a little looking after. I think I have saved one or two of them from being spoilt by an error in taste. Still if the weather should promise fair for a good run in the boat on Saturday night, I am rather inclined to think I shall leave for home—<u>Sweet Home</u>. The weather may ^{be} such that I should not like to venture in the boat at this season of the year; so that I should be glad to have you write, especially if there is anything important which I ought to know every day till you see me, as I shall give directions if any letters arrive after I leave to have them returned to Portland.[45] With affection, unspeakable, I remain yours,

S. S.

You will tell the dear children I do not forget to love them, and want them to be good.

Thursday Portland Nov. 15 1833[46]

Another day has passed, my dear husband, and I must confess with some degree of disappointment, for I had indulged a little hope that you would come this morning. I am ready, quite ready, to relinquish

---

[44] See notes 15 and 36 above. Davis's letters first appeared in the *New York Advertiser* on June 25, 1833.

[45] Envelopes to Smith with postmarks forwarded to Portland indicate this necessity in Oakes Smith's last letters to her husband.

[46] To Seba Smith, in Boston.

my Editorial chair the moment you arrive. This morning P. H. Greenleaf[47] and Abbott sent in an Address to the Citizens of Maine on the subject of abolishing Slav. in the Dis. Colum. Mr. Davis handed it to me. It occupies four pages, and they desire an immediate insertion. I have put them off with a few remarks as there was no room in to day's paper. I hate to feel so much responsibility, superadded to so much ignorance, inexperience, &c., and the more grievous offence of wearing petticoats.[48] A poor ignorant thing like me sitting in judgement upon the productions of men like the above. Do come home husband. Last evening Manly went and returned with me to the Lecture of Dr. McMurtrie.[49] It was very interesting. I could not possibly have obtained so good an insight to anatomy by a long course of hard reading. Appleton is sitting by me trying to write to you. Sidney sits very quietly looking at us. We are quite well. The proclamation affair is the fault of Mr. Davis. It came first in the Boston Transcript, and Mr. Davis brought it in Sabbath evening; I was not quite certain it was published by authority, but thought it best to republish it. Accordingly I mustered strength enough to write a short paragraph, stating we could hardly determine whether it was by the authority of the Major &c. I think it would have done very well. But when the Mail arrived Mr. Davis

[47] P. H. Greenleaf, graduate of Bowdoin College and son of Harvard Law professor Simon Greenleaf, became an Episcopal minister. In 1833, he was secretary of the Portland Anti-Slavery Society.

[48] The tone of Oakes Smith's combination of self-doubt and sarcasm is difficult to read here, but the phrase "grievous offense," along with her casual report that she has "put [the men] off with a few remarks," indicates that anything like real modesty here is feigned. This letter should be read in light of her earlier report of Davis's offense at her taking on editorial duties along with her husband's advice on how to handle the men's prejudice.

[49] Having translated several works by the noted zoologist and "father of paleontology" Georges Cuvier, who had died the previous year, Henry McMurtrie lectured in several cities, including Portland, in 1833. In a review for *The Literary Journal* of Providence the following February, editor Albert Greene welcomed McMurtrie's public lectures in a relatively "neglected" branch of natural history, in which the lecturer provided "a condensed view of the whole animal kingdom; from Man to the minute animalculae with which all creation is swarming, invisible to the eye unassisted by the microscope."

LETTERS

without consulting me cut it from the Journal. Holden has the Proclamation struck up about his shop received from Boston. You have
never told me how many they would publish for the first edition. To
make it profitable for you it ought to be pretty numerous. I regret
much the anxiety you suffered in consequence of receiving no letters
from home. I was told they would certainly put the letters in the
Post Office or I should have written by mail.[50] You must pardon me
if I say good night as little Alvin is awake and crying for me.

E. O. S.

Friday Nov 16 1833[51]

It is of no use to be so very reasonable any longer, dear husband, I
have thought of the good of the public, the necessity for your absence, and tried to feel contented and resigned at the length of time
you must be gone, but now I have ᵇᵉᵉⁿ so good a girl, so very self-
denying, I mean to treat my resolution, and begin to urge you to
come home. Do come, dear husband, next Sabbath in the Steam
boat if you have to go right back again. The time is so long and the
house so gloomy unless you can come in and say, well how do you
get along? Besides I grow somewhat nervous about you. I sometimes
fancy you sick, or that some accident has befallen you and then I
become so anxious I must to my work to drive it off. I am putting
my mouth into the prettiest pucker by the time you come, and I
begin to hope another ten years or longer may elapse before it will
be necessary for you to leave me again. I had no letter this morning
and I fear some of mine I have sent by the Steam boat may not have
reached you. We bought a barrel of flour to day at Mr. Winship,
and I am making some mince pies. I have been so used to talking
with you and telling you all I think and feel that my brain will run

---

[50] Due to the high cost of postage through the US Post Office, until the
mid-nineteenth century, letters were often sent privately outside the mail between
cities.

[51] Postmarked "Portland" with Oakes Smith's original address to her husband in Boston crossed out, this letter only reached her husband days after he had
returned.

31

over if you don't come home and let me empty my budget. We are all well. The children are delighted to think Father will come soon. I have nothing to write only you may tell Mr. Thatcher I fear he has made you love a bachelor's life, and if you are not as good, as kind and domestic as formerly, I shall think he is in fault or somebody else for keeping you in Boston so long. Tell him to never mind if people do steal from him Editorially, he can afford to lose it, and the poor wretches who take are guiltless, for they steal for bread. The paper grows rather wishy washy, it needs you. Good night my beloved husband. Appleton says tell my Father I am a good boy.

Your Affectionate Wife,
E. O. S.

Boston Sunday November 17, 1833
My dear wife,

I suppose you have been looking for me all this morning in the Steam boat, and I fear you will pass an anxious day and an anxious night, as you cannot hear from me before tomorrow morning, when I hope you will receive this line.

I had made up my mind to go in the Macdonough last evening, as the weather looked favorable and they told me at noon she would certainly go at five o'clock. I ran round over the pavements to get ready till my feet were so lame I could but just walk, and went down to the boat at five, and was told that she was not going. They had discharged their crew the day before and had not been able to get another. I was much disappointed and so were many others. The Chancellor arrived here this morning about nine o'clock. I have been down to her, about a mile from where I stop, and learn she is going again tomorrow night at seven o'clock. I have felt much hesitation whether to take the stage today, in which case I should have to ride all night, or wait till tomorrow for the boat. The boat would be the most comfortable, and at this season of the year the roads are bad and the waters are stormy, so that both modes of conveyance have their risks. I have concluded however to take the boat should the weather continue tomorrow to look favourable. If not I shall perhaps take the stage tomorrow. I write this in haste, to relieve your anxiety, and as it is time for the mail to close I can add no more. I am in hopes I have a letter in the Office from you, but if I have I shall not be able to get it till five o'clock this afternoon.

May Heaven's blessing rest on you and the dear children, and its kind protection be over us all till we meet.

Your affectionate husband,
S. S.

Sunday November 18, 1833
My dear husband,

This morning little Alvin and I were awake before daylight of course thinking of you. The children were taken up and dressed, everything put to rights and myself dressed in as becoming a manner as is consistent with my homely duties, and all was in readiness, by the time the Steam boat should arrive, for your reception. Hour after hour passed, I fidgeted from window to window, the boys went up garret to see if the boat was signalized, the furniture was readjusted, the baby's face rewashed, and then I looked again. But no letter, no husband came and I sat down in disappointment. The furniture is displaced, my ruffle tumbled, the children's faces dirtied, and the chicken pie eaten, and you have not come. What a catalogue of evils. But seriously when may we expect you? I have been reasonable long enough, and you must come home. I am very sorry to write that dear Sidney is behaving rather naughty this moment. I told him I should write it down and he feels somewhat hurt. I went to meeting this forenoon and carried the children. Mr. Meginnis asked if you were returned. I wrote last evening with scarcely a thought that you would receive the letter in Boston. This morning Mr. and Mrs. Evans called. They were married about a week since. Mrs. E looked all complacency. Mr. Evans quite gallant, his eyes twinkled with pleasure, and his step as brisk as a bridegroom's of 70 could well be. His cue was combed down to the most desirable state of sleekness and stuck out above his collar in the most approved style. They went to

ELIZABETH OAKES SMITH

our meeting today, after which Mr. Evans says they are going to separate, but this was said with some considerable glee, as much as to say I know you won't believe me. But Mrs. E with commendable zeal says, no, if he won't go with me I will go with him. What charming patterns of conjugal felicity these old couples are! But they are happy and I ought not to ridicule them. Mr. Davis has just gone out from here, and he tells me the Chancellor Livingstone will be here tomorrow morning.[52] I shall again hope to see you in the morning. I have no time to write more tonight.

Affectionately yours,
E. O. S.

---

[52] Seba Smith did arrive in Portland the next morning, crossing the mail, as evidenced by the postmark on Oakes Smith's letter, which has redirected it from Boston back to Portland.

B. Correspondence of Elizabeth Oakes Smith to Seba Smith, 1836–1837

If it was Seba Smith's first collection of *Major Jack Downing* letters and his trip to Boston to see his work through the press that gives us our first extended view of Oakes Smith's life as a wife, mother, and stand-in editor in 1833, it was arguably the target of Seba Smith's satiric work—President Andrew Jackson—who brought about the conditions by which the couple would be separated several more times three years later, between August 1836 and October 1837.

Oakes Smith and her husband were born in the District of Maine, a part of Massachusetts which was not accorded its own statehood until 1820. As with other areas of the growing nation, in the District, banks had made public lands available for sale on credit to encourage development and population growth, first to qualify for statehood, and later to encourage the building of an economic infrastructure (e.g., roads to access the land purchased). Through friends or on his own, Seba Smith was one who invested heavily in the opportunity. Several decades later, when the towns across the region designated as "No. 8" in Piscataquis County became exporters of some of the best slate in the United States, the investment would have made Smith a rich man, but without roads, resident labor, or associated markets to make this possible in 1836, and banks failing or foreclosing on loans across the country in their attempts to survive President Jackson's raid on the Bank of the United States, Smith's investment would remain worthless longer than the finances of a newspaper editor could withstand.

Only Oakes Smith's side of this correspondence has survived, documenting her recovery from the birth of her last child, Edward, sometime in early September 1836, her continued balance of work between her husband's publishing ventures and her domestic responsibilities, and, above all, her repeated attempts to buoy her husband's spirits as his speculations in land northeast of Bangor, Maine, left the family destitute in the wake of the Panic of 1837.

ELIZABETH OAKES SMITH

It is traditional to point out that without Seba Smith's financial failure at this moment in their lives, Elizabeth Oakes Smith may never have emerged as a professional writer. Already the mother of four young sons, by 1837, according to later comments in her autobiography, she had disciplined herself to a life of domesticity, which as the wives of ministers of the period vividly demonstrated, in many cases included far more than the maintenance or support of the home and family. Women's unpaid work varied widely in the transition to market capitalism, but what distinguished such a life specifically was a woman's exclusion—both in body and representation—from "public" circulation. Seba Smith's financial ruin in the Panic made such a life for his wife imprudent, if not impossible. As John Neal so brutally described the situation in one of the many prefaces to Oakes Smith's *The Sinless Child and Other Poems* (1843), Seba Smith

> took it into his head to bait a trap with his own fingers— in other words, to dabble in Eastern lands. The result was just what such a man, if he had a tithe of the shrewdness people credit him for as Major Jack, ought to have foreseen. He was ruined—lock, stock and barrel—horse, foot and dragoons—sinker and line; gave up his paper—or sold out, which—in a losing concern...amounts pretty much to the same thing. Thence to New York went he, bag and baggage—three children and a wife, the most delightful baggage on earth, under tolerable circumstances. There, husband and wife, having entered into copartnership for another term—though the first was forever—are trying to support themselves by their pen.

LETTERS

Portland Thursday August 24th 1836[1]
My dear Husband,

Here you have been gone almost a week, and not one line have I
received from you. It seems a long time, and every enjoyment seems
imperfect without you. Miss Hale says "we are having a very pleasant time, but I wish Mr. Smith were here." Tuesday evening we took
tea at Judge Ware's and spent the time very pleasantly. Harriet staid
all night, and the Judge came home with Francis and myself. Yesterday we called upon Mrs. Warren and Rachael Neal. I never realized before that Rachael was such an exact counterpart to John. She
seemed very glad to see us and gave us a fine [ ]. In the evening we
made use of the remainder of the treat you provided, by having a
few young ladies and Mr. Springer and the Cousins [Banks?]. We
played Blind Man's Buff and should have enjoyed it much except
that I kept all the time thinking of you away down east, exposed and
lonely.

I felt more like weeping than playing. Frances [?] is a lovely
little girl, and we love her better every day. I asked her what I should
say to you and she says tell him I am very sorry that I cant see him
before I go home. We should enjoy ourselves much better if he were
here. Hum, I replied, you don't send love to the Gentleman. O! that
she says, is understood. The children are all well, and very obedient.
Appleton says he can get you a good boat to carry down on the Pond
for $18, and that, he says is cheaper than you can get one any where
else. He is very desirous for you to select a house-lot for us to move
on to, so he can go down there and work to help you. I am perfectly
willing to move this fall, if you can make arrangements to that effect.
Aunt Child will leave tomorrow night. She was disappointed in not
seeing you again.

Harriet sends love to Mr. Smith. I am going to the P.O. this
morning and if I don't find a letter from you I shall be very much
disappointed and anxious. Shall either fear you are sick, or my own

---

[1] Addressed to Seba Smith, Sebec, Maine, 12 ½ cents. Postmarked "Aug
25."

ELIZABETH OAKES SMITH

Eliza (by which I mean the prettiest compliment in the world) is not so attentive as common. Come home soon and see your affectionate and

devoted Wife,
E. O. Smith

Friday[2]
Dear husband,

We all hardly know what to do without Father. Appleton wants to see you very much and wants you to bring him home a young bear. Sidney desires a young bear, tiger, or something else. Little Al had quite a cry this morning for Dear Father. I am sitting up to write this I have been up two hours this morning and half hour now. The baby is one of the best. Captain Mason and wife dined here yesterday, Cousin Ann and a Miss Snow, who is rather brown, by the way, today. When shall I hear from you. I find I cannot write more—my hand wont go

affectionately yours,
E. O. Smith

Thursday Sept 22 1836[3]
Dear husband,

Last night we fastened the doors at dark—so many of the "weaker vessels" and no "Lords of Creation" to protect us, it was best to be cautious. Mrs. Drinkwater spent a part of the evening with us. I was awake a part of the night, and thought of you this morn. Wonder if you did of me?

This morning Alexander [tugged?] from the Steamer a wooden box about half yd square addressed to Seba Smith &c. What do you

---

[2] Postmarked "Sept 21." Mention of Oakes Smith's "sitting up" after the birth of their last child, Edward, dates this letter in the year 1836. Envelope addressed to Seba Smith, Monson, Maine.

[3] Written in pencil, perhaps on a lap desk, this letter is addressed to Seba Smith, Monson, Maine. Oakes Smith is recovering after the birth of Edward, described here as "little chuck."

think it contained? Guess. A live Rattlesnake? No. A loaf of wedding cake for the Editor? No. The splendid Annuals, all silk and gold? No. I shall have to tell. A wheel. A great iron wheel. Phoebus! What a downfall to our expectations! What can it be for? To grind out editorial? After sitting in judgement upon it, I gravely determined to send it to C. Chase, Esq, as it might possibly be a "Token" from the Mt. Desert Humbug. Was that right?

I sat up almost two hours to day.

Little chuck grows like any thing, as Alvin says. We all behave beautifully. I am too tired to write more. Take good care of yourself.

Fondly,

E. O. Smith

[undated][4]
My dear Husband,

I regret very much the melancholy state of your mind, which your letter indicated. I trust it is nothing more than fatigue, and the influence of a rainy day upon your sensitive nerves; still I shall feel anxious until another welcome letter assures me you are not sick. I know your extreme anxiety about your pecuniary matters, and that your disquietude is more on our account than your own. Do not let it be so—do not let those who are dear to each other be a source of uneasiness. We can bear poverty as well now as in times past—and I trust better. For myself, I have really felt as though it would be no trial to me—indeed, it would be nothing, could you survive it cheerfully, and with affections unchanged. I dread it only as it will cause you grief and anxiety, and prevent you from devoting yourself to those pursuits congenial to your taste. But with health, industry and a will to work, we need fear nothing. A good Providence will always befriend us. And should this trial be in store for us, I trust we can bear it patiently, and even arise, made stronger for the trial.

I have had so much to do since you went away, that I have had no time to be sad. Edward S. has been rather sick but is better to

---

[4] Envelope addressed to Seba Smith, Monson, Maine, postmark April 20. The context indicates this was from their correspondence in 1837.

day. But I will give you a record. Saturday was a week long. The children were lonely, and poor little Alvin, wept half a dozen times for dear Father. Sabbath day morning was very beautiful—Chloe went to the school, at nine o'clock, and all the rest to church. In the afternoon, I went with the children in what I thought to be an April shower, but it proved to be a regular rain storm. We read as usual in the evening and retired at ten. Monday evening we took tea at Judge Ware's[5]—had an agreeable time. Charlotte Hale was there. The Judge was very gracious, enquired particularly for you, and said when you returned he should come & spend an evening. Dr. Jackson's Lecture was very interesting and fully attended.[6] His Theory respecting the change of the earth's axis, he explains in a very plausible manner, to say the least. It is in this way, that if an extensive range of mountains were thrown up on one side of the earth, by powerful volcanic action, that side of the earth would preponderate, the equilibrium be destroyed, and the axis be changed. A Deluge likewise would ensue. He made some very good experiments with Carbonic acid gas, which he supposed at one time to have been vastly more abundant than it is at present, which would account for the rapidity of vegetable growth. It was for ages being absorbed in the productions which form our coal basins, and in lime stone. Tuesday Charlotte Hale spent the day with us and Mr. and Mrs. Warren and two children took tea with us. They both desired me to remember them to you when I wrote, and Mr. Warren says he has a visit in store when you return. They went home just after eight. Yesterday was a smashing time for the merchants, Cushman & Phillips, Talford & Drinkwater, and Clark & Brown have all failed others are hourly expected. Judge Ware thinks this is but the commencement of disasters to the mercantile community, & he doubts

---

[5] Ashur Ware (1782–1873) was editor of *The Eastern Argus* in Portland before Smith, from 1817–1820. Appointed to the Federal District Court for the District of Maine in 1822, he served on the bench for forty-four years.

[6] Charles T. Jackson (1805–1880) studied chemistry, mineralogy, and geology at Harvard and in Europe and was appointed state geologist in Maine in the early 1830s, working on the state's geological survey for three years with James T. Hodge.

LETTERS

if it will be essentially better for two years to come. So you see, my dear husband, we shall have plenty of company if we go down.

Ann leaves to night in the boat she looked somewhat blank when I presented her one dollar.

She has been on a steady [ ] ever since you went away making calls. Chloe does very well. Appleton says give my love to Father, and ask him to bring me home a coin from some strange kind of wood or some minerals. The children are very good, obedient and pleasant. Sidney says give my love to Father, and I can't think of anything else—only I wish [you] would bring me a little Bear, or a great bear's foot. I think we shall get along very well in your absence and with little expense. Mr. Springer has just called and says he will let me have a five dollar bill if I need it—but I declined. He asked if I had company to attend me to the Lecture and I told him I proposed taking Appleton.

Do take good care of your health, keep your feet dry, and eat a plenty. Feel no anxiety about us—we do very well—are not at all afraid. Things go on very well.

My head aches violently. But rest will restore me I trust, yet I have rather a busy time of it.

Do write after and tell me where to write.

Your affectionate Wife,

E. O. Smith

Portland 23rd April 1837[7]
My dear Husband,

Your letter of the 18th was duly received and gave me great uneasiness, as its melancholy tenor gave me serious pause for your health. I would not fatigue myself by listening to the senseless tattle and

---

[7] Envelope addressed to "Seba Smith, Elliotsville Maine"—postage written is 18 ¾ cents. Writing in 1886, George Varney described the history of Elliotsville this way: "E. G. Vaughan built a saw-mill on the Little Wilson Stream, and E. T. Bridge built a gristmill on the Wilson. Hoping to hasten settlements thereby, he procured a town incorporation for the township in 1835, giving it his Christian

ELIZABETH OAKES SMITH

foolish quarrels of No. 8, for once I would exercise sufficient indifference to tell them, to "shut up their glab" as Alvin once said. I should hope that the air and exercise of your journey might do you good, but I fear the fare will be rather scant.

I wish you could have ~~made~~ heard the concluding lecture of Dr. Jackson "Geology of Maine." To my mind, it made No. 8 look right up. I saw in it inexhaustible mines of wealth. Mr. Chase's golden calf[8] literally raised on its pedestal of Slate. He stated we are importing Slate, at the rate of $27 a ton? was it (for I was inattentive), when there are immense quantities of it in our own State, of the very best quality, free from pyrites and that might be afforded at $6. About 40 miles to the north west of Bangor commences an extensive range of Slate formation, so easily quarried that with a common chisel and mallet perfect blocks of six feet square can be split out and always of the size required for roofing. He spoke particularly of the slate of Williamsburg, Brownville and Foxcroft. Now don't you think, thus, something might be done with the No. 8. I have half-mind to go to work, and prepare papers, get up a company, hire men, charter a vessel, sell stock, &c, so that when you return you will find yourself perfectly easy, rub your eyes, and behold you are a rich man. But seriously don't you think a summer's work might be done in this way. This don't' appear to me like the Mount Desert humbug.[9] Mr.

---

name. A county road was opened to Monson, school districts established, and a school fund secured by the sale of the reserved lands, but the incorporation proved premature. The inhabitants decreased, and in 1858, in response to their petition, the act of incorporation was repealed; since which time the township has been without an independent civil organization. The population in 1870 was 42. In 1880 it was 55."

[8] A reference to the biblical edict against worshiping idols of material wealth. Although the biblical warning is the basic theme of Oakes Smith's first novel, *Riches without Wings*, the reference here is at least partly ironic. "Mr. Chase" may refer to Samuel Chase, a Portland minister who brought suit against Reuben Ruby for his establishment of a church for black parishioners in Portland in the late 1820s.

[9] Mount Desert was then a crude maritime village north of Portland. The reference indicates another land speculation gone wrong in the 1820s or early '30s. Through the mid-nineteenth century, the island community became known as a

Jackson has been invited, I understand, a great deal in the upper part of the city, and to J. Neal's of course. Yet he only incidentally named the Kennebunk granite; if the quality were as good as it has been represented, don't you think he would have given it more of a <u>puff</u>?

I have received a line from Mansfield & Bigelow in which the[y] desire you to transmit their bill, as they are about changing their business. I have also received a letter from Mrs. Hale. Mr. Waterhouse has sent me one dollar. We get along very well, I assure you, boiled rice and molasses for dinner, hasty pudding for supper, and fried pudding for breakfast. The lb of butter holds out like the widow's oil. If we had no visitors it would be pretty cheap living.

Erastus Brooks I am told is here editing the Advertiser.[10] So says Mr. Springer.[11] He called here a few days since with Mary Bradford [?], but I was engaged and did not see him. I assure you I find a plenty to do notwithstanding our family is small. Edward is very heavy and very restless. The children behave very well, but want to see Father every day. Little Edward will laugh and turn his head whenever I call Father. Fast day and this forenoon I carried all the children to church with me. Alvin behaves very well, and is delighted with his new clothes. Mr. Springer is reporting the trial of Brown for the paper, with all the <u>particulars</u>. I admired his taste. Did I tell you Charles Moody has failed? I believe I have written all the news, but I am not in the way of hearing much, for we are as still here as a mouse in a cheese. Do try to write again and let me know that you are well.

Yours, affectionately and sincerely
Your Wife,
E. O. Smith

---

summer artist community, with painters of the Hudson River School paying local fisherman for "rustic" lodging. Only in the 1880s did Mount Desert become the affluent resort of the financial magnates of the day.

[10] The *Portland Advertiser* was a Whig organ which, under Brooks's editorship, led the campaign for William Henry Harrison's candidacy for president in 1840.

[11] Possibly John S. Springer, naturalist and author of *Forest Life and Forest Trees* (1851).

Portland May 30th 1837[12]
My dear Husband,

I am lonely enough I assure you in your absence. We have had fog and rain and a little sunshine. Tuesday was the finest day we have had for the season. Monday afternoon I went out to attend to a few things, and the children cut up didoes.[13] On my return, they were missing, and I went in pursuit. On nearing the water down on Mayo Street I caught a glimpse of the old washing machine swashing up and down in the water. And there were the two boys enjoying life in high glee, with about twenty noisy little tykes about them. I ordered them and the machine home and it was a pretty tough job to get the great box up hill, and they tried hard to induce me to let them trafic it away in the road, but no, it was carried home. I then gave them their suppers, then a smart whipping and put them to bed. Appleton is a noble boy—I gave him his punishment first, and he, when it came Sidney's turn, begged me to whip him instead of Sidney, for he was most to blame. Nor did he merely offer but begged, and intreated me to do it. Sidney, little scamp, I thought looked pleased at the suggestion, but I thought it best for each to suffer for his own sins. I then asked Appleton if he felt willing to take a part of little Alvin's—he readily consented. I then asked Sidney if he would take the rest—No, I believe not, said the little wag. I've had enough of it. And I don't want any, said Alvin, springing into bed.

This afternoon I attended the Maternal Association. Mr. Lincoln had gone to Boston, and I was obliged, without any preparation, to address the children. I succeeded much better than I anticipated—and I doubt whether any of the "lords of creation" ever had a more attentive audience, and that too for nearly an hour, including some notes which they took.

---

[12] Envelope addressed to Seba Smith, Sebec, Maine, at 12 ½ cents. Sebec is another small village in Piscataquis County in the section referred to as "No. 8."

[13] Mischievous pranks.

LETTERS

We have had no callers except Mr. Springer once—and a few young ladies. I called yesterday with Hepzibah[14] upon her relatives, and had an invitation to take tea on Friday next at Mrs. Hinman's, but declined.

Today a letter was brought from brother Abiel, he feels rather sad at not hearing from you.

Shall you select your location for a house this time? I believe I am quite willing to move, though I sometimes think there might be other situations, equally remote from corrupting influences, with regard to our children, and where the talents, such as they are, imparted to us, might be more usefully exercised. But I yield to your better judgment.

Do take good care of your health and return soon as may be. The children all desire love to dear Father.

Your affectionate wife,
E. O. Smith

PS. a heavy thunder shower came up last night and continued till after nine, so I couldn't get my letter into the office. I fear you will be disappointed and anxious.

Sincerely affectionately yours
E. O. S.

Sabbath day June 4, 1837[15]
My dear Husband,

It is a clear beautiful Sabbath after a night of rain and storms. Last evening we had some very severe thunder showers. The lightning I think was as vivid as I ever beheld it. Oh how I wished you were at home it was so lonely and so dismal. I lost all sense of its grandeur in the feeling of loneliness and terror. Did you have it at No. 8? How the deep thunder must reverberate amongst those ancient forests, with their "everlasting hills." How instantly the imagination would

---

[14] Unidentified. Oakes Smith's elder sister Hepzibah died in 1823.
[15] Addressed to Seba Smith, Sebec, Maine, at 12 ½ cents.

people it with warriors stern, ^{armed} with bow and spear, and the stealthy tread of the old and rightful masters of the soil.

I am willing to break away from the trammels of artificial life and go into the lone wilderness, and methinks we might rear there, another Eden, and bring up our sons to manliness and virtue. You shall be Adam, and I Eve, a little antique to be sure, and our sons shall be all Enochs. So please select our habitation.

I have had a letter from M & Bigelow in which they ask for an extension and renewment of notes, also an answer by return of Mail. I was in a dreadful quandary—but at last mustered courage to drop them a line, telling where you were gone, and desiring them to write to you if necessary, or to me and I would inform you. Did I do right? I did not dare consult anyone for the letter appeared confidential, &c.

Times are hard as ever, and it is quite sickly here—the throat distemper prevails—but thanks to a good Providence we are all well.

Sarah Dorrance expired on Friday last, was taken sick on Tuesday.

We have had no callers, for it has rained almost all the time since you went away.

How do you get along down there? Mr. Mansfield says his stumpage won't yield him "one mill." I do think we had better go to a farm, or something of the kind, for our boys need a tighter rein than I can always carry. I have engaged me a bonnet, which will cost me about $3, but I have had a great many compunctions of conscience about it, for I am afraid it is more than we can afford.

Do you have enough to eat, dear? If you have I fear it is [dry?] stuff. How do you pass your time? Do you find anything to read? Try to sit down on a stump and write me a piece of poetry—Fourteen years ago, such a request would have inspired your muse, and why not now?

Our friends are all well here except poor Mrs. Chase, she is very low, and her recovery rather doubtful. She has had an attack of pleurisy.

This afternoon at church a young man of not more than 25, came in and sat a half hour or so, he was insane occasioned by the loss of property in this pressure.

I cannot see to write more Do come home soon.

Your affectionate & faithful
Wife
E. O. Smith

Wednesday October [12,] 1837.[16]
My dear Husband,

I have just returned from the P.O. where I found, not a letter from you as I expected, but a notice from Mr. Clapp desiring us to vacate the house thirty days from sale. We have had some very cold weather since you left, and a little shower of rain last night, when it cleared off and left as beautiful a sky as I ever beheld. Today it is warm as June, and a most lovely day. We are lonely enough I assure you. Scarcely a soul has looked in upon us since you left. This afternoon I ran into Mrs. Gerrish's a few minutes and she told me she should send for us tomorrow or next day. I told her you were gone and she seemed very much disappointed. Have you ordered the old house to be shingled and the "bed-rooms" to be fixed for us? I wish we could know what we are to do, for this suspense is irksome enough. I believe our neighbors will really regret to part with us—and if we are obliged to leave Portland, it is pleasant to feel we shall leave many friends, and I trust no enemies.

I wrote a note to Franklin desiring an order on some money, and he gave me an order to the amount of $6.73 on G. [ ] which of course I have presented—you know my promptitude. The children learn their lessons every day and behave very well. Eddy grows as fat as a porpoise, and is every day astonishing us with some fresh proof of intelligence, but as to walking—he won't risque the bumps. As I came home from up in town today, I heard the little boys all in great commotion calling to each other and looking upon Alvin with

---

[16] Envelope addressed to Seba Smith, Sebec, Maine, postmarked "Oct 12."

something of the kind of admiration they would behold a young tiger, or a half tamed bear. "Come here" I heard one say, "come see this little Alvin Smith, he's been giving David Jones a real flogging, and made him scream like everything." In truth Alvin did look somewhat formidable rubbing his hands and his head thrown back. I called him into the house and talked with him. "Why didn't David flog you, when you flogged him?" "Flogg me—I gueth he couldn't do it, emphasizing the <u>do it</u>."

We sit in the chamber, go to bed early and rise early. I shall look for you next Tuesday. Do take good care of your health, and make such arrangements as you may think best as to moving this fall, and I shall be satisfied. Present my respects to Mrs. Greeley and family.

Your affectionate wife
E. O. Smith

Saturday Oct 15th 1837[17]
Dear Husband,

I know you were thinking of me last night, for I went to sleep at half past twelve feeling as if your head were resting on the same pillow— if you were not with me, bodily, I am sure you were spiritually, for never was a countenance more palpably visable. I got frightened a little too, and half grew superstitious, but suspect what caused me so much trouble at the witching hour of night was nothing less or more than a poor fly in the toils of a spider. But never were groans more distinctly audible, or more unearthly, and Mrs. Radcliffe-like than those that fell upon my ear—I went to every child and into all the chambers, but the sleep of each inmate was sweet and undisturbed—I began to feel an indescribable crawling and soon jumped into bed, first casting a wary glance into every half-obscured recess to be quite sure no sheeted ghost was there. Strange how the crude superstitions of childhood will sometimes revive, and make us children again.

---

[17] Addressed to Seba Smith, Bangor, Maine, with postage marked 12 ½ cents.

Do you know I sometimes think you will return and start for the West this winter, and abandon No 8 in toto? It must be dreadful cold down there now for the weather is very winter like here—yesterday morning we had a flight of snow—it looked so dismally that I could have wept—and the cold is worse to me than ever—I don't know what to think of my lungs. I have coughed nearly half the night ever since you left—yet I am not sick, I even think I gain flesh—but this cough is very troublesome to night. Mrs. Drinkwater advises me to take Laudanum.

When I went to the P.O. the other ~~night~~ day I took a one cent letter and offered a twenty five cent piece to pay with—they couldn't change it, and asked if I had not a cent, no said I, with one of my best smiles, except a Van Buren cent[18] which I want to keep—I wish you could have seen the vinegar aspect—you would have thought I had spoken high treason.

We are all very well, and quiet as church mice. I hope you will return soon—I shall look for you on Tuesday next. Take good care of yourself, and come as soon as possible.

Your devoted Wife,
E. O. Smith

---

[18] Democrat Martin Van Buren had been inaugurated as president earlier in 1837.

POETRY

"The Sinless Child" (1842–45)

Elizabeth Oakes Smith's move from a position as a valuable but unpaid contributor and editorial stand-in for her husband's publishing ventures to her role as a wage-earning professional writer in the literary marketplace of the 1840s is yet to be clearly documented, but the publication of her narrative poem "The Sinless Child" in *The Southern Literary Messenger* in its January and February issues of 1842[1] seems to mark the beginning of her full emergence as an "author"—a name and image circulating in the marketplace as a saleable commodity. As John Keese noted eighteen months later in his preface to the first collection of her poetry, he had "long known" Oakes Smith and even published her work previously,[2] but "it was only the frequent demand for the 'The Sinless Child' at his publishing office, under the presumption that it had already assumed the form of a book" that led him first to "procure a copy" and, finding none available, produce one himself.[3] While he would have liked to take credit for the "literary discernment" that ensured his success as a publisher, he admitted, here he was only following a market that had elevated his townswoman to popularity.

Critical notices of "The Sinless Child" set the tone for a decade of responses to Oakes Smith's writing, approving those qualities expected in women's writing in which the "mind and the affections are harmoniously...blended," or where "worthy utterance" is given to "sentiments of faith and duty," and quietly passing over passages that challenged gendered stereotypes pertaining to either the author or her work. Indeed, remarked one reviewer after the work's publication in book form in 1843, "what extent of attainment in a female mind can ever compensate for the lack of those sympathetic qualities

---

[1] *The Southern Literary Messenger* (January 1842): 86–89 and (February 1842): 121–29.

[2] See Keese, The Poets of America Illustrated by Their Painters, volume 2 (1840).

[3] *The Sinless Child and Other Poems*, ed. John Keese (New York: Wiley and Putnam, 1843) appeared in July 1843, with prefatory remarks by Keese, John Neal, and Henry Tuckerman.

in which consists the charm of the sex?"[4] In "editorial remarks" inserted over the publication of the first two parts of the poem in January 1842, editor of the *The Southern Literary Messenger* Thomas White called Oakes Smith "a lady of great literary merits" and the work an "exquisite little gem indeed," adding that he looked forward to "announcing the services of Mrs. Smith...as a regular contributor to our pages." The Boston *Notion* was the first to provide a proper review, comparing Oakes Smith's work to that of Wordsworth while withholding the male poet's capacity for invention, calling the poem "an unconscious eulogy on the purity of her mind," and politely excusing its lack of "brilliant points of expression or imagery" by pointing out how it demanded "more in its composition than mere imagination or intellect could furnish." For his part, Edgar Allan Poe respected Oakes Smith's effort enough to point out the poem's formal imperfections (as he did with any work he deemed worthy of notice), calling attention to what he considered the poor choice to include narrative summaries for each part that disturbed the "unity" of the whole, and the inclusion of "stories" shared between mother and daughter that, without "any natural connexion with the true theme," strike the reader as obviously "written long before the narrative was projected" and thus detrimental to any unified effect. But even if its conception was in many cases "superior to its execution," Poe concluded, "the originality of [the poem] would cover a multitude of greater defects than Mrs. Smith ever committed, and must forever entitle it to the admiration and respect of every competent critic."

For her part, it seems Oakes Smith was content at this early stage to accept the reputation male publishers and editors were willing to construct for her as long as the demand for her work grew steadily, which it did, garnering the notice of anthologist and current editor of *Graham's Magazine*, Rufus Griswold, who began to solicit her work for nearly every issue. "As to the manner in which

---

[4] Henry Tuckerman, in comments reprinted from *Graham's Magazine* 22 (April 1843) in the preface to *The Sinless Child and Other Poems*, ed. John Keese, xxvii–xxxii.

the poems are presented to the public" she admitted to Griswold, "that was no arrangement of mine. My good friends exercised their own judgement."[5] In this explanation, she likely had in mind John Neal's prefatory comments in Keese's volume, reprinted from an earlier review written soon after her arrival in New York with her husband, which, by emphasizing her eagerness and ability to help recover the fortune of her husband, emasculated him as a hapless and naïve businessman. Adding insult to injury was Neal's surmise that "one wouldn't much wonder perhaps to find the character of Major Downing himself, the joint product of husband and wife." But even if these comments were considered "not in the best taste," she wrote to Griswold, Neal "is a generous-hearted man, and somewhat popular.... [B]eside all this I did not feel prepared to <u>have my life taken</u>, yet a while."[6]

In the modern era, Oakes Smith's first and longest narrative poem has received the most scholarly attention of any of her works. On the surface, it seems to participate in a domestic sentimental tradition that empowered women only within patriarchal limits, providing them leadership over the "spiritual" destiny of society from within the home, while men, working in the public sphere, were held responsible (in theory) for the material needs of the family day to day. As literary historian Jane Tompkins has noted, understanding such gender roles as anything but the disenfranchisement and trivialization of women's lives requires us to reimagine a society for which eternal destiny (salvation or damnation) was very real— where men's political wrangling and economic maneuvering as agents of change looked silly in comparison to religious conversion or, in more secular terms, "a change of heart." Even if the text Tompkins is well known for historicizing in these terms is not "The Sinless Child" but *Uncle Tom's Cabin*, published eight years later in 1850, the massive popularity of the latter work, selling millions of copies in its first year, is a testament to the durability of the notion

---

[5] Elizabeth Oakes Smith to Rufus Griswold, undated, Gratz American Poets Collection, Case 7, Box 9, Historical Society of Pennsylvania.

[6] Ibid.

of "sentimental power" decades beyond the vaunted Age of Reason and the supposed secularization of American culture at mid-century. It follows that in 1842, it was not just Oakes Smith's East Coast audience who recognized the "work" of Eva, the sinless child in Oakes Smith's poem, but likely then-Ohio resident Harriet Beecher Stowe, whose character Little Eva, in her blockbuster novel, recalls Oakes Smith's character distinctly—a child doing the teaching instead of the parent,[7] modeling Christ's sacrifice in dying to save the unbelieving from their secular blindness. Many readers in Oakes Smith's time read "The Sinless Child" in these religious terms—according to a logic which, while providing the female poet with special authority, limited that authority to the spiritual realm.[8]

It is notable, however, that Oakes Smith did not merely choose a female child as her protagonist. However "sinless" she is, Eva is also a child uniquely aligned with and inspired by nature. In this regard, some scholars have argued that beyond the poem's recognizable appeal to conservative readers looking for religious allegory, "The Sinless Child" also participates in what was then the relatively new and radical philosophical tradition of transcendentalism.[9] Equally poised as a philosophical position and a political critique of the shallow materialism of the age, as Margaret Fuller demonstrated in *Woman in the Nineteenth Century* (1845), the transcendentalist view did not limit the expanded possibilities it made available for

---

[7] The role of child as teacher of the parent is explored in Oakes Smith's earlier work, notably in poems such as "Ministry of Childhood," *The Ladies' Companion* 10 (May 1839): 269.

[8] In "Elizabeth Oakes Smith's Unspeakable Eloquence," Eliza Richards argues that in its search for a ground of authority appropriate to women, Oakes Smith's poem "embarks on the pedagogic enterprise of introducing the public to a model of inventive female authorship by showcasing that model as a divine intervention," thereby "undermining [her own] claim to originary powers." See *Gender and the Poetics of Reception in Poe's Circle* (London: Cambridge University Press, 2004): 158 and passim.

[9] See, for example, Mary Louise Kete, "Gender Valences of Transcendentalism: The Pursuit of Idealism in Elizabeth Oakes-Smith's 'The Sinless Child,'" *Separate Spheres No More*, ed. Monika Elbert (Tuscaloosa: University of Alabama Press, 2000).

POETRY

our conceptions of selfhood to men or women. Indeed, as Ralph Waldo Emerson argued in *Nature* (1836), those trying to access the truth of self and their relation to world needed precisely to transcend the limits of the social roles they were taught to occupy:

> To speak truly, few adult persons can see nature. Most persons do not see the sun. At least they have a very superficial seeing. The sun illuminates only the eye of the man, but shines into the eye and the heart of the child. The lover of nature is he whose inward and outward senses are still truly adjusted to each other; who has retained the spirit of infancy even into the era of manhood.[10]

Without a father, Oakes Smith's Eva is "sinless" in that she has not fallen into a limited vision of herself and her social role as prescribed by men, as her mother clearly has, and much of the poem is dedicated to the child's attempt to impart to her remaining parent the lessons nature has freely taught her.[11] Indeed, the most powerful readings of the poem over the past two decades have suggested that

---

[10] Ralph Waldo Emerson, *Nature* (Boston: James Munroe and Company, 1836) 11. Leslie Ginsberg elaborates on the legal and political significance of the child in Oakes Smith's work in "Minority/Majority: Childhood Studies and Antebellum American Literature," *The Children's Table: Childhood Studies and the Humanities* (Athens: University Georgia Press, 2013): 105–23. Since it is during the early to mid-nineteenth century that the child becomes the "discursive mark" of inequitable power relations, Ginsberg argues, the ranking of women and slaves as of comparable legal status under patriarchy brings new meaning to the literary presence of "the child" as character and intended reader in Oakes Smith's first writings in the early 1830s through the 1840s, where "minors" reveal to their elders the limits of their social and political vision.

[11] In terms that might evidence Oakes Smith's reading of Emerson's 1836 essay, these lessons constitute a literal if not "superficial" seeing, comprising every dimension of nature argued by Emerson in his work: well beyond her mother's understanding of nature as a *commodity* to provide for material needs, Eva delights from the time of infancy in nature's *beauty* and gradually finds in it a new *language*. Over time, she learns from nature to value the unseen, a *discipline* that trains her for duties beyond any age and gender-appropriate chores her mother can imagine—the redemption of mankind in the person of Albert Linne. Completing her mission of awakening others to truth and beauty, Eva's *spirit* can transcend the material world entirely.

ELIZABETH OAKES SMITH

by implying a creative subjectivity behind the poem's child-heroine, "The Sinless Child" might lay claim to the liberal humanist subjectivity legally and politically denied to women of the time.[12]

The lingering question for many critics, however, is whether Oakes Smith's mid-nineteenth-century readers (male or female) were ready to acknowledge a woman's specifically *creative* role—or if the identity of woman poet herself was fated to be absorbed into her role as a spiritual medium, the uncorrupted but disembodied voice of a child, or even the transcendent truth of nature passed through the alembic of a woman's mind *for the betterment of men*.[13] That is, if Eva, as Oakes Smith's "original" creation, is invoked not to resist her world, but only to quietly disappear, indeed, Nina Baym's early feminist description of the poem as a political "dead end" would be more apt. As Eliza Richards has pointed out, however, though notable as Oakes Smith's only extended narrative poem, and one for which she quickly achieved the status of a celebrity in New York society, "The Sinless Child," is an early work that we isolate at the risk of reducing Oakes Smith's contributions to the poetic tradition specifically[14] and to the achievement of political

---

[12] See Elissa Zellinger, "Elizabeth Oakes Smith's Lyrical Activism" in *Lyrical Strains: Liberalism and Women's Poetry in Nineteenth-Century America* (Chapel Hill: University of North Carolina Press, 2020) 62–97.

[13] Eliza Richards's work cited above is the most extensive and detailed of any addressing the poetics of Elizabeth Oakes Smith, featuring close readings of not only "The Sinless Child" (often the limit of studies on Oakes Smith's poetry) but also a succession of Oakes Smith's poetry from succeeding decades, published and unpublished. The phrase "unspeakable eloquence," taken from Oakes Smith's remarks on Margaret Fuller, but fitting for both women's works, expresses Richards's strong argument for the hard limits of the woman writer's individual voice and effect in a nineteenth-century culture for which publicly authorized "poetic genius" was perceived (as Richards demonstrates, even by women writers themselves) as an exclusively masculine trait. As noted above, John Neal seems to have been one of Oakes Smith's contemporaries, at least, who "didn't get the memo," ascribing to his protégée a share of creativity and subjectivity equal to that of her husband.

[14] The bibliography of Oakes Smith's work in this genre is far from complete, but a broader view of Oakes Smith's career as a poet is already available in Eliza Richard's work, along with Cheryl Walker's *American Women Poets of the*

POETRY

voice for women more generally. More recently, Rebecca Jaroff has even suggested that in neglecting the mysterious gothic stories of violence and betrayal narrated between mother and child in parts IV and V (still following Poe's assessment of the way they only "intrude" on the unity of Eva's story), most modern readings of "The Sinless Child" idealize a poem that purposely grounded itself (and its narrative voice) with references to the real world Oakes Smith would address more and more directly as her career progressed.[15] Revealing in this first major effort mostly evidence of Oakes Smith's accommodation of popular forms and ideas, we should keep foremost in mind the identity she quite consciously left in reserve—the life she preferred not to be "taken yet awhile."

A Note on the Text

Between its first publication in *The Southern Literary Messenger* in 1842 (here designated *SLM*) and its last in 1845, Oakes Smith had two opportunities to revise her poem, designated here as *SC* (*The Sinless Child and Other Poems*, 1843) and *PW* (*The Poetical Writings of Elizabeth Oakes Smith*, 1845). The later version is supplied here, with notes to major changes made from earlier versions (e.g., addition or deletion of whole stanzas or lines). A full comparative edition, setting each text side by side in landscape format, is available on the Oakes Smith website.[16]

Nineteenth Century: An Anthology, and her introduction to Oakes Smith in her description of a "composite" biography of the female poet of the period in *The Nightingale's Burden: Women Poets and American Culture before 1900*.

[15] Jaroff's "To Understand the Hidden Things: Uncovering the Gothic, Recovering the Aesthetic, in Elizabeth Oakes Smith's 'The Sinless Child'" (2013) is the only work to date that has addressed the gothic elements of Oakes Smith's poem in detail.

[16] Minor changes, including changes to individual words and formatting, can be traced in Rebecca Gawo's comparative "master" transcript of Oakes Smith's poem on the Oakes Smith website: https://static1.squarespace. com/static/5422a3cee4b0ef23d87b 5310/t/62acbc1c5f67765488334b4e/1655487 517439/TSC+Master—Comparative.pdf .

"THE SINLESS CHILD"

"I say unto you, that in heaven their angels do always behold the face of my Father, which is in Heaven."
—Matthew, xviii.10.[1]

INSCRIPTION

SWEET EVA! shall I send thee forth, to other
    hearts to speak?
With all thy timidness and love, companionship
    to seek?
Send thee with all thy abstract ways, thy more
    than earthly tone—
An exile, dearest, send thee forth, thou, who art
    all mine own!

Thou art my spirit's cherished dream, its pure
    ideal birth;
And thou hast nestled in my heart, with love
    that's not of earth.
Alas! for I have failed, methinks, thy mystic life
    to trace;
Thy holiness of thought and soul, thy wild enchanting grace.

---

[1] This epigram is included in *PW* only.

THE

POETICAL WRITINGS

OF

ELIZABETH OAKES SMITH.

FIRST COMPLETE EDITION.

NEW YORK:

J. S. REDFIELD, CLINTON HALL.

1845.

Title page of *The Political Writings of Elizabeth Oakes Smith.*
Courtesy Albert and Shirley Small Special Collections Library, University of Virginia

POETRY

Thou dwellest still within my heart, thy beauty
    all unsung;
Like bells that wake the village ear, by echo
    sweeter rung;
And as thy graces one by one upon my fancy steal,
There lingereth yet another grace the soul alone
    can feel.[2]
With thee I've wandered, cherished one, at
    twilight's dreamy hour,
To learn the language of the bird, the mystery
    of the flower;
And gloomy must that sorrow be, which thou
    couldst not dispel,
As thoughtfully we loitered on by stream or shel-
    tered dell.

Thou fond Ideal! vital made, the trusting, earn-
    est, true;
Who fostered sacred, undefiled, my hearts pure,
    youthful dew;
Thou woman-soul, all tender, meek, thou wilt
    not leave me now
To bear alone the weary thoughts that stamp an
    aching brow![3]
Yet go! I may not say farewell, for thou wilt
    not forsake,
Thou'lt linger, Eva, wilt thou not, all hallowed
    thoughts to wake?
Then go; and speak to kindred hearts in purity
    and truth;
And win the spirit back again, to Love, and
    Peace, and Youth.

---

[2] The first half of this stanza was added to *PW*.

[3] The first four lines of this stanza were added to the text of *SC* and retained
in *PW*.

PART I

EVA, a simple cottage maiden, given to the world in the widowhood of one parent, and the angelic existence of the other, like a bud developed amid the sad sweet sunshine of autumn, when its sister-flowers are all sleeping, is found from her birth to be as meek and gentle as are those pale flowers that look imploringly upon us, blooming as they do apart from the season destined for their existence, and when those that should hold tender companionship with them have ceased to be. She is gifted with the power of interpreting much of the beautiful mysteries of our earth. The delicate penciling found upon the petals of the flowers, she finds full of gentle wisdom, as well as beauty. The song of the bird is not merely the gushing forth of a nature too full of blessedness to be silent, but she finds it responsive to the great harp of the universe, whose every tone is wisdom and goodness. The humblest plant, the simplest insect, is each alive with truth. More than this, she beholds a divine agency in all things, carrying on the great purposes of love and wisdom by the aid of innumerable happy spirits, each delighting in the part assigned to it. She sees the world, not merely with mortal eyes, but looks within to the pure internal life, of which the outward is but a type. Her mother, endowed with ordinary perceptions, fails to understand the pure spiritual character of her daughter, but feels daily the truthfulness and purity of her life. The neighbors, too, feel that Eva is unlike her sex only in greater truth and elevation.

WHILOM ago, in lowly life,
Young Eva lived and smiled,
A fair-haired girl, of wondrous truth,
And blameless from a child.
Gentle she was, and full of love,
With voice exceeding sweet,
And eyes of dove-like tenderness,
Where joy and sadness meet.

No Father's lip her brow had kissed,

Or breathed for her a prayer;
The widowed breast on which she slept,
Was full of doubt and care;
And oft was Eva's little cheek
Heaved by her mother's sigh—
And oft the widow shrunk in fear
From her sweet baby's eye,

For she would lift her pillowed head
To look within her face,
With something of reproachfulness,
As well as infant grace,—
A trembling lip, an earnest eye,
Half smiling, half in tears,
As she would seek to comprehend
The secret of her fears.

Her ways were gentle while a babe,
With calm and tranquil eye,
That turned instinctively to seek
The blueness of the sky.
A holy smile was on her lip
Whenever sleep was there,
She slept, as sleeps the blossom, hushed
Amid the silent air.

And ere she left with tottling steps
The low-roofed cottage door,
The beetle and the cricket loved
The young child on the floor;
And every insect dwelt secure
Where little Eva played;
And piped for her its blithest song
When she in greenwood strayed;

With wing of gauze and mailèd coat
They gathered round her feet,
Rejoiced, as are all gladsome things,
A truthful soul to greet.
They taught her infant lips to sing
With them a hymn of praise,
The song that in the woods is heard,
Through the long summer days.

And everywhere the child was traced
By snatches of wild song,
That marked her feet along the vale,
Or hill-side, fleet and strong.
She knew the haunts of every bird—
Where bloomed the sheltered flower,
So sheltered, that the searching frost
Might scarcely find its bower.

No loneliness young Eva knew,
Though playmates she had none;
Such·sweet companionship was hers,
She could not be alone;
For everything in earth or sky
Caressed the little child,
The joyous bird upon the wing,
The blossom in the wild:

Much dwelt she on the green hill-side,
And under forest tree;
Beside the running, babbling brook,
Where lithe trout sported free—
She saw them dart, like stringed gems,
Where the tangled roots were deep,
And learned that love for evermore
The heart will joyful keep.

She loved all simple flowers that spring
In grove or sun-lit dell,
And of each streak and varied hue,
Would pretty meanings tell.
For her a language was impressed
On every leaf that grew,
And lines revealing brighter worlds
That seraph fingers drew.

The opening bud that lightly swung
Upon the dewy air,
Moved in its very sportiveness
Beneath angelic care;
She saw that pearly fingers oped
Each curved and painted leaf,
And where the canker-worm had been
Were looks of angel grief.[4]

Each tiny leaf became a scroll
Inscribed with holy truth,
A lesson that around the heart
Should keep the dew of youth;
Bright missals from angelic throngs
In every by-way left,
How were the earth of glory shorn,
Were it of flowers bereft!

They tremble on the Alpine height;
The fissured rock they press;
The desert wild, with heat and sand,
Shares too, their blessedness,
And wheresoe'er the weary heart
Turns in its dim despair,

---

[4] This stanza appeared above the previous stanza in *SLM*, moved here in *SC*
and *PW*.

ELIZABETH OAKES SMITH

The meek-eyed blossom upward looks
Inviting it to prayer.

The widow's cot was rude and low,
The sloping roof, moss-grown;
And it would seem its quietude
To every bird were known,
The winding vine its tendrils wove
Round roof and oaken door,
And by the flickering light, the leaves
Were painted on the floor.

No noxious reptile ever there
A kindred being sought,
The good and beautiful alone
Delighted in the spot.
The very winds were hushed to peace
Within the quiet dell,
Or murmured through the rustling bough
Like breathings of a shell.

The red-breast sang from sheltering tree,
Gay blossoms clustered round,
And one small brook came dancing by,
With its sweet tinkling sound.
Staining the far-off meadow green
It leaped a rocky dell
And resting by the cottage door,
In liquid music fell.

Upon its breast white lilies slept,
Of pure and wax-like hue,
And brilliant flowers upon the marge
Luxuriantly grew.
They were of rare and changeless birth,
Nor needed toil nor care;

And many marvelled earth could yield
Aught so exceeding fair.

Young Eva said, all noisome weeds
Would pass from earth away,
When virtue in the human heart
Held its predestined sway;
Exalted thoughts were alway hers,
Some deemed them strange and wild;
And hence in all the hamlets round,
Her name of SINLESS CHILD.

Her mother said that Eva's lips
Had never falsehood known;
No angry word had ever marred
The music of their tone.
And truth spake out in every line
Of her fair tranquil face,
Where Love and Peace, twin-dwelling pair,
Had found a resting-place.

She felt the freedom and the light
The pure in heart may know—
Whose blessed privilege it is
To walk with God below;
Who see a hidden beauty traced,
That others may not see,
Who feel a life within the heart,
And love and mystery.

PART II

THE widow, accustomed to forms, and content with the faith in
which she has been reared, a faith which is habitual, rather than
earnest and soul-requiring, leaves Eva to learn the wants and

ELIZABETH OAKES SMITH

tendencies of the soul, by observing the harmony and beauty of the external world. Even from infancy she seems to have penetrated the spiritual through the material; to have beheld the heavenly, not through a glass darkly, but face to face, by means of that singleness and truth, that look within the veil.[5] To the pure in heart alone is the promise, "They shall see God."

UNTIRING all the weary day
The widow toiled with care,
And scarcely cleared her furrowed brow
When came the hour of prayer;
The voices, that on every side,
The prisoned soul call forth,
And bid it in its freedom walk,
Rejoicing in the earth;

Fall idly on a deafened ear,
A heart untaught to thrill
When music gusheth from the bird,
Or from the crystal rill;
She moves unheeding by the flower
With its ministry of love,
And feels no sweet companionship,
With silent stars above.

Alas! that round the human soul
The cords of earth should bind,
That they should bind in darkness down
The light—discerning mind—
That all its freshness, freedom, gone,
Its destiny forgot,

---

[5] Corinthians 13:12: "For now we see through a glass, darkly; but then face to face: now I know in part; but then shall I know even as also I am known." This and all subsequent references to biblical verses are to the King James Bible.

POETRY

It should, in gloomy discontent,
Bewail its bitter lot.

But Eva, while she turned the wheel,
Or toiled in homely guise,
With buoyant life was all abroad,
Beneath the pleasant skies;
And sang all day from lightsome heart,
From joy that in her dwelt,
That evermore the soul is free,
To go where joy is felt.

All lowly and familiar things
In earth, or air, or sky,
A lesson brought to Eva's mind
Of import deep and high;
She learned, from blossom in the wild,
From bird upon the wing,
From silence and the midnight stars,
Truth dwells in everything.

The careless winds that round her played
Brought voices to her ear,
But Eva, pure in thought and soul,
Dreamed never once of fear—
The whispered words of angel lips
She heard in forest wild,
And many a holy spell they wrought,
About the Sinless Child.

And much she loved the forest walk,
Where round the shadows fell,
The solitude of mountain height,
Or green and lovely dell;
The brook dispensing verdure round,
And singing on its way,

69

Now coyly hid in fringe of green,
Now wild in sparkling play.

She early marked the butterfly,
That gay, mysterious thing,
That, bursting from its prison-house
Appeared on golden wing;
It had no voice to speak delight,
Yet on the floweret's breast,
She saw it mute and motionless,
In long, long rapture rest.

She said, that while the little shroud
Beneath the casement hung,
A kindly spirit lingered near,
As dimly there it swung;
That music sweet and low was heard
To hail the perfect life,
And Eva felt that insect strange
With wondrous truth was rife.

It crawled no more a sluggish thing
Upon the lowly earth;
A brief, brief sleep, and then she saw
A new and radiant birth;
And thus she learned without a doubt,
That man from death would rise,
As did the butterfly on wings,
To claim its native skies.

The rainbow, bending o'er the storm,
A beauteous language told;
For angels, twined with loving arms,
She plainly might behold,
And in their glorious robes they bent
To earth in wondrous love,

POETRY

As they would lure the human soul
To brighter things above.

The bird would leave the rocking branch
Upon her hand to sing,
And upward turn its fearless eye
And plume its glossy wing,
And Eva listened to its song,
Till all the sense concealed
In that deep gushing forth of joy,
Became to her revealed.

And when the bird a nest would build,
A spirit from above
Directed all the pretty work,
And filled its heart with love.
And she within the nest would peep
The colored eggs to see,
But never touch the dainty things,
For a thoughtful child was she.

Much Eva loved the twilight hour,
When shadows gather round,
And softer sings the little bird,
And insect from the ground;
She felt that this within the heart
Must be the hour of prayer,
For earth in its deep quietude
Did own its Maker there.

The still moon in the saffron sky
Hung out her silver thread,
And the bannered clouds in gorgeous folds
A mantle round her spread.
The gentle stars came smiling out
Upon the brilliant sky,

ELIZABETH OAKES SMITH

That looked a meet and glorious dome,
For worship pure and high;

And Eva lingered, though the gloom
Had deepened into shade;
And many thought that spirits came
To teach the Sinless Maid,
For oft her mother sought the child
Amid the forest glade,
And marvelled that in darksome glen,
So tranquilly she stayed.

For every jagged limb to her
A shadowy semblance hath,
Of spectres and distorted shapes,
That frown upon her path,
And mock her with their hideous eyes;
For when the soul is blind
To freedom, truth, and inward light,
Vague fears debase the mind:

But Eva like a dreamer waked,
Looked off upon the hill,
And murmured words of strange, sweet sound,
As if there lingered still
Ethereal forms with whom she talked,
Unseen by all beside;
And she, with earnest looks, besought
The vision to abide.

POETRY

'Oh Mother! Mother! do not speak,[6]
Or all will pass away,
The spirits leave the green-hill side,
Where light the breezes play;
They sport no more by ringing brook,
With daisy dreaming by;
Nor float upon the fleecy cloud
That steals along the sky.

It grieves me much they never will
A human look abide,
But veil themselves in silver mist
By vale or mountain side.
I feel their presence round me still,
Though none to sight appear;
I feel the motion of their wings,
Their whispered language hear.

With silvery robe, and wings outspread,
They passed me even now;
And gems and starry diadem
Decked every radiant brow.
Intent were each on some kind work
Of pity or of love,

---

[6] Demonstrating "typographical errors" that Poe noted "very often mar the sense" of Oakes Smith's work, here and in several passages that follow, Oakes Smith, her editor, and the printer of the volume appear to have omitted close quotations that would more clearly separate the voices of Eva, her mother, the lyric speaker, and the poet herself. This edition retains the feel of Oakes Smith's final edition of the poem and even what may be an extension of her intention, as several critics have noted, to blur the boundaries between her own motivations, capacities, and even liabilities and those of the figures in her poem. For Elissa Zellinger's discussion of Oakes Smith's strategy, see *Lyrical Strains* (79–88) and *passim*.

ELIZABETH OAKES SMITH

Dispensing from their healing wings
The blessings from above.[7]

With downy pinion they enfold
The heart surcharged with wo,
And fan with balmy wing the eye
Whence floods of sorrow flow;
They bear, in golden censers up,
That sacred gift, a tear;
By which is registered the griefs,
Hearts may have suffered here.[8]

No inward pang, no yearning love
Is lost to human hearts,
No anguish that the spirit feels,
When bright-winged hope departs;
Though in the mystery of life
Discordant powers prevail;
That life itself be weariness,
And sympathy may fail:

Yet all becomes a discipline,
To lure us to the sky;
And angels bear the good it brings
With fostering care on high;
Though human hearts may weary grow,

---

[7] In *SLM* and *SC*, the following stanza followed, later deleted in *PW*:
For angels fold their wings of love
Round hearts surcharged with woe,
And fan with balmy wing the eye
Whence tears of sorrow flow;
And bear, in golden censors up,
That sacred thing, a tear;
By which is registered the griefs,
Hearts may have suffered here.

[8] This stanza and the subsequent three were added to *SC* and retained in *PW*.

POETRY

And sink to toil-spent sleep,
And we are left in solitude,
And agony to weep:

Yet *they* with ministering zeal,
The cup of healing bring,
And bear our love and gratitude
Away, on heavenward wing;
And thus the inner life is wrought,
The blending earth and heaven;
The love more earnest in its glow,
Where much has been forgiven!

I would, dear Mother, thou couldst see
Within this darksome veil,
That hides the spirit-land from thee,
And makes our sunlight pale;
The toil of earth, its doubt and care,
Would trifles seem to thee;
Repose would rest upon thy soul,
And holy mystery.

Thou wouldst behold protecting care
To shield thee on thy way,
And ministers to guard thy feet,
Lest erring, they should stray;
And order, sympathy, and love,
Would open to thine eye,
From simplest creatures of the earth
To seraph throned on high.

E'en now I marked a radiant throng,
On soft wing sailing by,
To soothe with hope the trembling heart,
And cheer the dying eye;
They smiling passed the lesser sprites,

Each on his work intent;
And love and holy joy I saw
In every face were blent.

The tender violets bent in smiles
To elves that sported nigh,
Tossing the drops of fragrant dew
To scent the evening sky.
They kissed the rose in love and mirth,
And its petals fairer grew,
A shower of pearly dust they brought,
And o'er the lily threw.

A host flew round the mowing field,
And they were showering down
The cooling spray on the early grass
Like diamonds o'er it thrown;
They gemmed each leaf and quivering spear
With pearls of liquid dew,
And bathed the stately forest tree,
Till his robe was fresh and new.

I saw a meek-eyed creature curve
The tulip's painted cup,
And bless with one soft kiss the urn,
Then fold its petals up.
A finger rocked the young bird's nest
As high on a branch it hung.
And the gleaming night-dew rattled down
Where the old dry leaf was flung.

Each and all, as its task is done,
Soars up with a joyous eye,
Bearing aloft some treasured gift—
An offering ON HIGH.
They bear the breath of the odorous flower,

The sound of the bright-sea shell;
And thus they add to the holy joys
Of the home where spirits dwell.

PART III

THE grace of the soul is sure to impart expressiveness and beauty
to the face. It must beam through its external veil; and daily, as the
material becomes subordinate to the spiritual, will its transparency
increase. Eva was lovely, for the spirit of love folded its wings upon
her breast. All nature administered to her beauty; and angelic teachings revealed whence came the power that winneth all hearts. The
mother is aware of the spell resting upon her daughter, or rather,
that which seemed a spell to her, but which, in truth, was nothing
more than fidelity to the rights of the soul, obedience to the voice
uttered in that holy of holies. Unable to comprehend the truthfulness of her character, she almost recoils from its gentle revealments.
Alas! that to assimilate to the good and the beautiful should debar
us from human sympathy! Eva walked in an atmosphere of light,
and images of surpassing sweetness were ever presented to her eye.
The dark and distorted shapes that haunt the vision of the unen-
lightened and the erring, dared not approach her. She wept over the
blindness of her mother, and tenderly revealed to her the great truths
pressed upon her own mind, and the freedom and the light in which
the soul might be preserved. She blamed not the errors into which
weak humanity is prone to be betrayed, but deplored that it should
thus blind its own spiritual vision, thus impress dark and ineffacea-
ble characters upon the soul; thus sink, where it should soar.

AS years passed on, no wonder, each
An inward grace revealed;
For where the soul is peace and love,
It may not be concealed.
They stamp a beauty on the brow,
A softness on the face,

ELIZABETH OAKES SMITH

And give to every wavy line
A tenderness and grace.

Long golden hair in many curls
Waved o'er young Eva's brow;
Imparted depth to her soft eye,
And pressed her neck of snow:
Her cheek was pale with lofty thought,
And calm her maiden air;
And all who heard her birdlike voice,
Felt harmony was there.

For winning were her household ways,
Her step was prompt and light,
To save her mother's weary tread,
Till came the welcome night;
And though the toil might useless be,
The housewife's busy skill,
Enough for Eva that it bore
Inscribed a mother's will;

All humble things exalted grow
By sentiment impressed—
The love that bathes the way worn-feet,
Or leans upon the breast;
For love, whate'er the offering be,
Lives in a hallowed air,
And holy hearts before its shrine,
Alone may worship there.

Young Eva's cheek was lily pale,
Her look was scarce of earth,
And doubtingly the mother spoke,
Who gave to Eva birth.
"O Eva, leave thy thoughtful ways,
And dance and sing, my child;

For thy pallid cheek is tinged with blue,
Thy words are strange and wild.

Thy father died—a widow left,
An orphan birth was thine,
I longed to see thy baby eyes
Look upward into mine.
I hoped upon thy sweet young face,
Thy father's look to see;
But Eva, Eva, sadly strange
Are all thy ways to me.

While yet a child, thy look would hold
Communion with the sky;
Too tranquil is thy maiden air;
The glances of thine eye
Are such as make me turn away,
E'en with a shuddering dread,
As if my very soul might be
By thy pure spirit read."

Slow swelled a tear from Eva's lid,
She kissed her mother's cheek,
She answered with an earnest look,
And accents low and meek:—
"Dear mother, why should mortals seek
Emotions to conceal?
As if to be revealed were worse
Than inwardly to feel.

The human eye I may not fear,
It is the light within,
That traces on the growing soul
All thought, and every sin.
That mystic book, the human soul,
Where every trace remains

ELIZABETH OAKES SMITH

The record of all thoughts and deeds,
The record of all stains.

Dear mother! in ourselves is hid
The holy spirit-land,
Where thought, the flaming cherub, stands
With its relentless brand;
We feel the pang when that dread sword
Inscribes the hidden sin,
And turneth everywhere to guard
The paradise within."

"Nay, Eva, leave these solemn words,
Fit for a churchman's tongue,
And let me see thee deck thy hair,
A maiden blithe and young.
When others win admiring eyes,
And looks that speak of love,
Why dost thou stand in thoughtful guise?
Why cold and silent move?

Thy beauty sure should win for thee
Full many a lover's sigh,
But on thy brow there is no pride,
Nor in thy placid eye.
Dear Eva! learn to look and love,
And claim a lover's prayer,
Thou art too cold for one so young,
So gentle and so fair."

"Nay, mother! I must be alone,
With no companion here,
None, none to joy when I am glad,
With me to shed a tear:
For who would clasp a maiden's hand
In grot or sheltering grove,

80

If one unearthly gift debar
From sympathy and love!

Such gift is mine, the gift of thought,
Whence all will shrink away,
E'en thou from thy poor child dost turn,
With doubting and dismay.
And who shall love, and who shall trust,
Since she who gave me birth,
Knows not the child that prattled once
Beside her lonely hearth?

I would I were, for thy dear sake,
What thou wouldst have me be;
Thou dost not comprehend the bliss
That's given unto me;
That union of the thought and soul
With all that's good and bright,
The blessedness of earth and sky,
The growing truth and light.

That reading of all hidden things
The mystery of life,
Its many hopes, its many fears,
The sorrow and the strife.
A spirit to behold in all,
To guide, admonish, cheer,
Forever in all time and place,
To feel an angel near."

"Dear Eva! lean upon my breast,
And let me press thy hand,
That I may hear thee talk awhile
Of thy own spirit-land.
And yet I would the pleasant sun
Were shining in the sky,

The blithe birds singing through the air,
And busy life, were by.

For when in converse, like to this,
Thy low, sweet voice I hear,
Strange shudderings o'er my senses creep,
Like touch of spirits near,
And fearful grow familiar things,
In silence and the night,
The cricket piping in the hearth,
Half fills me with affright.

I hear the old trees creak and sway,
And shiver in the blast;
I hear the wailing of the wind,
As if the dead swept past.
Dear Eva! 'tis a world of gloom,
The grave is dark and drear,
We scarce begin to taste of life
Ere death is standing near."

Then Eva kissed her mother's cheek,
And looked with saddened smile,
Upon her terror-stricken face,
And talked with her the while;
And O! her face was pale and sweet,
Though deep, deep thought was there,
And sadly calm her low-toned voice
For one so young and fair.

"Nay mother, everywhere is hid
A beauty and delight,
The shadow lies upon the heart,
The gloom upon the sight;
Send but the spirit on its way
Communion high to hold,

POETRY

And bursting from the earth and sky,
A glory we behold!

And did we but our primal state
Of purity retain,
We might as in our Eden days,
With angels walk again.
And memories strange of other times
Would break upon the mind,
The linkings, that the present join,
To what is left behind.

The little child at dawn of life
A holy impress bears,
The signet mark by Heaven affixed
Upon his forehead wears;
And naught that impress can efface,
Save his own wilful sin,
Which first begins to draw the veil
That shuts the spirit in.

And one by one his lights decay,
His visions tend to earth,
Till all those holy forms have fled
That gathered round his birth;
Or dim and faintly may they come
Like memories of a dream,
Or come to blanch his cheek with fear,
So shadow-like they seem.

And thus all doubtingly he lives
Amid his gloomy fears,
And feels within his inmost soul,
Earth is a vale of tears:
And scarce his darkened thoughts may trace
The mystery within;

For darkly gleams the spirit forth
When shadowed o'er by sin.

Unrobed, majestic, should the soul
Before its God appear,
Undimmed the image He affixed,
Unknowing doubt or fear;
And open converse should it hold,
With meek and trusting brow;
Such as man was in Paradise
He may be even now.

But when the deathless soul is sunk
To depths of guilt and wo,
It then a dark communion holds
With spirits from below."
And Eva shuddered as she told
How every heaven-born trace
Of goodness in the human soul
Might wickedness efface.

Alas! unknowing what he doth,
A judgment-seat man rears,
A stern tribunal throned within,
Before which he appears;
And conscience, minister of wrath,
Approves him or condemns;
He knoweth not the fearful risk,
Who inward light contemns.

"O veil thy face, pure child of God,"
With solemn tone she said,
"And judge not thou, but lowly weep,
That virtue should be dead!
Weep thou with prayer and holy fear,
That o'er thy brother's soul,

Effacing life, and light, and love,
Polluting waves should roll.

Weep for the fettered slave of sense,
For passion's minion weep!
For him who nurtureth the worm,
In death that may not sleep;
And tears of blood, if it may be,
For him, who plunged in guilt,
Perils his own and victim's soul,
When human blood is spilt.

For him no glory may abide
In earth or tranquil sky;
Fearful to him the human face,
The searching human eye.
A light beams on him everywhere;
Revealing in its ray,
An erring, terror-stricken soul,
Launched from its orb away.

Turn where he will, all day he meets
That cold and leaden stare;
His victim pale, and bathed in blood,
Is with him everywhere;
He sees that shape upon the cloud,
It glares from up the brook,
The mist upon the mountain side,
Assumes that fearful look.

He sees, in every simple flower,
Those dying eyes gleam out;
And starts to hear that dying groan,
Amid some merry shout.
The phantom comes to chill the warmth,
Of every sunlight ray,

He feels it slowly glide along,
Where forest shadows play.

And when the solemn night comes down,
With silence dark and drear,
His curdling blood and rising hair
Attest the victim near.
With hideous dreams and terrors wild,
His brain from sleep is kept,
For on his pillow, side by side,
A gory form hath slept."

"O Eva, Eva, say no more,
For I am filled with fear;
Dim shadows move along the wall;
Dost thou not see them here?—
Dost thou not mark the gleams of light,
The shadowy forms move by?"
"Yes, mother, beautiful to see!
And they are always nigh.

O, would the veil for thee were raised
That hides the spirit-land,
For we are spirits draped in flesh,
Communing with that band;
And it were weariness to me,
Were only human eyes
To meet my own with tenderness,
In earth or pleasant skies."

PART IV

THE widow, awe-struck at the revealments of her daughter, is desirous
to learn more; for it is the nature of the soul to search into its own
mysteries: however dim may be its spiritual perception, it still earnestly
seeks to look into the deep and the hidden. The light is within itself,

POETRY

and it becomes more and more clear at every step of its progress, in search of the true and the beautiful. The widow, hardly discerning this light, which is to grow brighter and brighter to the perfect day, calls for the material lights that minister to the external eye; that thus she may be hid from those other lights that delight the vision of her child. Eva tells of that mystic book—the human soul—upon which, thoughts, shaped into deeds, whether externally, or only in its own secret chambers, inscribes a character that must be eternal. But it is not every character that is thus clearly defined as good or evil. Few, indeed, seize upon thought, and bring its properties palpably before them. Impressions are allowed to come and go with a sort of lethargic indifference, leaving no definite lines behind, but only a moral haziness. The widow recollects the story of old Richard, and Eva enlarges upon the power of conscience, that fearful judge placed by the Infinite within the soul, with the two-fold power of decision and punishment.

"THEN trim the lights, my strange, strange child,
And let the fagots glow;
For more of these mysterious things
I fear, yet long, to know.
I glory in thy lofty thought,
Thy beauty and thy worth,
But, Eva, I should love thee more,
Didst thou seem more like earth."

A pang her words poor Eva gave,
And tears were in her eye,
She kissed her mother's anxious brow,
And answered with a sigh;
"Alas! I may not hope on earth
Companionship to find,
Alone must be the pure in heart,
Alone the high in mind!

We toil for earth, its shadowy veil
Envelops soul and thought,

And hides that discipline and life,
Within our being wrought.
We chain the thought, we shroud the soul,
And backward turn our glance,
When onward should its vision be,
And upward its advance.

I may not scorn the spirit's rights,
For I have seen it rise,
All written o'er with thought, thought, thought,
As with a thousand eyes!
The records dark of other years,
All uneffaced remain;
The unchecked wish forgotten long,
With its eternal stain.

Recorded thoughts, recorded deeds,
A character attest,
No garment hides the startling truth,
Nor screens the naked breast.
The thought, fore-shaping evil deeds,
The spirit may not hide,
It stands amid that searching light,
Which sin may not abide.

And never may spirit turn
From that effulgent ray,
It lives for ever in the glare
Of an eternal day;
Lives in that penetrating light,
A kindred glow to raise,
Or every withering sin to trace
Within its scorching blaze.

Few, few the shapely temple rear,
For God's abiding place—
That mystic temple, where no sound
Within the hallowed space

POETRY

Reveals the skill of builder's hand;
Yet with a silent care
That holy temple riseth up,
And God is dwelling there.

Then weep not when the infant lies
In its small grave to rest,
With scented flowers springing forth
From out its quiet breast;
A pure, pure soul to earth was given,
Yet may not thus remain;
Rejoice that it is rendered back,
Without a single stain.

Bright cherubs bear the babe away
With many a fond embrace,
And beauty, all unknown to earth,
Upon its features trace.
They teach it knowledge from the fount,
And holy truth and love;
The songs of praise the infant learns,
As angels sing above."

The widow rose, and on the blaze
The crackling fagots threw—
And then to her maternal breast
Her gentle daughter drew.
"Dear Eva! when old Richard died,
In madness fierce and wild,
Why did he in his phrensy rave
About a murdered child!"

"Dear mother, I have something heard
Of Richard's fearful life,
Hints of a child that disappeared,
And of heart-broken wife—
If thou the story wilt relate,
A light on me will grow

ELIZABETH OAKES SMITH

That I shall feel if guilt were his
Or only common wo."[9]

THE STORY OF OLD RICHARD.[10]

"HE died in beggary and rags, friendless, and grey, and old;
Yet he was once a thriving man, light-hearted too, I'm told.
Dark deeds were whispered years ago, but nothing came to light;
He seemed the victim of a spell, that nothing would go right.

His young wife died, and her last words were breathed to him
    alone,
But 'twas a piteous sound to hear her faint, heart-rending moan.
Some thought, in dreams he had divulged a secret hidden crime,
Which she concealed with breaking heart, unto her dying time."

"Ah, mother, tis a fearful thing,
When human bonds unite
Unwedded hearts, and they are doomed
For ever, day and night,
Companionship to hold,
Yet feeling every hour,
A beauty fading from the earth,
Thought losing half its power."[11]

"From that day forth he never smiled; morose and silent grown,
He wandered unfrequented ways, a moody man and lone.
The schoolboy shuddered in the wood, when he old Richard
    passed,
And hurried on, while fearful looks he o'er his shoulder cast.

---

[9] Stanza added to the text in *PW*.
[10] The header for the "story of Old Richard" appears only in *PW*.
[11] Stanza added to the text in *PW*.

90

POETRY

And naught could lure him from his mood, save his own trusting
    boy,
Who climbed the silent father's neck, with ministry of joy,
That gentle boy, unlike a child, companions never sought,
Content to share his father's crust, his father's gloomy lot.

With weary foot and tattered robe, beside him, day by day,
He roamed the forest and the hill, and o'er the rough highway;
And he would prattle all the time of things to childhood sweet;
Of singing bird or lovely flower, that sprang beneath their feet.

Sometimes he chid the moody man, with childhood's
    fond appeal:—
'Dear father, talk to me awhile, how very lone I feel!
My mother used to smile so sad, and talk and kiss my cheek,
And sing to me such pretty songs; so low and gently speak.'

Then Richard took him in his arms with passionate embrace,
And with an aching tenderness he gazed upon his face;—
Tears rushed unto his hollow eyes, he murmured soft and wild,
And kissed with more than woman's love the fond but
    frightened child.

He died, that worn and weary boy; and they that saw him die,
Said on his father's rigid brow was fixed his fading eye.
His little stiffening hand was laid within poor Richard's grasp;—
And when he stooped for one last kiss, he took his dying gasp.

It crazed his brain—poor Richard rose a maniac fierce and wild,
Who mouthed, and muttered everywhere, about a murdered
    child."

"And well he might," young Eva said,
"For conscience, day by day,
Commenced that retribution here,
That filled him with dismay.

A girl beguiled in her young years
From all of youthful joy,
And unto solitary life,
Is doomed her stricken boy."[12]

"Nor was this all," the widow said, "for in his early youth,
There was a tale of love and wrong, of vows and perjured truth.
The storm I do remember well that brought the bones to light;
I was a maiden then myself, with curly hair and bright.[13]

Unwedded, but a mother grown, poor Lucy pressed her child,
With blushing cheek and drooping lid, and lip that never smiled.
Their wants were few; but Richard's hand must buy them daily
    bread,
And fain would Lucy have been laid in silence with the dead.

For want, and scorn, and blighted fame, had done the work of
    years,
And oft she knelt in lowly prayer, in penitence and tears;
That undesired child of shame, brought comfort to her heart,
A childlike smile to her pale lip, by its sweet baby art.

And yet, as years their passage told, faint shadows slowly crept
Upon the blighted maiden's mind, and oft she knelt and wept
Unknowing why, her wavy form so thin and reed-like grew,
And so appealing her blue eyes, they tears from others drew.

Years passed away, and Lucy's child, a noble stripling grown;
A daring boy with chestnut hair, and eyes of changeful brown,
Had won the love of every heart, so gentle was his air,
All felt, whate'er might be his birth, a manly soul was there.

---

[12] The last four lines of this stanza added in *PW*.
[13] Stanza added to the text in *PW*.

POETRY

The boy was missing, none could tell where last he had been seen;
They searched the river many a day, and every forest screen;
But never more his filial voice poor Lucy's heart might cheer;
Lorn in her grief, and dull with wo, she never shed a tear.

And every day, whate'er the sky, with head upon her knees,
And hair neglected, streaming out upon the passing breeze,
She sat beneath a slender tree that near the river grew,
And on the stream its pendent limbs their penciled shadows threw.

The matron left her busy toil, and called her child from play,
And gifts for the lone mourner there she sent with him away.
The boy with nuts and fruit returned, found in the forest deep,
A portion of his little store would for poor Lucy keep.

That tree, with wonder all beheld, its growth was strange and rare;
The wintry winds, that wailing passed, scarce left its branches bare,
And round the roots a verdant spot knew neither change nor
    blight,
And so poor Lucy's resting place was alway green and bright.

Some said its bole more rapid grew from Lucy's bleeding heart,
For, sighs from out the heart, 'tis said, a drop of blood will start.[14]
It was an instinct deep and high which led the Mother there,
And that tall tree aspiring grew, by more than dew or air.

---

[14] Here Oakes Smith included a footnote in *SLM*, deleted in *SC* and *PW*:

It is a common belief amongst the vulgar, that a sigh always forces a drop of blood from the heart, and many curious stories are told to that effect; as, for instance: a man wishing to be rid of his wife, in order to marry one more seductive, promised her the gift of six new dresses and sundry other articles of female finery, provided she would sigh three times every morning before breakfast, for three months. She complied, and before the time expired, was in her grave. Many others of a like import might be recorded.

The winds were hushed, the little bird scarce gave a nestling
    sound,
The warm air slept along the hill, the blossoms drooped around;
The shrill-toned insect hardly stirred the dry and crispéd leaf;
The laborer laid his sickle down beside the bending sheaf.

A dark, portentous cloud is seen to mount the eastern sky,
The deep-toned thunder rolling on, proclaims the tempest nigh!
And now it breaks with deafening crash, and lightning's livid glow;
The torrents leap from mountain crags and wildly dash below.

Behold the tree! its strength is bowed, a shattered mass it lies;
What brings old Richard to the spot, with wild and blood-shot
    eyes?
Poor Lucy's form is lifeless there, and yet he turns away,
To where a heap of mouldering bones beneath the strong roots lay.

Why takes he up, with shrivelled hands, the riven root and stone,
And spreads them with a trembling haste upon each damp, grey
    bone.
It may not be, the whirlwind's rage again hath left them bare,
All bare, and mingled with the locks of Lucy's tangled hair."

Of wife, and child, and friends bereft,
And all that inward light,
Which calmly guides the white-haired man,
Who listens to the right;
Old Richard laid him down to die,
Himself his only foe
His baffled nature groaning out
Its weight of inward wo.

Oh there are wrongs that selfish hearts
Inflict on every side,
And swell the depths of human ill
Unto a surging tide,

And there are things that blight the soul,
As with a mildew blight,
And in the temple of the Lord
Put out the blessed light."[15]

There are, who mindless God hath given,
To mark each human soul,
Distinctive laws, distinctive rights,
Its being to control,
Would, in their blind and selfish zeal,
Remove God's wondrous gift,
And, that their image might have place,
God's altar veil would lift:

They call it Love, forgetful they,
That 'twas this hallowed screen,
Concealing, half revealing too,
The seen and the unseen.
That first suggested deathless love,
The infinite in grace,
This inward and seraphic charm,
That floated o'er the face.

PART V

THE storm is raging without the dwelling of the widow, but all is tranquil within. Eva hath gone forth in spiritual vision, and beheld the cruelty engendered by wealth and luxury—the cruelty of a selfish and unsympathizing heart. Her mother tells the story of the neglected children and their affluent stepmother. Sins of omission are often as terrible in their consequences, and as frightful in the retribution as crimes committed intentionally. Certain qualities of the heart are of such a nature, that, when in excess, they resolve themselves into appropriate forms. The symbol of evil becomes mentally

---

[15] This stanza and the subsequent two were added in *SC* and retained in *PW*.

identified with its substance, and the fearful shapes thus created haunt the vision like realities. The injurer is always fearful of the injured. No wrong is ever done with a sense of security; least of all, wrong to the innocent and unoffending. The belief of a Protecting Power watching over infancy, is almost universal; its agency being recognized even by those who have forgone the blessing in their own behalf. The little child is a mystery of gentleness and love, while it is preserved in its own atmosphere; and it is a fearful thing to turn its young heart to bitterness; to infuse sorrow and fear, where the elements should be only joy and faith. In maturer years, it is ever the state of the soul, the prevailing motive—the essential character that involves human peace or wretchedness. "The Kingdom of Heaven is within you," said the Great Teacher;[16] and as we wander from the innocence of children, and allow selfishness or vice to increase upon the domain of the holy, distrust usurps the place of confidence and joy.

The pair wile away the hours in domestic chat, Eva ever uttering her sweet mission of truth and fidelity to the internal life. The story of the Miser follows. No human law may be violated, all the claims of justice, and the common observances of society respected, and yet the soul be dead to its own real needs: may be defrauded of its "bread of life."[17] The miser wakes to a perception of these things, and bewildered in his helpless gloom and ignorance commits suicide.[18]

THE loud winds rattled at the door—
The shutters creaked and shook,
While Eva, by the cottage hearth,
Sat with abstracted look.

---

[16] Luke 17:21: "Neither shall they say, Lo here! or, lo there! for, behold, the kingdom of God is within you."

[17] John 6:35: "And Jesus said unto them, I am the bread of life: he that cometh to me shall never hunger; and he that believeth on me shall never thirst."

[18] This paragraph added to the text in *PW*.

With every gust, the big rain-drops
Upon the casement beat,
How doubly, on a night like this,
Are homes and comfort sweet!

The maiden slowly raised her eyes,
And pressed her pallid brow:—
"Dear mother! I have been far hence:
My sight is absent now!
O mother! 'tis a fearful thing,
A human heart to wrong,
To plant a sadness on the lip,
Where smiles and peace belong.

In selfishness or callous pride,
The sacred tear to start,
Or lightest finger dare to press
Upon the burdened heart.
And doubly fearful, when a child
Lifts its imploring eye,
And deprecates the cruel wrath
With childhood's pleading cry.

The child is made for smiles and joy,
Sweet emigrant from Heaven,
The sinless brow and trusting heart,
To lure us there, were given.
Then who shall dare the simple faith
And loving heart to chill,
Or its frank, upward, beaming eye
With sorrowing tears to fill!"

'Twas thus young Eva silence broke,
While still the dame, intent
On household thrift, croned at her work—
Her soundless needles blent

With flapping of the eager flame,
Nor raised she once her eyes,
But to her daughter's musing thought,
In answering tale replies.[19]

THE STEPMOTHER.[20]

You speak of Hobert's second wife, a lofty dame and bold,
I like not her forbidding air and forehead high and cold,
The orphans have no cause for grief, she dare not give it now,
Though nothing but a ghostly fear, her heart of pride could bow.

One night the boy his mother called, they heard him weeping say,
"Sweet mother, kiss poor Eddy's cheek, and wipe his tears away."
Red grew the lady's brow with rage, and yet she feels a strife
Of anger and of terror too, at thought of that dead wife.

---

[19] Stanza added to the text in *PW*, replacing two stanzas from *SLM*, which
read:
I look within a gorgeous room
A lofty dame behold—
A lady with forbidding air,
And forehead, high and cold—
I hear an infant's plaintive voice,
For grief hath brought it fears—
None soothe it with a kind caress,
Nor wipe away its tears.

His sister hears with pitying heart
Her brother's wailing cry,
And to the stately matron turns
Her earnest tearful eye.
'O mother, chilling is the air,
And fearful is the night—
Dear brother fears to be alone—
I'll bring him to the light.'
[20] Header for "The Stepmother" added in *PW*.

Wild roars the wind, the lights burn blue, the watch-dog howls
    with fear,
Loud neighs the steed from out the stall: what form is gliding
    near?
No latch is raised, no step is heard, but a phantom fills the space—
A sheeted spectre from the dead, with cold and leaden face.

What boots it that no other eye beheld the shade appear!
The guilty lady's guilty soul beheld it plain and clear,
It slowly glides within the room, and sadly looks around—
And stooping, kissed her daughter's cheek with lips that gave no
    sound.

Then softly on the step-dame's arm she laid a death-cold hand,
Yet it hath scorched within the flesh like to a burning brand.
And gliding on with noiseless foot, o'er winding stair and hall,
She nears the chamber where is heard her infant's trembling call.

She smoothed the pillow where he lay, she warmly tucked the bed,
She wiped his tears, and stroked the curls that clustered round his
    head.
The child, caressed, unknowing fear, hath nestled him to rest;
The Mother folds her wings beside—the Mother from the Blest!

"Fast by the eternal throne of God
Celestial beings stand,
Beings, who guide the little child
With kind and loving hand:
And wo to him who dares to turn
The infant foot aside,
Or shroud the light that ever should
Within his soul abide.

All evils of the outer world,
The strong heart learns to bear,
Bears proudly up the heavy weight,

Or makes it light by prayer;
But when it passes through the door,
To touch the life within,
God shield the soul that dared to give
An impulse unto sin."[21]

'Twas thus the pair the hours beguiled,
In lowliness content,
For Eva to the humblest things,
A grace and beauty lent,
And half she wiled the thrifty dame
From toil and vapid thought,
To see how much of mystery
In common life is wrought;

And daily learning deeper truth,
She Eva ceased to chide;
Whose simple mission only sought
The lowly fireside;
To cleanse the heart from selfishness,
From coldness, pride, and hate;
That Love might be a dweller there,
And Peace his dove-eyed mate.

She saw that round her daughter grew,
In all her guileless youth,
The depth and grace of womanhood,
The nobleness of truth;
And coarser natures shrank away,
Awed by a strange rebuke,
That lived within the purity
Of every tone and look.

---

[21] This stanza and the subsequent twelve stanzas, including "The Defrauded Heart," were added to the text in *PW*.

And something like instinctive light,
Broke feebly on her mind,
That Love, the love of common hearts,
Might not young Eva bind;
That she was made for ministry,
To lofty cheer impart,
And yet live on in tranquilness,
And maidenhood of heart.

And thence content around her grew,
Content, that placid grace
That clears the furrows of the cheek,
And smooths the matron face;
And now she laid her knitting by,
And quaint old legends told,
About a miser years agone,
A miser dull and old.

THE DEFRAUDED HEART

For fifty years the old man's feet had crossed the oaken sill,
No human eye his own to greet—the room is damp and chill—
Silent he comes and silent goes, with cold and covert air,
Around a scorching look he throws, then mounts the creaking
    stair.
He's a sallow man, with narrow heart, and feelings all of self—
His thoughts he may to none impart; they all are thoughts of pelf.
But now he enters not the door, he lingers on the stone,
What think you has come the old man o'er, that he loiters in the
    sun?

"Come hither, child,"—he stretched his hand and held a boy from
    play—
"The green old woods throughout the land—are they passing all
    away?

I remember now 'tis a bye-gone joy since birds were singing
    here—
'Twas a merry time, and I a boy to list their spring-time cheer."
And then he loosed the wondering child, and fiercely closed the
    door,
For there was something new and wild, that come his nature
    o'er—
A crowding of unwonted thought, that might not be repressed,
An inward pang that aching sought a sympathizing breast.

The long-lost years of sullen life apart from human kind,
Long torpid powers awaked to strife are struggling in his mind:
The child still near the threshold stays and ponders o'er and o'er,
With a perplexed and dull amaze the words of him of yore.
A stealthy foot beneath the sill—a dry hand pale and thin—
And thus the old man hushed and still has drawn he boy within.
"How long is't, child, since that cross-road the greenwoods severed
    wide?
A pool there was—'twas dark and broad with black and sluggish
    tide.

It seems but yesterday that I was hunting bird's eggs there—
To-day it chanced to meet mine eye, a dusty thoroughfare."
Breathed freely once again the child, "That road was always so."
And half in fear the urchin smiled, and made as he would go.
"Nay once a goodly wood was there—wild blossoms in the spring,
And darted thence the crouching hare and bird upon the wing,
But now a lengthened dusty way—a crossroad—mile-stone too—
Things that to you have been alway, to me are strange and new."

"I have not slept these long blank years, for store of gold is here,
Apart from joy, apart from tears, with neither grief nor cheer,
And never on my conscience left the stain of any wrong,
Why should I feel as one bereft, with yearnings new and strong?
Why hear a voice for ever cry, 'Unfaithful steward thou!'
Come tell me, child, the sun is high—do chills oppress *thee* now?"

POETRY

The boy glanced wistfully about the damp and lonely place,
Then at the warm bright sun without, then in the old man's face.

A moment shook his wasted frame as by a palsy touch,
The white hair thither went and came, the bony fingers clutch
Each other with an eager speed; and then his thin lips part—
"Come, child, canst thou the omen read? cheer up an old man's
 heart."
The boy, half pitying, half in dread, looked in his pale cold face,
"My grandam says, when footsteps tread upon our burial-place,
Tread on the spot our grave to be, we feel a sudden cold;
She's often said the thing to me, and she is very old."

"Now get thee hence," the old man cried, "thou bringest little
 cheer."
And then he thrust the boy aside as with a deadly fear;
Who wondering cast his eyes about to drink in life and air,
And burst his lips in one wild shout, for both were buoyant there.
Three days from thence a mound of earth the cross road marked
 anew,
And children stayed their voice of mirth when they beside it
 drew—
Unhallowed though the old man's rest, where men pass to and fro,
The rudest foot aside is pressed from him who sleeps below.

PART VI

IT is the noon of summer, and the noonday of Eva's earthly existence. She hath held communion with all that is great and beautiful
in nature, till it hath become a part of her being; till her spirit hath
acquired strength and maturity, and been reared to a beautiful and
harmonious temple, in which the true and the good delight to dwell.
Then cometh the mystery of womanhood; its gentle going forth of
the affections seeking for that holiest of companionship, a kindred
spirit, responding to all its finer essences, and yet lifting it above
itself. Eva had listened to this voice of her woman's nature; and

ELIZABETH OAKES SMITH

sweet visions had visited her pillow. Unknown to the external vision,
there was one ever present to the soul; and when he erred, she had
felt a lowly sorrow that, while it still more perfected her own nature,
went forth to swell likewise the amount of good in the great universe
of God. At length Albert Linne, a gay youth, whose errors are those
of an ardent and inexperienced nature, rather than of an assenting
will, meets Eva sleeping under the canopy of the great woods, and
he is at once awed by the purity that enshrouds her. He is lifted to
the contemplation of the good—to a sense of the wants of his better
nature. Eva awakes and recognizes the spirit that forever and ever is
to be one with hers; that is to complete that mystic marriage, known
in the Paradise of God; that marriage of soul with soul. Eva the pure
minded, the lofty in thought, and great in soul, recoiled not from
the errors of him who was to be made mete for the kingdom of
Heaven, through her gentle agency; for the mission of the good and
the loving is not to the good, but to the erring.

'TIS the summer prime, when the noiseless air
In perfumed chalice lies,
And the bee goes by with a lazy hum,
Beneath the sleeping skies:
When the brook is low, and the ripples bright,
As down the stream they go;
The pebbles are dry on the upper side,
And dark and wet below.

The tree that stood where the soil's athirst,
And the mulleins first appear,
Hath a dry and rusty colored bark,
And its leaves are curled and sere;
But the dog-wood and the hazel bush,
Have clustered round the brook—
Their roots have stricken deep beneath,
And they have a verdant look.

104

To the juicy leaf the grasshopper clings,
And be gnaws it like a file,
The naked stalks are withering by,
Where he has been erewhile.
The cricket hops on the glistering rock,
Or pipes in the faded grass,
The beetle's wing is folded mute,
Where the steps of the idler pass.

The widow donned her russet robe,
Her cap of snowy hue,
And o'er her staid maternal form
A sober mantle threw;
And she, while fresh the morning light,
Hath gone to pass the day,
And ease an ailing neighbor's pain
Across the meadow way.

Young Eva closed the cottage-door;
And wooed by bird and flower,
She loitered on beneath the wood,
Till came the noon-tide hour.
The sloping bank is cool and green,
Beside the sparkling rill;
The cloud that slumbers in the sky,
Is painted on the hill.

The spirits poised their purple wings
O'er blossom, brook, and dell,
And loitered in the quiet nook,
As if they loved it well.
Young Eva laid one snowy arm
Upon a violet bank,
And pillowed there her downy cheek
While she to slumber sank.

A smile is on her gentle lip,
For she the angels saw,
And felt their wings a covert make
As round her head they draw.
A maiden's sleep, how pure it is!
The innocent repose
That knows no dark nor troublous dream,
Nor love's wild waking knows!

A huntsman's whistle; and anon
The dogs come fawning round,
And now they raise the pendent ear,
And crouch along the ground.
The hunter leaped the shrunken brook,
The dogs hold back with awe,
For they upon the violet bank
The slumbering maiden saw.

A reckless youth was Albert Linne,
With licensed oath and jest,
Who little cared for woman's fame,
Or peaceful maiden's rest.
Light things to him, were broken vows—
The blush, the sigh, the tear;
What hinders he should steal a kiss,
From sleeping damsel here?

He looks, yet stays his eager foot;
For, on that spotless brow,
And that closed lid, a something rests
He never saw till now;
He gazes, yet he shrinks with awe
From that fair wondrous face,
Those limbs so quietly disposed,
With more than maiden grace.

POETRY

He seats himself upon the bank
And turns his face away,
And Albert Linne, the hair-brained youth,
Wished in his heart to pray.
He looked within his very soul,
Its hidden chamber saw,
Inscribed with records dark and deep
Of many a broken law.

For thronging came his former life,
What once he called delight,
The goblet, oath, and stolen joy,
How palled they on the sight!
No more he thinks of maiden fair,
No more of ravished kiss,
Forgets he that pure sleeper nigh
Hath brought his thoughts to this.

Unwonted thought it was for him
Whose eager stirring life,
Panted for action and renown,
High deeds and daring strife;
Who scorning times of work-day zeal
When thought may power impart;
In manly pastime sought to quell,
The beatings of his heart.[22]

Unwonted thought, unwonted calm,
Upon his spirit fell;
For he unwittingly had sought
Young Eva's hallowed dell,
And breathed that atmosphere of love,
Around her path that grew;
That evil from her steps repelled,

---

[22] This stanza and the next were added to the text in *PW*.

ELIZABETH OAKES SMITH

The good unto her drew.

Now Eva opes her childlike eyes
And lifts her tranquil head;
And Albert, like a guilty thing,
Had from her presence fled.
But Eva marked his troubled brow,
His sad and thoughtful eyes,
As if they sought, yet shrank to hold
Their converse with the skies.

And all her kindly nature stirred,
She prayed him to remain;
Well conscious that the pure have power,
To balm much human pain.
There mingled too, as in a dream,
About brave Albert Linne,
A real and ideal form.
Her soul had framed within.[23]

And he whose ready jest had met
The worldling in her pride,
Felt all his reckless nature hushed,
By hallowed Eva's side;
And when she held her wavy hand,
And bade him stay awhile;
He looked into her sinless eyes,
And marked her child-like smile:

And that so pure and winning beamed,
So calm and holy too,
That o'er his troubled thoughts at once
A quiet charm it threw.
Light thoughts, light words were all forgot,

---

[23] Ibid.

He breathed a holier air,
He felt the power of womanhood—
Its purity was there.

And soft beneath their silken fringe
Beamed Eva's dovelike eyes,
That seemed to claim a sisterhood,
With something in the skies.
Her gentle voice a part become
Of air, and brook, and bird,
And Albert listened, as if he
Such music only heard.

O Eva! thou the pure in heart,
Why falls thy trembling voice?
A blush is on thy maiden cheek,
And yet thine eyes rejoice.
Another glory wakes for thee
Where'er thine eyes may rest;
And deeper, holier thoughts arise
Within thy peaceful breast.

Thine eyelids droop in tenderness,
New smiles thy lips combine,
For thou dost feel another soul
Is blending into thine.
Thou upward raisest thy meek eyes,
And it is sweet to thee;
To feel the weakness of thy sex,
Is more than majesty.

To feel thy shrinking nature claim
The stronger arm and brow;
Thy weapons, smiles, and tears, and prayers,
And blushes such as now.
A woman, gentle Eva thou,

Thy lot were incomplete,
Did not all sympathies of soul
Within thy being meet.

But Faith was thine, the angel gift,
And Love untouched by earth,
For Albert was the crown affixed
To think immortal birth;
And not for thee the heavy pangs
Of those, who, doomed by fate,
Learn, though the lapse of weary years,
To love, to watch, and wait.[24]

Oh not for thee for such as thee,
To tremble with dismay,
Lest baser hands pollute they crown,
And rieve its light away.
Oh not for thee, the anguished prayer,
The struggle long and late,
The pleading of the still small voice,
That bids thee trust and wait.

Thou didst o'er step this fleeting space,
And grasp the higher world;
And angel-like they pinions here,
Their glory half unfurled.
All evil to thy clear, calm eyes,
Was but of transient date.
'Tis not for such, like us to sit,
And weep and love and wait;

Wait with a vain and mournful gaze
For feet that linger long,
Wait for the voice more dear to us,

---

[24] This and the next four stanzas were added to the text in PW.

Than aught of mirth and song;
And grieving much, lest over-wronged,
The spirit lost its mate;
And sit in deathful solitude,
Alone to watch and wait.

No Eva, for those eyes, that brow,
That proud and manly air,
Have often mingled with thy dreams,
And with thine earnest prayer!
And how has thou, all timidly,
Cast down thy maiden eye,
When visions have revealed to thee
That figure standing nigh!

Two spirits launched companionless,
A kindred essence sought,
And one in all its wanderings
Of such as Eva thought.
The good, the beautiful, the true,
Should nestle in his heart,
Should lure him by her gentle voice,
To choose the better part.

And he that kindred being sought,
Had searched with restless care
For that true, earnest, woman-soul
Among the bright and fair—
He might not rest, he felt for him,
One such had been created,
Whose maiden soul in quietude
For his call meekly waited.[25]

---

[25] This stanza and the subsequent four were added to the text in *SC* and
retained in *PW*.

ELIZABETH OAKES SMITH

And oft when beaming eyes were nigh,
And beauty's lip was smiling,
And bird-like tones were breathing round
That fevered sense beguiling;
He felt this was not what he sought—
The soul such mockery spurned,
And evermore with aching zeal,
For that one being yearned.

And she whose loving soul went forth
Wherever beauty dwelt;
Who with the truthful and the good
A genial essence felt,
Oh! often in her solitude,
By her own soul oppressed,
She fain had nestled like a dove
Within one stronger breast.

Though higher, holier far than those
Who listening to her voice,
A something caught of better things,
That make the heart rejoice;
Yet *teaching* thus her spirit lone
Aweary would have knelt,
And *learned* with child-like reverence,
Where deeper wisdom dwelt.

And now that will of stronger growth,
That spirit firmer made,
Instinctive holds her own in check,
Her timid footsteps stayed;
And Eva in her maidenhood,
Half trembles with new fear,
And on her lip that strange, deep smile,
The handmaid of a tear.

Oh, Eva, child of life and light,
Did angel missions part,
When half way in its flight to God,
Was stayed thy maiden heart?
Thine eyes, that unarrested sought
Their kindred in the sky,
Now, with a gentle searchingness,
Read first brave Albert's eye.[26]

And was their glance undimmed from thence?
Was heaven as near to thee?
Did folding pinions guard thee still,
Thou child of mystery?
Did no dim shadows from without
Darken thine inner light?
Didst thou in thy white meekness stand,
As ever, calm and bright?

Oh, human Love! thou seal of life,
Link to the good and true,
Strength to the fainting and infirm,
And youth's perpetual dew;
So oft art thou allied to tears,
To deep and hidden pain,
That in our weakness we are prone,
To deem thy mission vain:

Too much remembering of thy griefs,
Thy wildness and despair,
We seek to God with streaming eyes,
And agony of prayer.
Far better did we fold our hands,
The blessed boon above,
Nor, heeding incidental pangs,

---

[26] This stanza and the subsequent three were added to the text in *PW*.

Shield thus the gift of Love.

While doubting thus, a seraph stayed
His radiant course awhile;
And with a heavenly sympathy,
Looked on with beaming smile:
And thus his words of spirit-love
Trust and assurance brought,
And bade her where the soul finds birth,
To weakly question not.[27]

"Content to feel—care not to know,
The sacred source whence LOVE arise—
Respect in *modesty* of *soul*,
This mystery of mysteries:
Mere mind with all its subtle arts,
Hath only learned when thus it gazed
The inmost veil of human hearts,
E'en to themselves must not be raised!"

But Eva doubted, questioned not,
Content to only feel,
The music of a manly voice,
Upon her senses steal—
To find one heart instinctive learn
The beatings of her own,
And read afar unuttered thought
Known unto his alone.[28]

And firmer grew her heavenward life,
Thus with another blent;
They, twin-born souls, the wedded twain,
One in God's covenant:

---

[27] This stanza and the next were added to the text of *SC* and retained in *PW*.
[28] This stanza and the next were added to the text in *PW*.

POETRY

And she in modesty of soul,
Received the seal and smiled;
The crowning grace of womanhood,
Upon the sinless child.

Her trusting hand fair Eva laid
In that of Albert Linne,
And for one trembling moment turned
Her gentle thoughts within.
Deep tenderness was in the glance
That rested on his face,
As if her woman-heart had found
Its own abiding place.

And evermore to him it seemed
Her voice more liquid grew,
"Dear youth, thy soul and mine are one;
Once source their being drew!
Our souls must mingle evermore—
Thy thoughts of love and me,
Will, as a light, thy footsteps guide
To life and mystery."[29]

There was no sadness in her tone,
But Love unfathomed deep;
As from the centre of the soul,
Where the Divine may sleep:
Prophetic was the tone and look,
And Albert's noble heart,

---

[29] *SLM* included the following stanza at this point, deleted from *SC* and *PW:*
And then she bent her timid eyes,
And as beside she knelt,
The pressure of her sinless lips
Upon his brow he felt.
Low heart-breathed words she uttered then:
For him she breathed a prayer—
He turned to look upon her face,—
The maiden was not there.

Sank with a strange foreboding dread,
Lest Eva should depart.[30]

And when she bent her timid eyes
As she beside him knelt,
The pressure of her sinless lips
Upon his brow he felt,
And all of earth, and all of sin,
Fled from her sainted side;
She, the pure virgin of the soul,
Ordained young Albert's bride.

Low were her sweet and heart-breathed words,
Low was her voice of prayer,
Balmy and gentle was her love,
Like dew in summer air;
And Love, unto the Infinite,
Like Eva's is allied,
We say of such, "'tis gone before,"
But not that it hath died.

PART VII

Eva hath fulfilled her destiny. Material things can no further minister to the growth of her spirit. That waking of the soul to its own
deep mysteries—its oneness with another—has been accomplished.
A human soul is perfected. She had moved amid the beings around
her one, but unlike them—in the world, but not of it. Those who
had felt the wisdom of her sweet teachings, yet felt repelled, as by a
sacred influence. They dared not crave companionship with a spirit
so lofty, and yet so meek. And thus, though the crowd, as it were,
might press upon her, she was yet alone in her true spiritual atmosphere. To them she became a light, a guide, but to Albert Linne
alone, was her mission of Womanhood. In her he learned that no

---

[30] This stanza and the subsequent two were added to the text in *PW*.

one seeketh in vain, the good and the true—that as our faith is, it is given unto us. He confidently sought for the Divine, and it was given unto him. He but touched her garment and she perceived the soul test.[31]

Sorrow and pain—hope, with its kin-spirit fear, are not for the sinless. She hath walked in an atmosphere of light, and her faith hath looked within the veil. The true woman, with woman's love and gentleness, and trust and childlike simplicity, yet with all her noble aspirations and spiritual discernments, she hath known them all without sin, and sorrow may not visit such. She ceased to be present—she passed away like the petal that hath dropped from the rose—like the last sweet note of the singing bird, or the dying close of the wind harp. Eva is the lost pleiad in the sky of womanhood. Has her spirit ceased to be upon the earth? Does it not still brood over our woman hearts?—and doth not her voice blend ever with the sweet utterance of Nature! Eva, mine own, my beautiful, I may not say—farewell.

'TWAS night—bright beamed the silver moon,
And all the stars were dim;
The widow heard within the dell
Sweet voices of a hymn,
As loitering winds were made to sound
Her sinless daughter's name,
While to the roof a rare-toned bird
With wondrous music came.

And long it sat upon the cot
And poured its mellow song,
That rose upon the stilly air,
And swelled the vales along.
It was no earthly thing she deemed,
That, in the clear moonlight,

---

[31] The text from "She had moved" in paragraph one of this section to the end of this paragraph was added to the text in *PW*.

ELIZABETH OAKES SMITH

Sat on the lowly cottage roof,
And charmed the ear of night.[32]

The sun is up, the flowerets raise
Their folded leaves from rest;
The bird is singing in the branch
Hard by its dewy nest.
The spider's thread, from twig to twig,
Is glittering in the light,
With dew-drops has the web been hung
Through all the starry night.

Why tarries Eva long in bed,
For she is wont to be
The first to greet the early bird,
The waking bud to see?
Fresh as the dew of rose-lipped morn
Her sweet young face was seen,
Early amid the clustering blooms.

---

[32] At this point *SLM* includes the following footnote, omitted from *SC* and *PW*. Oakes Smith concludes her novel *The Western Captive*, published later in 1842 and included in *Elizabeth Oakes Smith: Selected Writings* Volume III, with another reference to this tradition:

We are indebted to the Aborigines for this beautiful superstition. The Indian believes that if the wekolis or whippoorwill alights upon the roof of his cabin and sings its sweet plaintive song, it portends death to one of its inmates. The omen is almost universally regarded in New England. The author recollects once hearing an elderly lady relate with singular pathos an incident of the kind. She was blest with a son of rare endowments and great piety. In the absence of his father he was wont to minister at the family altar; and unlike the stern practices of the Pilgrims, from whose stock he was lineally descended, he prostrated himself in prayer in the lowliest humility. It was touching to hear his clear low voice, and see his spiritual face while kneeling at this holy duty. One quiet moonlight night while thus engaged, the mother's heart sank within her to hear the plaintive notes of the whippoorwill blending with the voice of prayer. It sat upon the roof and continued its song long after the devotions had ceased. The tears rushed to her eyes, and she embraced her son in a transport of grief. She felt it must be ominous. In one week he was borne away, and the daisies grew, and the birds sang over his grave.

And woodbine's tendrilled screen.[33]

Why tarries she in secret bower,
Where lightly to and fro,
The curtain rustles in the air,
And shadows come and go?
Why stoops her mother o'er the couch
With half-suppresséd breath,
And lifts the deep-fringed eyelid up?—
That frozen orb is death![34]

Why raises she the small pale hand,
And holds it to the light?
There is no clear transparent hue
To meet her dizzy sight.
She holds the mirror to her lips
To catch the moistened air:
The widowed mother stands alone
With her dead daughter there!

And yet so placid is the face,
So sweet its lingering smile,
That one might deem the sleep to be
The maiden's playful wile.
No pain the quiet limbs had racked,
No sorrow dimmed the brow,
So tranquil had the life gone forth,
She seemed but slumbering now.

---

[33] These last four lines, in *PW*, revised those in *SLM*, which read:
Why stops her mother o'er the couch
With half suppressed breath,
And lifts the deep-fringed eyelid up?—
That frozen orb is death.
[34] Stanza added to the text in *PW*.

They laid her down beside the brook
Upon the sloping hill,
And that strange bird with its rare note,
Is singing o'er her still.
The sunbeam warmer loves to rest
Upon the heaving mound,
And those unearthly blossoms spring,
Uncultured from the ground.

There Albert Linne, an altered man,
Oft bowed in lowly prayer,
And pondered o'er those mystic words
Which Eva uttered there.
That pure compassion, angel-like,
Which touched her soul when he,
A guilty and heart-stricken man,
Would from her presence flee;

Her sinless lips from earthly love,
So tranquil and so free;
And that low, fervent prayer for him,
She breathed on bended knee.
As Eva's words and spirit sank
More deeply in his heart,
Young Albert Linne went forth to act
The better human part.

Oft in the stillness of the night
Sweet Eva's Jove-like eyes,
Beamed through the darkness of his room
Like stars in dusky skies.
Oft came a tranquil light diffused
The darkness to beguile,
And Albert felt within his heart,
It was but Eva's smile.[35]

---

[35] This stanza added to the text of PW.

POETRY

Not lost, his Eva, though her form
The elements concealed,
Within the chambers of the soul,
Her meek form stood revealed;
And there he felt her heavenly eye,
Her downy arms caressed,
And like a living presence there,
She stole into his breast.[36]

Oh not alone did Albert strive;
For, blending with his own,
In every voice of prayer or praise,
Was heard young Eva's tone.
He felt her lips upon his brow,
Her angel form beside;
And nestling nearest to his heart,
Was she—THE SPIRIT-BRIDE.

The sinless Child, with mission high,
Awhile to Earth was given,
To show us that our world should be
The vestibule of Heaven.
Did we but in the holy light
Of truth and goodness rise,
We might communion hold with God
And spirits from the skies

FOR FURTHER READING

Beam, Dorri. "Fuller, Feminism, Pantheism." In *Margaret Fuller and Her Circles*. Edited by Brigitte Bailey, Katheryn P. Viens, and Conrad Edick Wright. Durham: University of New Hampshire Press, 2013: 52–76.

Kete, Mary Louise. "Gender Valences of Transcendentalism: The Pursuit of Idealism in Elizabeth Oakes-Smith's 'The Sinless

---

[36] Ibid.

Child.'" In *Separate Spheres No More*. Edited by Monika Elbert. Tuscaloosa: University of Alabama Press, 2000: 245–60.

Larson, Kerry. "The Passion for Poetry in Lydia Sigourney and Elizabeth Oakes Smith." In *A History of Nineteenth-Century American Women's Poetry*. Edited by Jennifer Putzl and Alexandria Socarides. New York: Cambridge University Press, 2017: 53–67.

Prins, Yopie. *Victorian Sappho*. Princeton, NJ: Princeton University Press, 1999.

Prins, Yopie and Virginia Jackson. "Lyrical Studies." *Victorian Literature and Culture*. 27/2 (1999): 521–30.

Richards, Eliza. "Elizabeth Oakes Smith's Unspeakable Eloquence." In *Gender and the Poetics of Reception in Poe's Circle*. Cambridge University Press, 2004.

Walker, Cheryl. *The Nightingale's Burden: Women Poets and American Culture before 1900*. Bloomington: Indiana University Press, 1982.

Watts, Emily Stipes. "1800–1850: Sigourney, Smith and Osgood." In *The Poetry of American Women from 1632 to 1945*. Austin: University of Texas Press, 1977: 83–120.

Zellinger, Elissa. "Elizabeth Oakes Smith's Lyrical Activism." In *Lyrical Strains: Liberalism and Women's Poetry in Nineteenth-Century America*. Chapel Hill: University of North Carolina Press, 2020: 62–97.

FICTION

"THE BLACK FORTUNE-TELLER"

Published in her husband's weekly, *The Family Reader*, on March 8, 1831, "The Black Fortune-Teller" may be Oakes Smith's first published piece of fiction. Although she would allude to slavery, abolition, and the condition of freedpersons in several other contexts during her career,[1] this is the only known story by Oakes Smith featuring a black female protagonist. Given the fact that fewer black people live in the state of Maine today than in South Dakota, one might suspect that Oakes Smith's story was inspired from what she'd read or heard from others, but by the 1820s, the black population of Portland, Maine, was substantial and active on their own behalf—so much so that a group led by hack driver and abolitionist leader Reuben Ruby, frustrated by policies of segregation in Portland churches, formed the Abyssinian Society, bought land, and built their own place of worship. On September 19, 1826, Seba Smith published a letter written by Chris Manuel, his brother-in-law Reuben Ruby, Caleb Jonson, Clement Thomson, Job L. Wentworth, and John Siggs in his *Eastern Argus* that explained the need for their own place of worship, given their reception in the established churches of the city: "Pardon our misapprehensions, if they be such," the men wrote, "[but] we have sometimes thought our attendance was not desired."[2] When the following year Oakes Smith's

---

[1] Oakes Smith was in no way immune from the racist assumptions of her day, which is evident in correspondence with friends in the north while living with her son Appleton in North Carolina during the 1870s and '80s. In 1874, however, she wrote a long editorial for New Berne (NC) *Republic Courier* in 1874 entitled "The White Man's Party" that castigated the ideas and actions of the KKK in uncompromising terms. Five years earlier, Oakes Smith published a poem celebrating her son's delivery of the Iron-Clad *Atlanta*, renamed *Triumph*, to support the revolutionary government of Haiti, with hopes that the ship will "leave a name in coming years/With Toussaint's name entwined."

[2] See Kelly Bouchard, "The Abyssinian and the Struggle to Save Black History in Maine," Portland *Press Herald*, June 22, 2020. Seba Smith sold his share of

mentor John Neal returned to Portland and opened the first public gymnasium in the United States, patrons complained when Neal permitted a black man to participate and invited others. Refusing to segregate, Neal closed the gym.[3] Surveys of Portland's economy in the first half of the nineteenth century generally reveal how the efforts of an active and often prosperous working class black community coexisted in tension with a powerful minority of local citizens who regarded them as inferior. Ira Gray, a black entrepreneur who, along with Chris Manuel, ran a prosperous barbershop in the 1810s and later opened a "Boarding House for People of Color" became the object of a race riot in 1825, but when tried for manslaughter for killing one of his white assailants, Gray's defense of his property was ruled justified. He opened an employment office for "SEAMEN AND COOKS" on the same wharf with his barbershop.[4]

Even if overt racism in Portland was no less uncommon in Oakes Smith's time than abolitionist resistance and activism, there is no question that the city's wealth—indeed, fortunes of Oakes Smith's own family—were derived from the exploitation of black labor, most of it from the West Indies, where in Haiti alone, plantations from which tons of sugar and other exports were imported by Portland shipowners worked thirty thousand slaves to death each year.[5] As one historian reminds us, "Paradoxically, Portlanders were structurally involved in the slave trade abroad, yet they were intolerant of it on their soil. This cognitive dissonance reveals moral standards that were malleable in the face of profits and comfort."[6]

The Eastern Argus in 1826 and started the Portland *Daily Courier* and *Family Reader* in 1829.

[3] William D. Barry, "Maine's Forgotten Men: State's father of athletics a multi-faceted figure." *Portland Monthly Magazine* (20 May 1979).

[4] Van Gosse, *The First Reconstruction: Black Politics in America from the Revolution to the Civil War* (Chapel Hill: University of North Carolina Press, 2021): 200–201.

[5] David Carey Jr., "Comunidad Escondida: Latin American Influences in Nineteenth- and Twentieth-Century Portland," in *Creating Portland: History and Place in Northern New England*, ed. Joseph A. Conforti (Hanover, NH: University Press of New England, 2005): 92–94.

[6] Ibid., 94.

FICTION

Even if the *Eastern Argus* published Reuben Ruby's appeal for black sovereignty in the Portland churches in 1826, a few years later it would also celebrate a West India Trade "by which constant and profitable employment is afforded to a large class of the community."[7]

When Abigail Harris-Culver discovered "Black Fortune-Teller" in the Maine Historical Society archives in 2013, she expanded her search for other sketches and stories in 1831 featuring abolition or plots involving African Americans for comparison with Oakes Smith's story.[8] Debates over slavery were rising in prominence with the burgeoning abolitionist movement in Portland, and Nat Turner's insurrection later that year would bring a rash of racist responses across the national news, but given the divisiveness of the issue, it is perhaps not surprising that newspapers like Smith's *Portland Courier*, *The Portland Advertiser*, and the *Portland Transcript* generally steered clear of content that might negatively impact their readership and income. Harris-Culver discovered three articles in Portland newspapers that display typical racist assumptions in their references to African Americans. The closest cognate to "The Black Fortune-Teller" is entitled "A Noble Action," which anticipates the common portrayal, by Thomas Nelson Page and others, of the "loyal" ex-slave in local color fiction during Reconstruction. In it, a wealthy woman grants her slave freedom for his many years of faithful service, along with funds to start a new life. According to the formula guiding such accounts, when the woman herself loses her

---

[7] Ibid., 93.

[8] Searching column by column through preserved hard copies of this now very rare journal, Harris-Culver notices several stories and poems over the signature "E" that had not been identified in William Jordan's index of Oakes Smith's work in the Portland *Daily Courier* and *Family Reader* held in the Brown Library, Maine Historical Society. Her paper, "Recovering the African Female Subject of Oakes Smith's Earliest Published Fiction," delivered at the American Literature Association conference in 2016, is available on the Oakes Smith website, www.oakes-smith.org, along with further details in "More Archive Adventures: More Context for 'The Black Fortune-Teller,'" Blog Post, November 8, 2016 http://www.oakes-smith.org/news.

fortune, the ex-slave invites her into his home and supports her in comfort to the end of her days—presumably in base gratitude for her earlier generosity. "Nowhere in this story," comments Harris-Culver, "is there any hint of the peculiar institution's inhumanity. Instead, it paints a sappy picture of the virtue of servility and reinforces the myth that slavery is a natural state of affairs. Its message is clear: emancipation is a nice gesture, but it cannot change the fact that there are those who were born to serve."[9]

Oakes Smith's story provides no radical antidote to the racial assumptions of "A Noble Action" (indeed, it is perhaps its lack of a clear radical edge that convinced Seba Smith that he might publish it). Again, we see an ex-slave, named, ironically, for one of the most powerful African women in recorded history, willingly return to an inferior position in the social hierarchy. Still, the differences Harris-Culver identifies between "The Black Fortune-Teller" and "A Noble Action" are important to note. In "The Black Fortune-Teller,"

> Cleopatra was not emancipated; she escaped from slavery on her own strength. Second, she does not provide her labor pro bono but demands what every working person deserves: payment for services rendered. The third and most compelling difference is the sympathies of its author. Rather than glide over how people are made into slaves or presenting it as an eternal, natural state of affairs, Oakes Smith describes how Cleopatra and her sister were stolen from their home and forcibly brought to America. There is nothing natural about this process, and Cleopatra's reluctance to leave her independence shows that no person in their right mind would brush aside their freedom to return to service, regardless of whatever kindnesses their old master showed.

To these distinctions might be added the deliberate recentering of cultural and historical authority here: wherever she chooses to go

---

[9] Harris-Culver, "More Archive Adventures: More Context for 'The Black Fortune-Teller.'"

FICTION

in the end, this is Patra's story, not one about the "lady dressed in black" who visits Patra's place of work, and in the economic order described, it is Patra who either controls the sought-after knowledge or who consciously takes advantage of others' need for certainty to support herself. To be sure, as Oakes Smith speaks for "those who had been particularly interested in [Patra's] welfare" (presumably abolitionists), she would have readers hear the frank tale of slavery's violence—a burning village, people paralyzed with terror, the murder of a young girl's father—details recalled by her principle character not with wistfulness or resignation but with "a fierce countenance" and "imprecations" upon the "white men" responsible that seem to shock even the sympathetic into silence.

Moreover, while Oakes Smith seems intent, in even a small sketch, to cure some of her readers' ignorance about the conditions of slavery, it would be a mistake to dismiss the work Patra has found to do as simply taking advantage of her townspeople's "bigoted" superstition. In the most basic terms, Patra is an example of a woman who has found gainful employment, something Oakes Smith would spend her career seeking out for herself, and later for other women to gain economic independence. Indeed, in representing a working black woman's story, Oakes Smith made visible a female counterpart to enterprising black men like Reuben Ruby, Ira Gray, or Christopher Manuel. Even more significant for Oakes Smith might be the content of Patra's profession—divination, fortune-telling, ministering to those with questions about the future—subjects that would remain central to Oakes Smith's thinking and writing from this very early point to the end of her life. "The Witch of Endor," also included in this volume, is only one of dozens of other pieces in which this fascination returns in her work,[10] and while Oakes Smith could

---

[10] Noting how Oakes Smith's use of spiritualism in her novel *Bertha and Lily* (excerpted in Volume III of *Elizabeth Oakes Smith: Selected Writing*) "enabled both formal and thematic innovation, extending the range of subject matter appropriate to women's novels," Ashley Reed is one of the rare scholars who has already begun to address the deep vein of spiritualist or parapsychological dimensions in Oakes Smith's work. Oakes Smith's voluminous writing on spiritualism as a critique of the material limits of perception—a subject clearly distinct from religious piety on

not possibly have known it in 1831, there would indeed be "much sorrow in her destiny," leaving her, toward the end of her life, in the position of the white woman of this early tale—a woman abandoned and nearly alone who seeks to know her fate.

---

one hand and the "spirit rapping" hoaxes of the post-Civil War period on the other. Her treatise on the subject, published by Fowler and Wells along with *Woman and Her Needs* and *Hints on Dress and Beauty* in the early 1850s, is entitled *Shadowland, or The Seer*, in the midst of which one can find "The Witch of Endor" (pages 147–153 below) as a central chapter. In addition, however, the notion of spiritual destiny, unseen motive forces in the world, divination, and the occult sciences can be found in nearly every one of her novels, including an unpublished manuscript left in her papers at the time of her death that concludes with a long imagined colloquy between her heroine, Rachel Vaughn, and a young Cotton Mather on the insights of Nostradamus. Along with "The Lover's Talisman, or The Spirit Bride" of 1839, her unpublished play, *Destiny* (1851), as well as an unrelated story "The Destiny," published in *The Oddfellows Offering* for 1852, display these themes, as do many passages in her journals and her MS autobiography, "A Human Life."

"THE BLACK FORTUNE-TELLER"
—E. [1]

In our country, where we boast so much of our enlightened population, our freedom from the shackles of bigotry and superstition, there is scarcely a town or village, but that has its witch, its fortune-teller or haunted-house. I have heard many almost incredible stories upon these subjects, that may perhaps sometime or other serve for an article, but at present I shall confine myself to the story of a single fortune-teller.

In the out skirts of one of our most populous towns stood a small building containing but one room, inhabited by an African female about forty years of age. Many singular stories were told respecting the history of this woman, which if they did not strengthen the belief of people in her occult science, at least excited an interest for her, which was never diminished by an introduction. To those who had been particularly interested in her welfare she would occasionally speak of the period of her childhood, of the golden sands and verdant plains of Africa, and the mute homage of her people, who bent the knee to the daughter of their king, of the horrors of the conflagration, of the terror and dismay, that paralyzed their efforts to flee, of the murder of her royal father in his cabin as he strove to protect his children from the kidnappers, and her own and little sister's voyage across the great waters; but he who had witnessed, as she dwelt upon these themes, the fierce expression of her countenance, or heard the imprecations which she pronounced upon the white men, was never willing to prolong or recur to the subject again. Of her fate, subsequent to her arrival in this country, she would say nothing; but it was reported that she had been a slave at the south, and it was inferred she had a kind master from the

---

[1] "The Black Fortune-Teller," Portland *Family Reader,* March 8, 1831. Smith's earlies publications were signed by the initial "E" only.

circumstance of her having been taught to read and write; but how or when she left his service was not known. She was known by the name of Cleopatra, or as some abridged it, Patra; and the extreme dignity and haughtiness of her manners might well have become that despotic princess.—Her form was taller and more slender than usually belongs to her people, and her skin clear and of the most glossy jet. Her teeth white and regular, her forehead narrow and re-treating, and always surmounted by a purple turban, so arranged as to entirely conceal her hair. She was scrupulously neat in her habits, and her flowing purple robe was always tastefully adjusted to her form. Indeed the appearance of Cleopatra was, always that of one, who might have been a queen in her own country. The equipages of the rich and fashionable were often to be seen at the door of this woman, while their owners strove to look into futurity, and often at the stealthy hour of twilight the good-wife would repair to the cabin of Patra, that she might through her means recover her stolen goods. The servant maid, before her lover went to sea, must consult the fortune-teller as to his return, and truth to say, her predictions were strangely verified, for the sailor was sometimes ship-wrecked, some-times lost, and sometimes he returned to find his love the pride of another. Whether Patra was aware that such calamities were inci-dental to a sailor's life, and therefore hazarded nothing in foretelling them, or her native penetration read proofs of fickleness and vanity in her visitor sufficient to warrant her foretelling she would never become his wife, I shall not take upon me to determine. Truth to say, such things often did occur, even or very nearly, as she foretold; and they always added to her reputation. She would never tell the fortune of one in the presence of another, and this gave an air of mystery to her proceedings, which those who visited her were always willing to enhance, when ever they referred to her. She never asso-ciated with people of her own colour, and scarcely ever crossed her own threshold to go abroad. She was remarkably sensitive, and the discerning might read almost every thought in her countenance. She would gaze upon that species of beauty with large black eyes and raven hair, with an intense expression of admiration, that seemed to absorb every other feeling; while to the clear white brow of the blue eyed maiden, the enchantress would incline her head as if she gazed on a being of superior purity. It was a bright moonlit evening, in the beginning of autumn, when a carriage stopped at the door of Patra, and a lady dressed in black alighted and entered the humble dwelling.

The fortune-teller threw open the back casement, and allowed the bright rays of the full moon to illuminate the little apartment. Throw back your veil, lady, and let the moon-beams fall upon your face, said she, at the same time leading her visitor to the window. The stranger did as she was desired, and without glancing at her hostess, raised a pair of large blue eyes to the clear orb in the heavens. As she threw aside her veil, she exhibited a brow of dazzling whiteness, and her youthful countenance exhibited the pale melancholy expression of one accustomed to sorrow. Patra remained for a few moments gazing upon her beautiful features, with a countenance expressive of a thousand varying emotions. At length she approached her side, and said in a low tremulous voice: "There can be nothing but goodness, though I fear there has been much of sorrow in thy destiny. Have you forgotten your old slave, my beautiful mistress?" The stranger started. "Is it thee, Patra? my old faithful slave, and obtaining a livelihood by the credulity of others?" Aye retorted the slave bitterly, and what was the object of my young mistress Julia, when she visited the unknown fortune-teller? True, Patra, true, I have seen so much of sorrow, I would fain know if heaven can have more in store for me. Parents, husband, children, all are dead, Patra, and I have come here to the north to spend the remainder of my days with the friends of my husband. But why did you leave me, Patra? Was I not kind, an indulgent mistress? Aye, replied Patra, with a tear in her eye, but you taught me to *think*, and I felt the degradation of being a *slave*, even to you. Had I remained in ignorance, I might have thought less of my situation; I will be your *servant*, lady, and a faithful one till death; but my soul revolts at the idea of being a slave, a degraded thing, to be bought and sold. Soon after this interview, Patra disposed of her little dwelling, and became the faithful servant of her former mistress, and ever after persisted in denying that she knew any thing more about futurity than her neighbors, and we may conclude likewise, that the discovery of the fortune-teller completely cured her mistress of credulity. –E

FOR FURTHER READING:

Barry, William D. "John Neal: The Man Who Knew Everything Else." *Portland Monthly Magazine* (July/August 1994): 9–17.
———. "Maine's Forgotten Men: State's father of athletics a multi-faceted figure." *Maine Sunday Telegram* (May 20, 1979).
Creating Portland: History and Place in Northern New England. Edited by Joseph A. Conforti. Hanover, NH: University Press of New England, 2005: 90–100.
Gosse, Van. *The First Reconstruction: Black Politics in America from the Revolution to the Civil War*. Chapel Hill: University of North Carolina Press, 2021: 200–17.
Kanes, Candace. "Slavery's Defenders." *Maine History Online*. Maine Historical Society.
———. "Uncomfortable History." *Maine History Online*. Maine Historical Society.
Reed, Ashley. *Heaven's Interpreters: Women Writers and Religious Agency in Nineteenth-Century America*. Ithaca, NY: Cornell University Press, 2020.
Ruby, Reuben. "To the Public." *The Eastern Argus* (September 15, 1826).
Rucker, Walter C. *The River Flows On: Black Resistance, Culture, and Identity Formation in Early America*. Baton Rouge: Louisiana State University Press, 2006: 85–86.

"HOW TO TELL A STORY"

Published in January 1843 in *Graham's Magazine*, "How to Tell a Story" seems to belong to the group of what John Neal called "little roguish local color stories...in Down East accents" written in Oakes Smith's early career that he praised in one of the many prefaces to Oakes Smith's first collected book of poems in 1843. Although this humorous style would never become Oakes Smith's brand, it does give readers a sense of her versatility and of her resistance to the limitations associated with the role of "poetess," the term George Graham and Rufus Griswold later used to market her during the 1840s. In terms she used in a letter to Benson Lossing in 1851, Oakes Smith was never willing to be seen solely as a "compounder of mawkish stories and sentimental poetry," and her penchant for humor and sarcasm was well known and appreciated by many in her lecture career and feminist writings.

By the early 1840s, other New York women writers such as Caroline Kirkland had already made dialect a part of their portrayal of regionally distinct characters,[1] but Oakes Smith's use of local accents here and elsewhere was likely viewed as more charitable; the joke here is not on the circumlocutious storyteller, but on readers duped by the expectations set up by Oakes Smith's narrator to desire the exciting details of "John Catamount's" eponymous feat. In another way, the speedy dialogue of the story (especially the parenthetical self-interruption of a busy housewife in the sketch) seems to prefigure moments in the work of Oakes Smith's fellow Portland writer Fanny Fern, but unlike "Mrs.

---

[1] Like Seba Smith, Kirkland's husband also speculated in land in the 1830s, though unlike Oakes Smith and her husband, the Kirklands actually moved to their "new home" in frontier Michigan in 1835, where William Kirkland founded the town of Pinkney. In three novels—*A New Home: Who'll Follow* (1839), *A Forest Life* (1842), and *Western Clearings* (1845)—Kirkland wrote of her sojourn on the western frontier, depicting the neighbors with whom she lived and worked with a "realism" relatively new to fiction of the time. However faithful or innovative, her portrayal of "local" speech patterns proved offensive to those depicted in her work.

Adolphus Smith Sporting the Blue Stocking,"[2] or "Tom Pax's Conjugal Soliloquy,"[3] Oakes Smith's sketch involves a metafictive frame, loudly announced by her title.

Thus, at least at first glance, one might think "How to Tell a Story" gives a rare insight into Oakes Smith's approach to *craft*, and even some hard evidence that her work—no less than that of other women writers of the time—is no more "spontaneous" than that of male writers of the period.[4] It is the piece's argument against "spontaneity" that might bring to mind Poe's criticism of readers' assumptions about the origin of great works of art in his "The Philosophy of Composition," an essay of 1846 which debunks the artist's claim for the "ecstatic intuition" out of which a work might magically emerge. As a counterpoint, in this essay Poe presents the conscious decisions he made—or says he made—in the process of writing his famous poem "The Raven"—not as some spontaneous overflow of emotional response, but with "all the precision of a mathematical problem." Even more than in Poe's case, however (and many have doubted the seriousness of Poe's essay), what is presented as "serious" consideration of effective story-telling in Oakes Smith's sketch proves to be a send-up of such explanations—or at least a frank admission that whatever the ideal conditions or process might be for how a tale should best be told, those conditions are rarely achievable, especially by women writers of the period such as Kirkland, Fern, or Oakes Smith herself, whose literary efforts, however conscious or skilled, were regularly interrupted by their "other" employment in the care of children and other domestic responsibilities.

---

[2] From *Fern Leaves from Fanny's Portfolio*, Second Series (Auburn, AL: Miller Orto and Mulligan, 1854) 101–102.

[3] *New York Ledger*, February 9, 1856. Printed in *Ruth Hall and Other Writings* ed. Joyce W. Warren (New Brunswick: Rutgers University Press, 1986) 268–69.

[4] Oakes Smith's attention to her craft is evident in her correspondence with Griswold the following month, complaining that in proof, "'The Way to Tell a Story'" [*sic*] was full of blunders, which marred the story out of all reason." Elizabeth Oakes Smith to Rufus Griswold, December 22, 1842, Gratz American Poets Collection, Case 7, Box 9, Historical Society of Pennsylvania.

"HOW TO TELL A STORY"[1]

Mrs. Seba Smith

No character is more genial to a child than a good story-teller—one that with a serene fullness pours out incident and narrative, peril and "hair-breadth 'scape," tale of enormous serpent or deadly beast, of wild or chivalric adventure, till the old clock behind the door is heard to tick with a solemn loudness, and the elders begin to yawn and stir the ashes in token of weariness. Most heartily do I pity either man or woman who has no such delicious reminiscence. It was my good fortune when a child to pass much of my time at an old country farm-house, where the many retainers, the primitive and exact ordering of the household had in it much of the baronial style of which we read amongst our Saxon ancestors. The principal apartment for ordinary occasions was a long hall, or dining-room in the centre of which was spread a table capable of holding the whole family—from the head down to the youngest servant. Our New England gentry are exact observers of precedence, and in the old families where any degree of state is observed, a single glance at the ordering of the table betrays the relative position of each member. At the head sit the master and mistress, then occasional visitors, next the children ranged according to the age of each, and then come the upper domestics, as they might be termed, old, respectable retainers, who sometimes join a few words in the conversation at the head of the table; but always in a subdued and respectful voice—followed next by the younger servants, "to the manor born" as it were, but as yet too young to share in its dignities.

After the morning and evening meal, which is announced by the blowing of a horn, each member places his chair to the wall, and the patriarch of the family reads a portion of scripture from the "big ha' bible, once his father's pride," and then,

"The saint, the husband, and the father prays."

---

[1] "How to Tell a Story," *Graham's Magazine* 22 (January 1843): 33–35.

ELIZABETH OAKES SMITH

At night, when the household arrangements were completed, this long room with its dim recesses, its antique furniture and quaint ornaments, was the place to give impressiveness to a story. Here might one shudder at the supernatural, stare at the marvelous, and thrill at the bold and magnanimous. Here was the place, too, to bemoan the cruelty of "Queen Eleanor" to "Fair Rosamond," to weep for the lover by "Yarrow flowing," and to rejoice in the retribution of the proud and "cruel Barbara Allen." These and many other ballads, such as the "Milk White Doe," "Fair Margaret and Sweet William," "Lord James and Fair Eleanor,"[2] were preserved in rude manuscript and learned orally, and most have been in this way preserved by tradition and brought over to this country by the first settlers; the writer having never seen them in print till she found them in Perry's reliques[3] and long after she had been familiar with them as chanted in the old farm-house.

The city is no place for story-telling—nothing is in harmony. A story to go well must be either in a rich antique room, or old-fashioned farm-house, where things have an air of quaintness and permanency; in our rough cottage with smoky rafters; or, better still, in some rude cabin upon the wild frontier. In such places we abandon ourselves to any fantastic illusion, and are not ashamed to yield faith, nor to be swayed by the emotions of the tale. A sea story need be told by some weather-beaten tar by the sea shore, or by a dim wood fire with a fierce tempest raging without; unless you have the good fortune to hear it by the forecastle itself. A good story-teller should be exceedingly careful to never mis-time, nor mis-place his narrative. If his miserable fortune afford him nothing better than a

---

[2] Titles of well-known English and Scottish ballads, with sources stretching in some cases to the Middle Ages. All are available in Francis James Child's English and Scottish Popular Ballads, in five volumes, published first in 1860 and reprinted to the present time. In Child, the ballads referenced are #156, "Queen Eleanor's Confession"; #214, "The Dowie Dens o' Yarrow"; #84, "Barbara Allen"; #15, "The Milk White Doe"; #74, "Fair Margaret and Sweet William"; and #73, "Lord James and Fair Eleanor."

[3] A misprint or mistaken memory of Percy's *Reliques*, a collection of 180 ballads by Bishop Thomas Percy and published in 1765.

FICTION

carpeted room, with sofas and chandeliers, be sure to make the light dim; let it come from behind some piece of statuary or heavy-stuffed chair, a rose bush, or large geranium, that outline and faint shadows be cast—then if he have a quiet voice, and not too much of the detail, a very good illusion may be produced.

Children, in whom the love of the marvelous is always predominant, and who never weary at the twice-told tale, will adopt all sorts of expedients to hear one. They may be found in the garret turning over musty relics and old records, in the desire for suggestion; and they drag forth triumphantly a rusty sword, a cocked hat, a worm-eaten log book, or time hallowed garment, any one of which may afford material for a story. The boy sits on the steps of the grocer, lolls upon the pump at the corner, or leans over the tafferel of the ship, and he is listening to some history of stirring adventure. Do not call him away, he is building up the materials for a man—a man firm, enterprising and self-sustained—the only wealth, the only true dignity.

A story-teller should never hurry, least of all be interrupted—as for himself he should think for the time being only of his story; give himself up and become a part of what he relates. Nothing mars a story like pre-occupation. I believe all I am writing was suggested to me when about eight years old, from the fact of having unfortunately asked Mrs. Smith, a respectable country woman, rejoicing in that rarest of names, to tell me the story of a Catamount.[4] Her husband was also happy in the name of John, but as these two favorite names happened to conjoin in union as well as many of his neighbors, it was not always easy to determine the individual specified. In a transition state of society, a man frequently receives a soubriquet, indicating some quality of mind, person or achievement, by which he is distinguished from those about him. It is an ancient practice sanctioned by history, and one mode by which names were created. The aborigines in this way named their chiefs and warriors. Mr. John Smith, of the country town of which I am speaking, was hence called Catamount Smith.

---

[4] One of more than forty names in English for "cougar" or "mountain lion."

Great was my curiosity to learn why. I questioned every one. Why is Mr. Smith called Catamount John?

"Why? Because he killed the Catamount."

There was the fact; but I wanted the story—all the details—the enormous size of the animal, his growl, his tremendous leap, the fierce contest, the peril, and finally to be in at the death. Once seduced by the good-natured face of Catamount John, I ventured to crave the story, blushing up to the eyes while I did so.

"Mr. Smith, will you tell me how you killed the Catamount?"

He turned his bland face full upon mine, placed his rough, broad palm upon my head and answered,

"My dear, I shot him."

"But how, Mr. Smith, how?"

"I took my gun and pointed, so—'suiting the action to the word,' and shot him through the ———." I ran out of the room to hide my vexation.

At this moment, Mrs. Catamount Smith passed by me, bearing an enormous pan of butter, fresh from the churn. Now Mrs. Smith would never have deluded any thing but a child into a belief that she could tell a story. She was entirely deficient in that quality of repose, so essential to the thing. She was a little, plump, bustling dame, forever on the alert to see that all was neat and tidy. Her sleeves were always up at the elbow, her apron white as snow, and the frill of her cap blowing back with her quick tread. Short people never stoop, and Mrs. Smith being very short and very round, tipped somewhat backward when she walked.

That night, when all the family were in bed, except a faithful domestic named Polly, I seated myself beside the good old lady, to hear the story of the Catamount. The reader must bear with me while I relate the thing just as it transpired.

Mrs. Smith gave one keen look about the apartment, to convince herself that all was right, and then stuck her needle into a sheath affixed to her belt, and commenced knitting and talking at the same moment.

"John and I began house-keeping in the log house down by the pond, about a mile from the place where this meeting-house now—

FICTION

(la, Polly, there's Jacob's buskins on the back of your chair, and they must be bound round to-night; do go right to work on them)—where did I leave off?—where the meeting-house now stands. 'Twas another thing to be fixed out then, to what it is now-a-days. I was considered very well off—my father gave me a cow and a pig—and I had spun and wove sheets and kiverlids, besides airning enough to buy a chist of draws, and a couple of chairs. Then my mother launched out a nice bed, a wheel, and some kettles. We hadn't much company in them times, our nighest neighbor was over the mountain, five mile off—(now did you ever—I liked to forgot them are trousis of Ephraim's—he's tied his handhercher round his knee all day, to kiver up the hole—Polly, get my wax and thimble, and the patches, and I'll go right to work.) Well, what was I sayin'? Oh, we hadn't much company, and my old man made a settle, with a high back, and bought chairs two at a time, as our family grew larger."

"But, my dear ma'am, you promised to tell me about the Catamount."

"Yes, yes, I'm comin along to it. Well, John had got together a yoke of oxen, some sheep, and other cattle, and we began to be pretty considerable fore-handed. He was a nice, smart man, and nobody should say he had a lazy wife. (Polly, just sweep the hearth up.)

We had no machines then to card our wool, and I had to card it all myself—for I never hired *help* till after our Jacob was—"

"Dear Mrs. Smith, the Catamount."

"Yes, child, I'm eeny most to it. Let me see—till after Jacob was born—then I hired Lydia Keene, as smart a girl she was, as ever wore shoe leather. By this time we had eighteen or twenty sheep, and John used to drive them into the pen and count them every night, to be sure that the wolves or panthers hadn't got any of 'em; for the beasts were pretty thick about the mountain, and many a time I've stood to the door, and heard them howl or cry, to say nothing of the foxes and screech-owls that kept up a rumpus all night long. (Dear me, this snappy wood now has burnt a hole in my apron—it looks jist like a pipe hole—I do so hate to see it. I'll mend it now, and then 'twill be done with. I never put off any thing till to-morrow, that can be done to-day—that's the way to—) Now

141

don't fidget, child, you see I'm almost to it; that's the way to get fore-handed, as I was saying. Well, one morning John went out, and found the sheep all huddled together into a corner, trembling piti-fully. He counted them, and one was missing. This was a loss, for I needed the wool for winter kiverlids. (There, Polly, you've forgot the apples you're a goin to pare for the pan-dowdy, now the buskins is done, you better get them under way.)

"Well, the next night John took Rover—now Rover was the largest dog I ever see, near about as large as a heifer, and the knowingest critter I ever laid eyes on. Well, John took him out to the pen, and told him to watch the sheep. John'll never forget how the critter looked up in his face, and licked his hand when he left him, just as if he knew what would come of it, and wanted to say good bye; nor how he crouched down before the bars, and laid his nose upon his paws, and looked after him solemn-like. Poor Rover! The next morning John was up airly, for he felt kind a worried. He went out to see the sheep pen, and sure enough the first thing he see, was—(Polly, you've just cut a worm-hole into your apples)—the first thing he see, was poor Rover dead by the bars, his head torn right open, and another sheep gone. John's dander was fairly up—he took down the gun, there it hangs on the hooks, took his powder-horn and bullets, and started off. I tried to coax him to set a trap, or to watch by the sheep-pen. But John always had a will of his own, and was the courageousest man in the town, and he declared he'd have nothing to do with any such cowardly tricks. He'd kill the crit-ter in the broad day-light, if 'twas only to revenge poor Rover. So he started off. He tracked the critter about a mile round by the moun-tain, which in them days was covered with trees to the very top. (Polly, jist take them are trousis, and lay them down by Ephraim's chamber door; he'll want them in the morning.)

Well, John now missed Rover dreadfully, to scent out the beast—he moved along carefully, searching into the trees—expectin he might be down upon him every minit. All at once he heard the bark ripped up from a tree almost over his head, and then a low, quick growl, and there was the Catamount jist ready for his spring—(my conscience, Polly, there's that new soap all running out o' the

FICTION

barrel into the cellar, I saw it had sprung a leak about supper time, and then I forgot all about it again.")

The word "spring" had been the unlucky association, and away she darted to the cellar, followed by the faithful Polly.

"Mrs. Smith, Mrs. Smith, do finish the story!"

"La! child—John shot him!" she screamed from the foot of the stairs.

"THE WITCH OF ENDOR"

Oakes Smith's story "The Witch of Endor" appeared no less than five times in print during the 1840s, then again as a central chapter of her treatise on spiritualism, *Shadowland, or The Seer*, in 1851.[1] The biblical story was well known to Oakes Smith's readers, but her rendering and argument make it not only a fine example of her early feminist revision of traditional narratives, but likewise a pivotal text that joins her earliest with her latest work.

The Old Testament version of the story recalled in Oakes Smith's sketch[2] finds Saul, king of the Israelites, distraught over his fate on the eve of his army's battle with the Philistines. Though he has outlawed the practice of divination, he disguises himself and secretly finds a spiritual medium, the witch of Endor, to summon the ghost of his predecessor, Samuel. At first, she refuses, citing the king's interdict, but realizing it is the king himself who requests her work, she complies, conjuring the ghost of Samuel, who gives Saul no hope, flatly reporting that he has sinned (scholars debate over whether it was his disobedience to God before this, or his lack of faith in seeking answers from a witch) and that in the battle that follows, he will pay with his life. Hearing this, Saul collapses in a heap, overwhelmed by his fate, and, incidentally, as the biblical text indicates, because he has not eaten all day and night.

And here, the witch of Endor, the sinful necromancer who has risked her life breaking the law to bring Saul the news of his fate, becomes something unexpected for readers associating the figure of the witch with the Salem trials or Shakespeare's *Macbeth*: the *woman*

---

[1] *Graham's Magazine* (April 1843): 225–27; *The Rover* 2/2 (1843): 42–44; *Dew Drops of the Nineteenth Century* ed. Seba Smith (New York: J. K. Wellman, 1845) 71–79; *The Mayflower for MDCCCXLVII* (Boston: Saxton and Kelt, 1846) 282–91; *The Christian Annual, a Miscellany for 1846* (Philadelphia: Henry F. Anners, 1846): 106–16; and *Shadowland, or The Seer* (New York: Fowler and Wells, 1851) 60–68.

[2] The story is found in 1 Samuel 28 and 1 Chronicles 10.

FICTION

of Endor, who takes pity on the failed king, and, without reminding him of his fate, asserts some power over him in his vulnerability (I have listened to you, now you listen to me, she tells him), kills her fatted calf, makes dinner for him and his consort, and sends them on their way. It's not as if this end to the story (and that, inconclusively enough, is how the biblical chapter ends) is something created or revised by Oakes Smith, thus allowing her to celebrate the "beauty," "wisdom," and "tenderness" of the Woman of Endor; Oakes Smith adds her commentary, but her paraphrase is faithful to the Old Testament text.

"The Witch of Endor" is another example of Oakes Smith's practice of revising the assumptions of her culture, but not in the sense of a "revisionist history" that alters or erases the terms of patriarchal culture for progressive ends. Rather, Oakes Smith has chosen a story from the patriarchal story *par excellence*—the Old Testament—that has always involved a woman who, when brought to the center of the reader's attention, changes yet another story of patriarchal succession to one that redeems, overturns, and transforms associations with "womanhood" that have accumulated over time. One might argue that even the term "witch" in Oakes Smith's title is calculated to lure certain readers toward the reconsideration that ends her recounting of the story. If, for nineteenth-century Americans, women were seen to occupy either the place of supporting Angel or threatening Monster, Oakes Smith found a model that denies the difference: the same woman whose name was translated in the Greek as the "Pythoness" of Endor—the animaga of the Devil—is also the one who demonstrated the most humanity in the story.

As Leigh Kirkland has pointed out, Oakes Smith's adoption of the name "Eva" in her poem "The Sinless Child" is supremely ironic in its remembrance of the original "temptress" still blamed literally in Oakes Smith's time for the fall of Man; citing this association and noting how many of her dearest friends began to address her as "Eva" after the success of her poem, Kirkland writes, "She is almost

145

gleeful when she mentions...that at an earlier time she would have been burned as a witch."[3]

---

[3] Leigh Kirkland, "A Human Life: Being the Autobiography of Elizabeth Oakes Smith—A Critical Edition and Introduction," PhD dissertation (Georgia State University, 1994): 21–22.

"THE WITCH OF ENDOR"

Mrs. Seba Smith

The unfortunate are always superstitious; just in proportion as the calamities of life impair the freedom of the human mind, do the elements of the dark and mysterious gather about it. The past has been embittered by care and disappointment; and, in the words of Scripture, their "way is hedged up," there is no hopeful vista to relieve the gloom of the present, and they appeal to omens, predictions, and the rude superstitions current among the vulgar.

Too feeble to boldly enter the precincts of Truth, grasping with a strong faith the very horns of the altar; and thus to learn how the temporary yields to that which is eternal; how the partial is lost in the universal; they linger about the threshold, perplexing themselves with dim shadows and faint intimations. They pause in the vestibule, where Superstition sits portress, rather than enter to worship Truth herself.

It is the error of their destiny more than their own. The light that is in them has become darkness. The clearness and vigor of perception is lost under the pressure of circumstances, in which human wisdom would seem to be of no avail, and they yield at length as to an irresistible fate.

The history of Saul, the first king of Israel, is an affecting record of this kind. Raised to the dignity of royal power, by no ambition of his own, but by Divine appointment, in compliance with the will of a people weary of their Theocracy, we look upon him from the first as an instrument, a being impelled rather than impelling.

Painful, indeed, is the contrast of the proud and handsome youth commencing his royal career in the freshness and freedom of early manhood, when life presented but a long perspective of sunshine and verdure, to that of the stricken man, weighed down by calamities, bereft of hope, bereft of faith, yet manfully marching to that fatal field where death only had been promised him.

From the commencement of his career the "choice young man and goodly" seems to have had a leaning to the occult, a willingness to avail himself of mysterious power, rather than to arrive at results through ordinary and recognized channels. We find him commissioned by his father, going forth in quest of three stray asses, which he seeks, not by hillsides and pastures of Israel, but by consulting the seer, Samuel. The holy man hails him king, and gently rebukes him as the object of his visit, by saying, "set not thy mind upon the asses which were lost three days, for they are found."

Ardent and impulsive, he now goeth up and down in the spirit of prophecy, with the strange men who expound its mysteries, and anon he sendeth the bloody tokens to the tribes of Israel, rousing them from the yoke of oppression.

Generous and heroic, he repels the foes of his people, and loads the chivalric David with princely favors. Yet beneath all this, like hidden waters, heard but unseen, lurked his dark and gloomy mysticism, that embittered even his proudest and brightest hours. An evil spirit troubled him, which only the melody of the sweet psalmist of Israel could beguile.

Moses had been familiar with all the forms of Egyptian worship, and all their many sources of knowledge: but, as the promulgator of a new and holier faith, he wished to draw his people from the subtleties of divination, and induce them to a direct and open reliance upon Him who alone "knoweth the end from the beginning." No insight to the future is needed by the strong in faith and the strong in action. Hence the divinely appointed legislator prohibited all intercourse with those who dealt in this forbidden lore—forbidden, as subversive of human hope and human happiness. For the mind loses its tone when once impressed with the belief that the "shadows of coming events" have fallen upon it.

The impetuous and vacillating Saul, impelled by an irresistible instinct to this species of knowledge, sought to protect himself from its influence by removing the sources of it from his kingdom. For this reason he put in force the severe enactments of Moses against dealers in what were termed "familiar spirits." Thus betraying the

FICTION

infirmity of his manhood, by removing temptation rather than bravely resisting it.

Vain and superstitious, oh "choice young man and goodly," thou wert no match for the rival found in the person of the chivalric David, the warrior poet, the king minstrel, the man of many crimes, yet redeeming all by the fervency of his penitence, and his unfaltering faith in the Highest. Yet the noble and the heroic did never quite desert thee, even when thou didst implore the holy prophet to honor thee in the presence "of the elders of the people," and he turned and worshiped with thee. A kingly pageant when the sceptre was departing from thee.

Disheartened by intestine troubles, appalled by foreign invasion, the spirit of the unhappy king for-sook him, and it is said "his heart greatly trembled." Samuel, the stern and uncompromising revealer of truth, was no more. Unsustained by a hearty reliance upon divine things, Saul was like a reed cast upon the waters, in this his hour of trial and perplexity.

"When Saul inquired of the Lord, the Lord answered him not, neither by dreams nor by prophets." Unhappy man, thy prayers were those of doubt, not of faith, and how could they enter that which is within the veil!

In the utterness of his despair, he consults the Woman of Endor. She might not control events, but she could reveal them. Perilous and appalling as his destiny threatened, he would yet know the worst.

There was majesty in thee, oh Saul! even in thy disguise and agony as thou didst confront thy stern counsellor brought from the land of shadows—"the old man covered with a mantle." When Samuel demands, "why hast thou disquieted me?" we share in the desolateness and sorrow which thy answer implies.

"God is departed from me, and answereth me no more, neither by prophets, nor by dreams, therefore have I called thee, that thou mayest make known unto me what I shall do."

The Woman of Endor! That is a strange perversion of taste that would represent her hideous in aspect. To me she seemeth all that is genial and lovely in womanhood.

149

ELIZABETH OAKES SMITH

So great had been the mental suffering of Saul, that he had fasted all that day and night, and at the terrible doom announced by the seer his strength utterly forsook him, and he fell all along upon the earth.

Now cometh the gentle ministry of the Woman of Endor. "Behold thou hast prevailed with me to hearken to thy voice, even at the peril of my life; now, also, I pray thee, hearken to the voice of thy handmaid, and let me set a morsel of bread before thee, and eat, that thou mayest have strength."

Can aught be more beautiful, more touching or womanly in its appeal? Aught more foreign from a cruel and treacherous nature, aloof from human sympathies, and dealing with forbidden or unholy knowledge?

To the Jew, trained to seek counsel only from Jehovah, the Woman of Endor was a dealer with spirits of evil. With us, who imbibe truth through a thousand channels made turbid by prejudice and error, she is a distorted being allied to the hags of a wild and fatal delusion. We confound her with the witches of Macbeth, the victims of Salem, and the Moll Pitchers of modern days.

Such is not the Woman of Endor—we have adopted the superstition of monk and priest through the long era of darkness and bigotry, and every age hath lent a shadow to the picture.

"Hearken to the voice of thine handmaid, and let me set a morsel of bread before thee." Beautiful picture of primitive and genial hospitality! The Woman of Endor riseth before me in the very attitude of her kind, correct entreaty. The braids of her dark hair mingle with the folds of her turban; her oriental robes spread from beneath the rich girdle, and the bust swells with her impassioned appeal. I behold the proud contour of features, the deep, spiritual eye, the chiseled nostril, and the lip shaming the ruby. The cold, haughty grace, becoming the daughter of the Magi, hath now yielded to the tenderness of her woman's heart.

Woman of Endor! thou hast gathered the sacred lotus for the worship of Isis; thou hast smothered the dark-winged Ibis in the temple of the gods; thou art familiar with the mysteries of the pyramids; thou hast quaffed the waters of the Nile, even where they

150

FICTION

well up in the cavernous vaults of the ancient Cheops; thou hast watched the stars, and learned their names and courses; art familiar with the sweet influences of the Pleiads, and the bands of Orion. Thy teacher was a reverent worshiper of nature, and thou a meek and earnest pupil. Thou heldst a more intimate communion with nature than we of a later and more worldly age. Thou workedest with her in her laboratory, creating the gem and the pearl, and all things whatsoever into which the breath of life entereth not.

There was nothing of falsehood, nothing of diabolic power in this. Men were nearer the primitive man, nearer the freshness of creation, and they who patiently and religiously dwelt in the temple of nature learned her secrets, and acquired power hidden from the vulgar, even as do the learned now, in their dim libraries, and amid their musty tomes.

Thus was it with the Woman of Endor. She was learned in all the wisdom of the East. She had studied the religion of Egypt, had listened to the sages of Brahma, and studied philosophy in the schools to which the accomplished Greeks afterwards resorted to learn truth and lofty aspiration; yet even here did the daughter of the Magi feel the goal of truth unattained.

She had heard of a new faith—that of Israel—a singular people, who at one time had sojourned in Egypt, and yet who went forth, leaving their gods and their vast worship behind, to adopt a new and strange belief. Hither had she come with a meek spirit of inquiry, to learn something more of those great truths for which the human soul yearneth forever.

Hence was it that her wisdom and her beauty became a shield to her when the mandates of Saul banished all familiar with mysterious knowledge from the country. She was no trifler with the fears and the credulities of men. She was an earnest disciple of Truth, and guilelessly using wisdom which patient genius had unfolded to her mind.

All night had she watched the stars, and firmly did she believe that human events were shadowed forth in their hushed movements.

She compounded rare fluids, and produced creations wondrous in their beauty.

There were angles described in the vast mechanism of nature, in the passage of the heavenly bodies, in the congealing of fluids, and the formation of gems, which were of stupendous power when used in conjunction with certain words of mystic meaning, derived from the vocabulary of spirits; spirits who once familiarly visited our earth, and left these symbols of their power behind them. These the learned, who did so in the spirit of truth and good-ness, were able to use, and great and marvelous were the results.

Such was the knowledge, and such the faith of the Woman of Endor, the wise and the beautiful daughter of the Magi. She was yet young and lovely; not the girl nor the child, but the full, intellectual, and glorious woman.

She had used a spell of great power in behalf of Saul, who was in disguise, and unknown to her; and thus had compelled the visible presence of one of the most devout servants of the Most High God. Even she was appalled, not at the sight of the "old man covered with a mantle," but that she saw "gods descending to the earth."

The fate of Saul would have been the same had not the prophet from the dead pronounced that fearful doom, "To-morrow shalt thou and thy sons be as I am," but he might till the last have realized that vague comfort to be found in the uncertainty of destiny, and in the faint incitements of hope. Fancy might have painted plains beyond the mountains of Gilboa, where the dread issues of battle were to be tried, and he would have been spared that period of agony, when the strong man was bowed to the earth at the certainty of doom.

Saul and the Woman of Endor, ages on ages since, fulfilled their earthly mission, leaving behind this simple record of the power and fidelity of human emotions in all times and places; we cannot regret even the trials of Saul, in the view of enlarged humanity, for had he been other than he was, the world had been unblessed with this episode of woman's grace and woman's tenderness, in the person of the Woman of Endor.

FICTION

FOR FURTHER READING:

Beam, Dorri. "Fuller, Feminism, Pantheism." In *Margaret Fuller and Her Circles*. Edited by Brigitte Bailey, Katheryn P. Viens, and Conrad Edick Wright. Durham: University of New Hampshire Press, 2013: 52–76.

Reed, Ashley. *Heaven's Interpreters: Women Writers and Religious Agency in Nineteenth-Century America*. Ithaca, NY: Cornell University Press, 2020.

"COMING TO GET MARRIED"

Published in *Graham's* in 1843, "Coming to Get Married" combines the example of a form of writing emerging from technological innovations of the 1830s with experiments in character and theme Oakes Smith would continue to develop into the 1850s.

Readers who remember or have heard tell of the internet before and after the regular circulation of images and video might easily imagine the impact of a similar revolution in Oakes Smith's time, when new print technologies made possible the inclusion of fine mezzotints by the day's most talented artists and engravers in popular magazines. Often removed and framed by subscribers (which is why they are so often missing in extant copies of these journals), one engraving by a celebrated artist sometimes cost the publisher as much as the entire "literary" contents of an issue of the magazine.[1] Given the new popularity and commercial priority of these images, editors began enlisting some writers—especially newer contributors such as Oakes Smith—to "embellish" their featured art with text, rather than the reverse. In this context, Oakes Smith's narrative, which "illustrates" Rawdon Wright and Hatch's engraving for the first page of her story, only to turn to another story behind the minister's brow, would seem to critique the culture of materialism leading to both premature marriages and the popularization of image over text.[2]

The mispreparation of young women for marriage was a central theme to which Oakes Smith returned throughout her career. In her novel *The Western Captive* (1842) her readers had already met a

---

[1] Frank Luther Mott, *The History of American Magazines* (Cambridge: Harvard University Press) I: 519, quoted in Cynthia Lee Patterson, "'Illustration of a Picture': Nineteenth-Century Writers and the Philadelphia Pictorials" *American Periodicals* 19/2 (2009).

[2] Other examples of Oakes Smith's work in this vein are not hard to find. The same month, she "illustrated" Alfred Jones's engraving of "The Village School" in *Godey's Lady's Book* 27 (July 1843): 39–41.

FICTION

heroine who refused to marry, and in stories like "The Defeated Life" (1846) Oakes Smith would dramatize in horrific detail the results of early or ill-sorted marriages, but "Coming to Get Married" is one of her first attempts to articulate, at least indirectly, her argument against divorce as a legal remedy—and thus how any marriage worth the name was currently for only "the very few." While quite a few readers may have nodded at the correspondence between the first page of the story and the fine artwork they received as part of their subscription, others may have noticed that Herman Vortenberg does not divorce his wife. More fully elaborated both in *Woman and Her Needs* (1851)[3] and in her articles on divorce in the New York *Tribune* in 1853, Oakes Smith's counterintuitive position *against* divorce was an attempt to cut a Gordian knot that plagued woman's rights advocates through the 1850s: would the relaxation of divorce laws free women from men's despotism or relieve men from all but the legal and material obligations of marriage? Rather than reduce the concept of marriage to what Margaret Fuller rated in "The Great Lawsuit"[4] a mere "household partnership" or "mutual idolatry" (and however Herman has suffered, it's actually not clear how the arranged marriage of the young immigrant couple here will turn out), Oakes Smith's radical solution was to make marriage so legally binding that not only were both parties enjoined to serious reflection before entering into such a contract, but ideally, women would be given opportunities for the intellectual, economic, and social equality on which a deeper relationship might be based. Until the "better

---

[3] Included in *Elizabeth Oakes Smith: Selected Writings*, Volume II.

[4] Margaret Fuller's early feminist treatise "The Great Lawsuit: Man vs. Men, Woman vs. Women," published in the *Dial* in 1843, includes a description of the range of marriage relations, from "the Household Partnership" of material convenience to the spiritual or "Religious Union" of partners sharing a mutual pilgrimage to a higher ideal. In a chapter dedicated to Oakes Smith in *Woman Thinking* (Lexington Books, 2007), Tiffany Wayne details the ways in which Oakes Smith's feminist work of the 1850s carried forward Fuller's work of the 1840s. Oakes Smith knew Fuller in New York and likely discussed their mutual concerns for woman's rights at Ann Lynch Botta's literary salon in 1845, but the subtext of "Coming to Get Married," published before Fuller's treatise, shows Oakes Smith working out positions on marriage before she knew of Fuller's work.

"Coming to Get Married" engraving by
Rawdon, Wright & Hatch from *Graham's Magazine*, July 1843.

Image from Scrapbook, Box 4.
Papers of Elizabeth Oakes Prince Smith, Accession #38-707.

Courtesy Albert and Shirley Small Special Collections Library, University of Virginia

time coming" in which such equality and more spiritual unions might become more common, Oakes Smith's story stood as an example of the pains endured by the majority.

Another item of interest for this story is Oakes Smith's use of a pseudonym. "Ernest Helfenstein" was not an unfamiliar name to readers of popular magazines in New York and Philadelphia in 1843. Oakes Smith had used it as early as 1840, soon after her arrival in New York, in order to submit, publish, and receive pay for multiple contributions in the same issues of *Godey's* and other magazines. As the letter copied below demonstrates, at least for some time publishers considered Helfenstein to be a real person, not to mention a male identity whose authority on "speculative" or philosophical matters might have been more easily accepted in light of the gender expectations of her readers.

It is significant that Oakes Smith killed Helfenstein off shortly before her full emergence as a feminist advocate, ascribing the authorship of *The Salamander* (1848) to "the late Ernest Helfenstein." The name "Bertha" would return along with Helfenstein, this time as a main character, in *Bertha and Lily*, her novel of 1854, where the example of a more fully developed female protagonist leads to a more progressive and hopeful resolution than readers saw in this early sketch.

"COMING TO GET MARRIED"[1]

Ernest Helfenstein

"Come to get married!" Dorothea was just on the point of lifting up the tea-urn, but she only held up both hands with such a queer smile, and looked at the pair as she would have done at a brace of nice ducks to be picked for her master's dinner.

Dear soul! Matrimony was a *terra incognita* to her, about which she had the most vague and grotesque ideas, as one might be supposed to have of the Fegee Islands. She had a just and conscientious sense of what was due to "creature comforts," presenting them in the best and most appropriate shape, and in this way she was of immense value to the worthy rector and his benign sister.

Indeed, so alive was she to all temporal concernments, that the good man at one time took occasion, when she was spreading the table for dinner, to read her an extra homily upon the interests of her soul. Poor Dolores began to cry first, which still more inspired the eloquence of the good man, and then she hung down her head and blushed, and then, to his utter amazement, went off into such a fit of laughter as really to endanger suffocation in the paroxysm. Upon recovering from this, she exclaimed,

"It's of no sort o' use. Soon's ever a man talks to me alone, I always think of Jacob Flanders, and that sets me to laughing."

At this moment, Aunt Jane looked grave, and directed some article to be carried to the kitchen, and then explained, with spinster-like propriety, how Jacob had even attempted the unseemly language of love to Dorothea, going so far as to kiss her hand, at the relation of which enormity, Aunt Jane slightly blushed, and the pastor's face departed very considerably from clerical gravity.

---

[1] "Coming to Get Married," *Graham's Magazine* (July 1843): 52–56; republished in *The Rover* (April 12, 1845): 50–54.

It is astonishing how much more complacently women regard the matrimonial intentions of others than do the other sex. Their sympathies are all alive upon the occasion, and they feel an interest and a tenderness, perfect for the time being. Aunt Jane had not one particle of vanity or selfishness in the world. She had never thought of a man, except when she thought of her brother, and never seemed to imagine that she existed otherwise than as an appendage to him.

When the pair determined upon the desperate measure of matrimony appeared at the parsonage, she fixed her benign regards upon them, mechanically placed her finger upon the side of her smooth cheek, as she was wont to do when the pranks of the poodle arrested her attention from the intricacies of "reed stich" or "tent," and happening to be nearest Dorothea, she leaned one hand upon her shoulder, as much as to say, "Dear souls, how nicely they look together," and then she had a confused image of the tenderness of a pair of birds she once kept in a cage, and that used to look so lovingly upon the same perch all night side by side, each with its head behind its wing.

"So you have come to get married?" said the pastor, half rising from his chair, and speaking much more severely than the occasion would seem to justify.

Ralph assented, looking a little blank at the sternness of the good man, and half began to think, as a man is pretty apt to do, that he was doing a very foolish thing. Sybil's pretty face grew crimson, and her eyes dropped, but then she looked as if she though it all quite natural, and she was content.

Ralph had come to Pennsylvania four years before, and settled in the village of _____, and, of course, became one of the parishioners of my friend. He had been betrothed to Sybil before leaving "faderland," and now that his enterprise and patient labor had met its reward of easy competence, he had sent for Sybil and her widowed mother to share it with him.

"Come get married!" there was a long pause, and the minister compressed his lips, and cast his eyes onward almost with an expression of scorn. It was unnoted by the inmates of that little room, the simple-hearted woman and that brave, loving pair whose hearts

FICTION

were unchanged by time, labor and separation, and soon the good man arose, and with even more than his wonted impressiveness, united two who should from henceforth be eternally one.

Those who have never known deep suffering are slow to detect its indication in others. Aunt Jane knew that her brother had in early life passed through a period of severe mental anguish, but he was now entirely calm, had been so for years, and she never imagined him to be otherwise than perfectly happy. Busied with the little genialities of every-day life, blessed with simple and ordinary desires, undisturbed by those ideal tendencies which so often embitter, at the same time that they ennoble the more imaginative, her life was as placid as a heart full of content could make it. She saw fearful lines stamped upon the face of her brother, and supposed that study and the sanctities of religion were making their busy impress—she never dreamed the sorrow of early life had been seared by the lapse of years into his very soul.

We have said he looked sternly upon the young people who stood before him. He did so, and yet Herman Vortenberg was a kind-hearted, genial man, who regarded the infirmities of others with the eye of true charity, while his own life was a perpetual reaching for that ideal standard recognized by the Great Master when he said, "Be ye, therefore, perfect, even as your Father in heaven is perfect."

Marriage to him was a solemn and beautiful mystery by which was typified that angelic existence in which the two were no longer twain, but one forever and forever in the Paradise of God.

A marriage, to his high and spiritual mind, must be a marriage of hearts; a union of soul with soul; a high and holy communion, by which the faculties of the soul were fully to be developed, its repose secured, and the whole nature with all its manifold attributes brought into harmonious action. He was no dreamer, but a deep spiritual thinker, basing his life upon his insight of the Ideal. The revealments of great truths, brought out by the fervency of prayer, by fidelity to the good, by meek obedience to the indications of all spiritual discernments, all of these were combined into great principles of action, earnest and unwavering.

He was now the meek, self-sacrificing apostle of truth, moving in a sphere of limited usefulness, yet content therein, inasmuch as it left him free from the stormier passions of his early youth. To most persons he seemed a man of calm, agreeable temperament, constitutionally incapable of strong emotion of any kind; but a close observer of the human face, or studier of human character, might detect the smouldering ashes of fierce and latent fires, once burning with a terrific violence, though now extinct it may be forever.

He was exact, almost stern in the discharge of his parochial duties, discoursing much upon the sanctity of all human affections, the care, the earnestness and devotion with which they should be fostered—the hazard of mistakes, the danger of abuse, and the fearful lethargy induced by worldliness and all ungenial influences. Upon subjects like these a strange eloquence grew upon him, a solemn majesty that went forth infusing itself amid his hearers, like the waving shadow of a great banner, moving to and fro, and giving boldness to the outlines of all things upon which the light falleth.

Herman Vortenberg was now a solitary man, waiting with patient faith for the good yet in store for him, and firmly and resolutely casting aside the shadows which the evils of early experience might rest upon his soul. He had once gathered the household gods about him; once, in the impetuosity of early passion, when the strong physical man is so apt to be misled by the seductions of beauty, it was then that beneath the green tree, like the idolaters of old, he set him up an altar and bowed in worship. Alas! for the highest divinity came not to the feast, and he quenched, even with his heart's blood and the soul's tears, the fires of the altar. Calmly, solemnly did he take it away, and alone in the sanctuary of his own soul bow down to the worship of the good and the true.

He had just left the University, high in honor, and full of that aimless enthusiasm that so often bewilders and disturbs the soul of early genius, as yet unrelieved by action or expression. The seclusion, too, of a student's life, while it afforded no opportunity for the exercise of early emotion, left ample room for the dreams of the imagination, and thus fostered the germ as yet dormant. Relieved from the routine of a collegiate life, he was conscious of a wild sense of freedom, an exulting power, a longing for action, a confused and aimless grandeur of existence, equal to all things, but undetermined as to what. He was like a steed of the desert, for awhile a captive, but now rejoicing in freedom, tossing its mane to the winds of heaven, with dilating nostril and spurning hoof "snuffing the battle afar off," and ready for the fierce encounter. Thus the study that had filled him with thought left him unready for action. Knowledge had become his own, but wisdom was to be the growth of painful experience, of soul-sickening, soul-withering contact and grapple with the hardness of human destiny.

What wonder, then, that the fascination of Bertha C—— should fire the brain of the youthful and romantic student? At the time of his departure for the University, she was a gay, beautiful girl, abounding in intellect, and holding as by a spell all who approached her. A mere boy, he had regarded her then with a sort of wonder, a something in which he had no concernment, beautiful but remote. A few years his senior, she scarcely bestowed a glance upon the studious boy, who had never directed a stray regard to her face. In the short vacations he had been equally indifferent. Absorbed in his studies, he heard of her seductions just as he read of those of Helen or Cleopatra, beings who hitherto raised no emotion of sympathy.

The day of his return from the University, a small party were invited to his father's house; Bertha was of the guests. Nothing but ordinary civilities passed between them, and yet, when the youth retired to his pillow, he found the low tones of her voice lingering upon his ear, like a stray chord of music.

For the first time in his life, he felt that the soul had other desires than that for knowledge, other pursuits than that of glory. He tried to arrest the unwonted current of thought, to compose himself to slumber, but in vain. At this moment, the faint notes of a song came to his ear. He listened with a tumultuous thrill. He barely breathed. He felt as if his soul had suddenly been dissolved, and mingled and became part of that sweet melody.

Trust it not, the idle story,
 Love hath no abiding here—
Bubbles all are fame and glory,
 Nothing real but the tear.

Smiles are false, and still deluding,
 Hiding withered hearts and sear,
Fleet are they, for sighs intruding
 Usher in the coming tear.

The words were sung to a listless air, and so low as to be almost undistinguished, but the melody thrilled the very soul of the young student, while the words were graven upon the memory unconsciously at the time, but to become the material for after years of bitter reflection. He listened till the words died away, and then, overcome by emotion, he stepped out upon the terrace.

The moon was calm and clear, and the night wind, fresh from the sweet south, gave another drop of intoxication to his bewildered senses. The building was a low one of stone, covered with vines, and sheltered by trees of a primitive growth, which the taste of his forefathers had preserved in making the "clearing." The long sweep of these gigantic trees, in the dim light, gave a cathedral-like grandeur to the scene, and inspired emotions of love and religion.

The old vines that draped the building had been suffered to grow almost without pruning, and, in some parts, the terrace was nearly encumbered by their growth. Lifting up these, at an angle of the building, the songster was revealed to him, half reclining on a low form, her eyes lifted to the moon, and bathed in tears. Obeying the first wild impulse of his heart, Herman rushed forward and knelt at her feet. She moved not, but her lustrous eyes fell slowly to the face of the youth, and their calm light entered his very soul.

"Bertha!"

She smiled faintly; there was more of sadness than tenderness in that faint smile, and yet it was a blending of both. Who does not know of the fearful power that lurks in the self-possessed gentleness,

FICTION

the half-dreamy tenderness of a beautiful and mature woman, when acting upon the young and inexperienced!

He seized her hand—he covered it with kisses. She did not repel him, and yet the smile died from her lips—a deep sigh escaped her, and she burst into tears.

The youth sprung to his feet. "Oh, God! I have offended you—you are unhappy, and I have added a new pang, I who would have died to serve you."

She took his hand in hers, and drew him to the seat beside her. Her tears dried away, and there, by that still light, her low, gentle tones of voice blended with the calm night, and "lapped him in Elysium." She spake of the fickleness of human hearts, of the mockery of life, of its weariness, soul-sickening vapidness. It was a new theme to the student, with his fresh and untried nature. It stirred the deep fountains of his sympathy. He looked into her tearful eyes, listened to the low voice, and drunk in a strange and wild bewilderment.

When, at length, she arose to leave him, and her long curls, shading her cheek, revealed yet her pure spiritual brow and deep eyes; the youth seemed to awake to a sense of life and bereavement.

"Go, Herman," she whispered, "forget this night, forget that you have seen me, and may God bless you."

The student slept none that night. A new life had been revealed to him. He wondered at his former existence, so cold and unreal, and hour after hour did he pace his lonely room, thinking of Bertha.

Bertha would have left the farmhouse the next day, but the good mother of Herman saw that he desired her stay, and she playfully commanded her to abide. Week after week the youth yielded to her fascinations. A new meaning was revealed to him in the aspect of nature, and the language of poetry, and Bertha seemed to hold the key that unlocked beautiful mysteries. At length their vows were plighted.

Herman was an only son, the heir to wealth. Bertha had more than a competence. Worldly calculations were unthought of. He lavished upon her the fullness and freshness of a heart whose fountains she only had stirred, and Bertha—

As yet, Herman had no plan for life. To live that he might elucidate great truths, that he might be as a city set upon a hill in the highway of goodness, had hitherto been his ideal. Now, why should he not live to impart happiness to a human soul. Why would not the vast destiny of life be accomplished with him by devoting himself to one human being; to foster the true and ennobling, to develop the hidden mysteries of his and her heart; to go out into the beautiful in nature and art, and thus build up the temple of God in their own souls.

Bertha's clear intellect and imaginative character seemed to have acquired a new strength by association with the impassioned youth. Yet that strange calmness, that touching sadness was ever the same. New *thought* had been elicited, but the foundations of emotion were unmoved. Her lustrous eyes met his with the same look of dreamy tenderness, the faint smile yet played upon her lips, and that self-possessed gentleness was all unchanged. Yet there, even these, might have aroused the suspicions of one versed in the hidden language of the heart, wrought with stupendous power upon the unsophisticated student. The elements of her character were unlike his own, but it was the contrast that results in harmony. Her repose was refreshing to him. It supplied what was wanting in his own nature. It was like the dew imparting life and vigor to the plant scorched by the meridian sun.

They were wed. No change grew upon the youth. Bertha's affluence of thought was a never failing source of interest. Her gentle manners, her sweet playfulness of fantasy, supplied an unfailing source of delight. Yet, in the midst of all this, a strange yearning grew upon the heart of the youth. A sense of chill even in the presence of his beautiful wife; a void unfilled even by her tenderness.

Prone to metaphysical subtleties, he began to question the nature of his emotions. He believed that perfect human love would result in entire content—in soul-fullness. More than once had Bertha hinted at a former attachment, which he, with mistaken magnanimity, had forborne to listen to, as a subject most painful to herself. He remembered, too, that he had more than once found her in tears, which she instantly suppressed, and met him with smile such as could dwell on no other lips.

It was now his turn to smile sadly, to meet the gaze of Bertha with an aching tenderness; to feel how awful, even here, are the mysteries and revealments of the soul.

One evening he found Bertha in the library, bending over an old Lutheran Bible, discolored by time, yet its velvet covering and silver clasps betokened the care with which it had been preserved. It had belonged to one of the early reformers, and was regarded with great reverence by the family. She did not look up when Herman entered, and he though her lost in pleasant reverie over the interesting relic.

When, however, he approached her, he saw her face was bathed in tears, and she was engaged in reading the answer of Jesus to the materialists of those days. Placing her finger upon the text, she raised her eyes slowly to his face, and repeated, in a voice scarcely above a whisper,

"Whose wife will she be in the resurrection?"[2]

Herman turned ghastly pale; a cold sweat started upon his brow, he staggered to a seat, and covered his face with his hands.

Bertha shuddered, she knelt down, and laid her head upon his knee, looking upward with that mysterious, sad face, now pale and passionless as marble. At length, she heaved a deep sigh, and fell senseless to the floor.

Herman placed her upon a couch and bathed her cold face, till the sad eyes opened and met his agonized expression.

"Oh, Herman, Herman! I have committed a deadly sin, in that I swore, before God, to love and honor you, while my love, aye, the deep love of a strong woman's strong nature, had been that of another. I have never dared call you husband. I have entreated you to

---

[2] Matthew 22:28: "Therefore in the resurrection whose wife shall she be of the seven?" The question refers to "levirate" marriage, which was meant to protect a poor widow, but which also ensured the deceased brother's property would stay within the family. The implication here is that Bertha has given herself to another.

call me Bertha, for the name wife has been too holy for me to respond to."

A fierce light grew in the eyes of the wronged man, as he listened to these fearful words. He grasped her wrist convulsively, and looked sternly into her pale face.

"Woman, tell me solemnly, before God, if you felt all of this at the time you consented to be mine."

"No, on my soul, dear Herman, I did not even know the extent of my love for another—another with all his worth and manhood, now in his grave;" and she covered her face with her hands and burst into tears.

"Bertha, you have mocked me; you have perjured your own soul, and plunged me into everlasting misery. You have bound us with cords death only can sever, while we must from henceforth be as strangers to each other."

A shriek, wild and piercing, burst from the lips of the wretched woman, and she once more relapsed into insensibility. Herman again bathed her brow, unconsciously murmuring "Oh, God, so beautiful, and yet so wretched—so noble, and yet so weak!"

"Weak, most weak!" responded Bertha, without unclosing her eyes. "But, Herman, even truth must be gradually unfolded to the mind. The blessed Savior recognized the weakness of human understanding when he said, 'I have yet many things to say unto you, but ye cannot bear them now,'[3] and he fulfilled his great mission, leaving these things unsaid. Is not the mystery of marriage one of these things? Is the human mind, even after the lapse of centuries, prepared to receive the true doctrine?"

Again, Herman found himself listening to the eloquence of those sweet lips, content to live upon the honey of words so purely framed, and again he forgot the mysterious sadness and the tranquilness of manner that revealed a soul whose destiny had been sealed.

"Dear Herman, those truths have been growing upon me; slowly but surely unfolding themselves to my mind. At the time of

---

[3] John 16:12.

FICTION

our contact, I was a solitary being, yearning for sympathy. I would have been content as your friend, your sister, but your vehemence forbade that. I was fearful of losing you altogether. I thought love was a thing to be conquered, to be transferred even."

"Bertha—"

"Herman, I must say all now, it is better for both."

"Go on, go on."

Again she shuddered and clasped her hands upon her breast, as if to keep back her emotion.

"I thought, Herman, that old things would pass away, forgetting that material things only perish in the using, while love is indestructible and eternal, growing brighter and brighter unto the perfect day."

"Bertha, you drive me mad. You, who love me not, can talk in this wise, while I, I who have expended my whole soul upon you—" And he paced the room with clenched hands.

Most gently did Bertha exercise her powerful ministry. "No, Herman, yours is not love. It is an intellectual admiration, a content in thought, a gratified imagination, but love is more than this. It is too intangible for definement, yet the soul knoweth its presence by its fullness of content in the beloved. Herman, let me say all. I had not been able to detect its tokens, till I found I would sooner lose you, Herman, than lose the memory even of my buried love."

"Oh, God! Oh, God! Is this life!" exclaimed the unhappy man.

"It is fearful, Herman, the weakness, not the vice, of our nature that has brought this upon us. I have endured this, dear Herman, and even more."

Both were, for a long time, silent.

"Then, this doctrine of the true marriage has been a gradual revealment," said Herman; "You did not, could not, understand these things in their present light, and yet consent to take such fearful vows upon yourself."

"Never, never. Oh, God! Herman, to souls like ours, made to discern the truth, such vows, where the two are not one in spirit, truly and entirely one before God, are a fearful desecration. It is a mockery of all Divine appointments."

"True, most true." He grasped her arm with a strong grasp, and replied, huskily, "and yet we are bound in the light of human institutions—bound till death, death, shall sever the bonds. Bound by human ties, though from henceforth strangers upon earth," and he fell headlong to the floor.

Long and fearful was the malady that followed this terrible explanation. Bertha watched over his couch with sister-like assiduity, preserving her calm gentleness of demeanor, even while the others were blanched with fear. Often and often, in the silence of his slumber, did she kneel down and pray that the bitterness of his cup might be assuaged. Often, in the wildness of his delirium, did she respond with some seasonable word of sympathy, that brought comfort to the inner soul.

Was there no strife in the soul of that strong woman, think ye? Had she no need of human sympathy under her load of suffering? Alas! no; she suffered but as she had brought suffering upon others; suffered for the infirmity of her woman-nature, but hers were divine ministrations, comfort from the Beloved, help from God.

Most beautiful grew she in her spiritual loneliness. Worn and stricken as she was, the true soul draped even mortality with angelic garments.

Herman slowly recovered from that long fever, and again listened to the soothing and elevating language of Bertha.

"Whose wife shall she be in the resurrection? Not mine, not mine, Bertha. I can think calmly of it now. But, oh, God! The agony I have suffered; surely, surely there is a fearful retribution here! No, not retribution, for mistakes are followed often by more severe and protracted misery than even vice. But then they do their office of discipline to the soul, while sin brandeth thereon a perpetual stain."

"Yes, dear Herman, we must be 'made perfect through suffering,'[4] and the dismay of darkness causeth us to turn in search of the light." She took his hand, and the tears slowly gathered in her eyes,

---

[4] From Hebrews 2:10: "For it was fitting for Him, for whom are all things and by whom are all things, in bringing many sons to glory, to make the captain of their salvation perfect through sufferings."

FICTION

for she had that to say that was most painful to be uttered. Herman closed his eyes, divining what was the nature of that mute, yet eloquent appeal.

"Speak, dear Bertha, I understand what you would say."

There was one wild gush of agony, and she buried her face in the pillow and sobbed aloud. Herman laid his hand gently upon her head, and thus, in silent and holy communion, each praying that comfort might come to the heart of the other, without the utterance of a single word, was the external bond reverently recognized between them, yet as reverently spurned by the spirit as no bond of union. Herman pressed his lips to her cold hand, and she arose from her kneeling posture, and implanted one last kiss upon his brow.

And thus they parted, she to cherish the image of the heavenly; he to wrestle in spirit, to strive as striveth the strong man for the mastery of self—to go out into high and holy pathways searching forevermore for the good promised to the faithful.

Here died out in his soul all the promptings of ambition. Here arose a noble desire to impress worthily some few minds in the great mass of humanity. Herman traveled many years; he sought the society of the gifted and the learned. Alas! He found sorrow lurking in every heart. He found that love alone is its own exceeding great reward; but that few, very few, are equal to the gift.

FOR FURTHER READING:

Patterson, Cynthia Lee. "'Illustration of a Picture': Nineteenth-Century Writers and the Philadelphia Pictorials." *American Periodicals* 19/2 (2009): 136–64.

Tuchinsky, Adam. "'Woman and Her Needs': Elizabeth Oakes Smith and the Divorce Question." *Journal of Women's History* 28/1 (Spring 2016): 38–59.

"THE DEFEATED LIFE"

Oakes Smith's story entitled "The Defeated Life" was published in a giftbook called *The Mayflower*, published by Saxton and Kelt, in 1847.[1] Oakes Smith also edited this volume, along with the following years' edition, including several texts from her own pen. One of Oakes Smith's most interesting literary productions in a formal sense, it blends four different genres—historical sketch, short story, and a woman's personal diary, at times written in poetry—to achieve horrifying psychological effects of a female character we might find in a tale written by her friend Edgar Allan Poe. As a narrative describing a woman's descent into madness, it also foreshadows the now commonly anthologized tale of female imprisonment "The Yellow Wallpaper," written by Charlotte Perkins Gilman nearly a half-century later, in 1892.

Readers of "The Defeated Life" familiar with Oakes Smith's autobiography can hardly be blamed for identifying her with her character Lizzie Brewster. If the name weren't enough of a tip-off, Oakes Smith's description of her marriage in the autobiography— the season, the weather, the dress, even the hairstyle—matches the story point for point. True, not much is said about Seba Smith's eyes in the autobiography, but like the creepy husband Mr. Malcolm, he is also described there as "bald and bespectacled." A closer inspection shows that whole passages from "The Defeated Life" seem to have been brought into the autobiography:

---

[1] By the mid-1830s, giftbooks or annuals combining shorter works (stories, sketches, poems) from a variety of up-and-coming authors had become a staple of the publishing industry. Editions became available for purchase in November or December, usually well-bound and decorated, with a variety of engraved illustrations to accompany printed material. Editors were often chosen for their ability to acquire recognized names for the year's table of contents, though it was also expected that, beyond what he or she could procure from literary friends and acquaintances, the editor would provide whatever additional material was needed to fill the volume.

FICTION

"The Defeated Life" (1847)	"A Human Life" (1881)
Dolly, the maid, gave the last touches to the dress of the fair girl, and then stood apart in wondering delight at her loveliness. There was a quiet dignity about Lizzie, which made it difficult for anyone to address her in the language of praise; but Dolly could not now restrain herself.	The maid who dressed me for the occasion stepped aside, and giving me a careful inspection, exclaimed, "You are the most beautifulest creature I ever laid eyes on," at which somehow, I did not smile. I was so foreign to all this: so unfit for the occasion.

Nor do the comparisons even end with the married pair. In the autobiography, more than ten pages are taken up with a description of the "Old Meeting House below the Ledge" in very much the same reverential tone as we find in "The Defeated Life," including a poetic elegy to the building that runs for several manuscript pages.[1]

And yet if we read the autobiography carefully, we find it is the historical references Oakes Smith makes here where one-to-one comparisons between her life and the story begin to break down. When we compare her description of the "Old Meeting House below the ledge" in the story to her description of it in the autobiography, we are still in recollection mode, but we find Oakes Smith addressing not her time but her grandparents' time. The setting of her vignette is "one hundred years ago (this 1881)" she writes, imagining herself on the "horse block" "before her *grandfather's house*:"[2] before which we see

---

[1] Oakes Smith's earliest version of the theme appeared in *The Southern Literary Messenger* in 1841: "The Old New England Meeting House" *The Southern Literary Messenger* 7 (September 1841): 607–608.

[2] Emphasis mine.

the Maidens in their long bodices framed upon whalebone and mercilessly indicating the proportions of full health and elegant beauty; arms cased in sleeves tight to the elbow, and terminating in a wilderness of ruffles, with gloves of silken net. A profusion of petticoat, short in front and trailing behind; the feet in pointed shoes and high heels. It behooves maidens thus dressed to be decorous in mirth. Many is the time I have masqueraded in these brocades and costumes of the long ago, nor did I doubt the truth of it when Grandma would say, "Ah! Elizabeth you are not so handsome as your mother was at your age."[3]

This critical voice, which we might recognize in the withering comments of Madam Brewster, "proud dame in every sense of the word," matches a woman in Oakes Smith's life, and that woman may be her own mother, Sophia Blanchard, but given the historical reference to 1781, the portrait may more accurately reflect a woman like Hephzibah Drinkwater Blanchard, Oakes Smith's maternal grandmother, remembered in the autobiography as a "haughty intellectual woman" with a high hand and an equally bold stance with her husband in the 1780s and '90s. That is to say, as much as the prematurely married Lizzie seems to resemble Oakes Smith herself, Lizzie also resembles Oakes Smith's mother, who, born in 1787, was married off to David Prince at the age of sixteen, not to mention Oakes Smith's older sister Hepzibah, two years old than Elizabeth, who was married at about the same age to Richard Loring Cutter, born in 1795 and thus also many years her senior. From Oakes Smith's perspective, premature marriage isn't personal, it's institutional. Indeed, if we read Oakes Smith's autobiography not as a simple recitation or "copy" of her life, but rather as a continuation of the arguments she had been making since the early 1840s about the impropriety and injustice of the marriage relation in the United States in her time—institutional drag even more frustrating for Oakes Smith as the Reconstruction era left women in a position

---

[3] "A Human Life," MS 44–45.

Section of the original image entitled "The Old Meeting House Below the Ledge," painted by A. Johnston and engraved by John Sartain, from Elizabeth Oakes Smith's copy of *The Mayflower*, 1847.

Courtesy Timothy H. Scherman

FICTION

little different than she had begun to work against in 1850—we might conclude that Oakes Smith took women's subjugation as a class personally, even if, in fact, she was never "Defeated" by it herself. Neither in 1847 nor even 1837 did Oakes Smith find herself the kind of helpless victim she describes in her story, and by 1850 she would change her strategy from negative critique to constructive prospect, admonishing women who would otherwise "stay at home and fret and dawdle, be miserable themselves and make all within their sphere miserable likewise" to " meet and...devise plans, explain difficulties, rehearse social oppressions and political disabilities, in the hope of evolving something permanently good."[4]

If it is ultimately impossible to say whether Oakes Smith's poem "The New England Meeting House" of 1841 demonstrates her own nostalgia for simpler times, her use of the same mode in "The Defeated Life" is certainly part of a familiar rhetorical strategy. Only by cultivating the sympathy and confidence of more conservative readers (especially those willing to offer to their mothers, daughters, or sisters a fine "Gift" for the year 1847) does the powerful shock that ends the tale achieve the potential to actually change minds. Like many of her stories, the nested narrative begins far from where we will end, and Oakes Smith's choice of a point of view outside Lizzie Brewster's perspective until the moment of the story's denouement cleverly interpellates the reader as a by-standing accomplice in her suffering and descent into madness. An antecedent to Charlotte Perkins Gilman's similar portrayal of a woman's mental dissolution in her story "The Yellow Wallpaper" forty-five years later, Oakes Smith's story has been figuratively "crawled over" repeatedly by feminist scholars tracing abundant references to the effects of isolation and self-denial in the writing of women of the nineteenth century on both sides of the Atlantic. Beyond many of her peers, however, Oakes Smith would pursue the fate of women like her protagonist from fiction into lived history in subsequent years, shocking conservative audiences in editorials by defending

---

[4] See *Woman and Her Needs*, chapter 1, printed in Volume II of *Elizabeth Oakes Smith: Selected Writings.*

women who, rather than conveniently dying like Lizzie Brewster, took the law into their own hands against real-life Mr. Malcolms in the 1850s.[5]

---

[5] Oakes Smith's editorial in August 1855 documenting her interviews with "The Veiled Murderess" Mrs. Robinson may have contributed to the commutation of Robinson's death sentence to life in prison.

"THE DEFEATED LIFE, OR

THE TIMES OF THE
OLD MEETING HOUSE"[1]

Elizabeth Oakes Smith

"It was a church low-built and square
With belfry perched on high;
And no unseemly carving there
To shock the pious eye."[2]

Upon the shores of Casco Bay, about ten miles from the city of Portland, is a long hilly range, of perhaps three quarters of a mile in length—a barren rocky spot partially covered with stinted pines. In one part where the grey granite "crops" out from the thin soil, may be seen a weather-beaten vane, which a few inhabitants of the district have elevated upon a rude frame and soldered into the rock, in the pious hope of thus preserving this only relic of the "Meeting House below the ledge."[3] Rarely might be found a more attractive spot for the worship of a new people, than the site of this old church, standing as it did, at the base of the ledge before named, upon a green esplanade, flanked upon every side by the forest, through the

---

[1] "The Defeated Life," *The Mayflower for MDCCCXLVII* (Boston: Saxton and Kelt, 1846) 36–75.

[2] Lines from Oakes Smith's poem "The Old Meeting House," republished in Potter's *American Monthly* 4 (1875).

[3] Built in 1729, the Old Meeting House served as a church and town house for the local settlers. The original structure was torn down in Oakes Smith's time, and the weather vane is now an exhibit in the Yarmouth History Center, but the base of the iron structure that held the weather vane as a marker can still be seen in the granite several hundred yards up the hill from where the meeting house stood.

openings of which arose the "Block House," the place of refuge of the colonists in periods of peril, fast by the altar of God, with here and there the humble dwellings of the worshipers, each in fact a citadel, built for strength, and armed for defence. In front was the Bay, a most lovely expanse of water, with Island and Cove, sloping hill, and rude promontory, all wearing the aspect of newness and beauty, to awaken the freshest impulses of the heart.

Though little can be said in defence of the architectural perfections of the "Old Meeting House," yet in the proud days thereof it might have been regarded as the model of excellence. Here came the staunch men and the stately dames of the olden time, to listen to the profound and subtle teachings of Parson Gilman as he stood reverently in his large white wig, and discoursed upon "predestination," "fore-knowledge," "free agency," and "eternal necessity," together with other doctrines abstruse and all-important in the eyes of the unflinching thinkers of that day. Then it was that a sermon held its all-important place as a part of the seventh day teaching; then it was that the theologian found wary hearers; then it was that the Teachers from the pulpit became "Boanarges,"[4] indeed, thundering forth their sublime intellectualities, to overawe the feebler minds, which were unable to penetrate these fearful mysteries, and could only cry trembling and in tears, "I believe, help thou mine unbelief."[5] Then it was that prayer, by which spirit maketh itself known to spirit, became a weapon of attack, a vehicle for the utterance of dogmas to be received by human ears, and lost its great purposes of supplication, confession and faith. Every man was supposed to have become "Priest unto the Lord," and the errors of heresy were more dreaded than errors of practice, amongst a people with so few temptations to evil from without. Hence the introversion of thought in that day; the anxious and pious ingenuity with which men searched for hidden evil; the monkish self-abasement; the severe nicety of

---

[4] Ancient Greek or Hebrew term meaning "sons of the tumult," or, more commonly, "fiery preacher." In the New Testament, this is a name given to James and John by Jesus.

[5] Mark 9:24.

FICTION

moral construction; and those terrible wrestlings and groanings of the spirit to be "delivered from the thorn in the flesh."[6] This was a part of the Pilgrim care to preserve themselves and their children from abuses, which they had braved peril in every shape to escape. They would keep themselves a pure people, "jealous of good works," and in order to do this, they laid the foundation in their own hearts, which they "guarded with diligence."[7] Far-seeing, earnest and true men, let us reverence the sanctity of their motives, although we may condemn the intolerance of their measures.

Parson Gilman[8] has long since been gathered to his fathers; and his hearers have nearly all departed, except a few venerable men, who still talk of the self-willed, independent old man, who for fifty years swayed the minds and consciences of the people about Casco Bay; whose great learning, severe piety and uncompromising logic found no rival, and have left their impress yet upon the minds of men, after the laps of nearly a century. Parson Gilman and his white wig are still held in affectionate remembrance, and the "elders" in North Yarmouth delight in reviving reminiscences of him and his ministry, when the Old Meeting House was the only place of worship in the town, and people came from the distance of ten miles to listen to the word of God, as delivered by Parson Gilman "below the ledge."

After standing more than a hundred years, it was pulled down in 1830, if I mistake not, having been long deserted as a place of prayer. Yet it was in excellent preservation up to the time of its fall, having been built of white oak. I cannot even think of this desecration without a pang. I remember the awe with which I once trod alone its deserted aisles. The quaint pulpit, with its antique, oaken carvings; the communion table, folded in its place, and covered with dust, from which the elements had been distributed to the pious and

---

[6] 2 Corinthians 12:7: "There was given to me a thorn in the flesh."

[7] Proverbs 4:23: "Keep thy heart with all diligence."

[8] Fourth pastor of the First Congregational Church of North Yarmouth, Rev. Tristram Gilman was ordained in 1769. His headstone is clearly visible in the Ledge Cemetery at the intersection of what is now Gilman Road and Lafayette Street.

believing, now no more; the crypt beneath the pulpit, in which had been kept the rude "communion service"—then the doors ajar, or slipped from their hinges—the seats once pressed by the young and the beautiful—the solemn galleries—the place for singers, the slender balustrade surmounting each pew, which left their tracery where the light fell through the small glass. I remember the sparrow and the swallow which found there a peaceful habitation—the whispered murmur of the pines, as the wind swept adown the ledge, and stole through the lone church—and the bleat of the sheep sheltered beneath its eaves.

Truly, I know not how human hands could have been raised against it. I know not what heart would not have been awed into remorse and grief, as the venerable rafters, so long audible to prayer and praise, were crushed to the earth. We have no ruins, and it may be never shall have, for the spirit of our people is opposed to associations of the kind—they reject the past, whether in experience, in sentiment, or architecture. A cobweb is monstrous to them—a cornice honored by dust, and made sacred by the swallow, is an offence—the grey beautiful tintings of time are unseemly, and they long for the tidy, painted wall, and the brisk white-wash.

Oh had they but spared the "Old Meeting House below the ledge!" Thither they might have brought their children, and have told them tales of blood and peril—have taught them there the sublime lessons of human freedom, and the more sublime lessons of order and good citizenship. Reverently pacing those old aisles, how impressive might have become the teachings of wisdom! How the bye-gone age had lived again! What though the bird sang above the sounding board, was it not a sweet harmony? What though the fox might pat upon the stairs, and look forth from the windows; would it not send solemn and earnest thoughts home to the heart? What though the vestibule became a fold for the sheep—is not Jesus called the lamb of God, and would not their meek innocent natures appeal for the like in our own? What though the green moss lay in tufts upon the roof, the grass nodded from the eaves, and the turf rolled itself like a fold about the tilted steps, yet most pleasantly had come down the sabbath sun to light each with a smile, and old men, too

FICTION

infirm for church-going, or it may be yearning too much over the past, would have loitered about the door-way, or leaning heavily upon their crutch, have walked along the aisles, with ears too deaf to be startled by the sepulchral echoes. Oh that a plea might be heard from the old meeting-houses in which our fathers worshiped, in times when each went armed to the house of God, lest the savage should find them unprepared for defence, when worship was a great human need, to be sought through peril and death, and not as now a luxury, an appendage to respectability.[9]

Chapter II

'Tis a new world—no more to maid,
Warrior, or bard, is homage paid;
The bay-tree's, laurel's, myrtle's shade,
Men's thoughts resign;
Heaven placed us here to vote and trade,
Twin tasks divine!

Halleck[10]

The site of the Old Meeting House is now a smooth green turf, and only the grasshopper and the cricket pipe a Sabbath day song to God. The road skirting the hill is overgrown with bushes, and the pines under the shelter of the 'Gilman rock,' those dear cool pines, which kept up such a whispering all day and seemed as if they were telling over what the lovers had said beneath them, and trying to sigh in the same style; those old pines, so hard and smooth underneath, where no reptiles ever came, and no bushes crowded themselves, and only the winter-green came up to show off its red berries, and the Indian pipe, so wax-like in its purity, as if it once thought to be a columbine, but found itself out of place, and grew pale and

---

[9] The nostalgic tone of the first chapter is retained and even amplified in Oakes Smith's treatment of the place in her autobiography. The story's shift to fiction occurs in this second chapter at a calculated pace.

[10] Fitz-Greene Halleck, from "A Poet's Daughter," published in *Alnwick Castle with Other Poems* (1835).

179

tenderly beautiful, like a pure heart breaking; those social, talkative pines are deserted now. You can still see the road, and a rough one it must have been, adown which every Sunday morning might be seen the Brewster family on their way to church.

There was Mr. Brewster, a short stout man, with a fresh good-natured face, whose ruffles and velvet gave him the appearance of an overgrown boy, and who bestrode his large sleek chestnut horse with the air of a clumsy master upon the nursery hobby. Behind him, stately, in lace and brocade, perched daintily upon a pillion, her fair but haughty head rising above him, sat Madam Brewster, her shapely figure almost courtly in its careless yet proud bearing. One hand, which slightly pressed his waist, allowed the many rows of lace to fall backward and expose the handsome arm, scarcely shielded by its glove of net. From the pocket peered out amid the masses of drapery a lawn handkerchief and a bible with clasps, while a fan of gauze, a half a yard in length, graced her fingers. A proud dame was Madam Brewster in every sense of the word, queening it over her household as few women were wont to do in those days of deference for manly prerogative—when the blessing at the board, the petition at the family altar, and the prayer in the pulpit were each and all worded in a way to make her feel that she was indeed the 'weaker vessel.'[11] Mr. Brewster, good man, knew better than to indulge in any such pious arrogance, and it was currently hinted that his very smooth, almost episcopal generalizing form of prayer was carefully prepared by his good dame, and duly committed to memory by himself; for it was generally believed in the neighborhood that Madam Brewster had a leaning to the old church of England worship, [12] 'a hankering for the flesh-pots of Egypt,'[13] a spice of

---

[11] 1 Peter 3:7.

[12] Madam Brewster is suspected by strict Calvinists of her time of both materialism and a social elitism the Puritans (at least according to doctrine) sought to "purify" from the first Reformation.

[13] Exodus 16:3: "Would to God we had died by the hand of the LORD in the land of Egypt, when we sat by the flesh pots."

FICTION

the 'old leaven' of abomination,[14] as it was called, and even Mr. Gilman, orthodox as his doctrines were believed to be, was not without censure for not curbing the pride of his parishioner, Madam Brewster.

We have said she was a proud woman, and proud she was in every sense. Indeed, it was a rare sight, the flutter caused by the family of a sabbath morning amongst the primitive congregation, as the cavalcade swept the side of the hill all in order, and the calm eye of the lady often quietly turned itself back to see that due decorum was preserved. Well might her pride be forgiven, for it was a goodly sight—those seven sons, each with his hair in a long braid at the back of the head, handsome boys were they, as they came two by two, into the Old Meeting House, following the steps of good Mr. Brewster and his comely wife, with the pretty Lizzie at their side. Proud was she of the beauty of this fair girl, and the shapeliness of her seven boys. Proud was she as she saw Parson Gilman rise to the service as if it had waited her coming. Proud was she to see how her simple neighbors blushed and looked gratified if she by chance gave them a smile or a slight bow of recognition, for she did not attempt anything like familiarity with them. Proud was she of her wealth, and the blood in her veins, allied to the best in England. Proud was she of the memory of her father, a staunch adherent of the Stewarts,[15] who had exiled himself for them, and died here in this new land, bequeathing to her as her best dowry, his own uncompromising principle.

Mr. Brewster certainly had little sympathy with the lofty notions of his wife, nor did she seem to expect that he should have. Whatever ambitious motives she and her family might once have

---

[14] This is most likely a reference to either 1 Corinthians 5:7 or 5:8: the first line speaks to purge out the old, and the second to feasting without sin or malice, leaving all wickedness behind.

[15] While Oakes Smith's allusion aligns Madam Brewster with the Stuarts, the royal line who adhered to France and the Roman Catholic faith even after Scotland adopted Protestantism in the sixteenth century, the dynamic of mother and daughter in the story in many ways echoes the relation between Elizabeth I and her cousin Mary, Queen of Scots.

entertained, had been long since abandoned, but the haughtiness which distinguished her was an ingredient of the blood, combined with a love of sway, which, if it be not altogether amiable, must have done much in the early settlement of the country, to preserve the fine old families of the colonists from degeneracy. She was pertinacious in her adherence to the forms and usages of household matters, such as they existed at her father's house in England. There was no lack of stateliness in her arrangements, which, however becoming in themselves in a wealthy household, savored too much of aristocracy, to please the hardy democrats of the neighborhood. Parson Gilman, it is true, settled himself in the midst of these courtly trappings with the aspect of a man entirely at home, and it may be the taste of the fine old aristocrat was too well gratified, to admit of anything like pastoral reprehension. Madam Brewster went on her own way, indifferent to the cavilings of her neighbors, and so long as she appeared regularly at church, she and her household, orderly and devout, so long as all the ordinary offices of good citizenship were well filled by the Brewster family, there really seemed no just cause for complaint.

Mr. Brewster sometimes encountered a sly shrug when the subserviency of wives became the topic of conversation, and the stout radicals of the day, sometimes relieved themselves by a covert allusion to the 'better horse,' and the like, but he, good man, took it all quite naturally, never once seeming to think he had the least to do with the matter; nor no more had he, for Madam relieved him of a world of care, managed the boys, reprimanded the servants, and made Lizzie cry, all in a stately and proper manner, thoroughly ladylike, and edifying. There was nothing left for him to do, but enjoy himself in his own way: go to church of a Sunday, with Mrs. Brewster behind him; say grace at the table; make prayers morning and evening; hold the babies for Parson Gilman to christen, and in all other ways, demean himself as a good plain honest man should.

It will be seen that in those days the family must have lived nearly apart. There was then no village nearer than Portland, which was twelve miles distant; there was no corner, no tavern then, nothing but the farm houses with long intervals between, the old

FICTION

Meeting House, the Parsonage and the block house. People were too much apart, and too much encompassed with peril to afford much time for neighborly interference. Excepting the Sabbath-day meetings, and the meetings for prayer, weekly, at the houses of the parish, in which the sermon of Parson Gilman the Sabbath before became the subject for discussion, people had few opportunities for social gatherings, and fewer still for country gossip. They were all orthodox in their religious opinions according even to strict Puritanic construction. They were all virtuous in their relations in life, or there would have been a gathering of the elders to inquire into the matter, and bring the parties to a right sense of the proprieties of things. There was in fact nothing left upon which gossip might expend itself, except the all-engrossing and never-ending subject of the pride of Madam Brewster, the extravagance of Madam Brewster, and the domination of Madame Brewster, varied by a change upon the good natured Mr. Brewster, the hen-pecked Mr. Brewster, the affable Mr. Brewster, &c.

Those were the days[16] of decorum and good order, every man knowing that his neighbor's eye was upon him, to read the thoughts of his heart. Those were the days when a marriageable youth and maiden were a sort of public property, scrutinized by the old people with watchful guardianship, and the objects of all the artillery of simple coquetry, covert smiles, and glances from the young, every one of which became the subject of comment or surmise and were duly registered as a part of the important little drama which was hereafter to terminate in a wedding or a heartbreak, either of which would relieve the monotony of the hamlet.

Ah! but these were great days for smiles and ogles, days when each became a matter of profound interest; pretty lips had weighty meanings hid within them, bright eyes sent no random glances abroad, but each were warily used, and only with the premeditated will and consent of the fair owners. Staid and decorous Dames were

---

[16] Repeated several times in this paragraph, the period referred to by "those days" remains unprecise, making it difficult for readers to limit the woman's situation she is about to describe to any particular historical moment.

they of those days, they with calm, steady eyes, compressed lips, and scanty words; they with firm step, and careful observation—they of proud humility, and many internal questionings which found no relief in words; they who bore daily the cross of ungenial ministry, of crushed and distorted sympathy silent and tearless.

Chapter III

Affections are as thoughts to her, the measure of her hours;
Her feelings have the fragrance and the freshness of young
    flowers;
And lonely passions changing oft, so fill her, she appears
The image of themselves by turns, the idol of past years.

Pinkney[17]

Hitherto we have said nothing of Lizzie Brewster, fair as she was, and living like a gem in its own brightness. Except her own roistering brothers, from whom she fled half in terror, she had no companions. Madam Brewster, though well aware of her loveliness, often marked her daughter with an anxious scrutiny, fearful that something might be a little wrong in the construction of her mind, a shade of imbecility—a chord slightly ajar, which while it imparted a grace and variety to all her thoughts made them in turn a trifle less reliable. She could not name this to Mr. Brewster, for the subject was altogether beyond his capacity of comprehension, and the thing was in reality too intangible to be well explained to any one.

In this dilemma, she laid the matter before Parson Gilman. The loud, incredulous laugh of the clear-minded good man grated upon the ears of the proud woman.

'Ah no, Madam Brewster,' he said, 'you shall not be-little and be-twist the pretty lamb in this way. 'There is one glory of the sun, and another glory of the stars, and one star differeth from another star in brightness,'[18] but you shall not make little Lizzie no star at

---

[17] Edward Coote Pinkney, from "A Health" (1825).
[18] 1 Corinthians 15:41.

FICTION

all, simply because she has not the power and effulgence of her mother. She is not the bright one amid others, but the one star alone in the twilight.'

'Yes, all that is finely said, my dear sir, but my daughter is so strangely gentle, so without any particular bias in any way, that really I do not see how I am ever to look for anything in her.'

Again the Parson laughed, and Madam Brewster, not at all satisfied, was quite glad when Lizzie came in leading Charles Edward by the hand to claim the greetings of the good Parson. He placed her in a chair beside him, and in a few moments they were absorbed in one of those interminable debates as to the nature of free will and fore-knowledge, with which the ladies of that day were in the habit of amusing their leisure moments, and employing any super-abundance of feminine fancy which might be in their possession. It was really surprising to observe the easy grace with which Lizzie wound herself in and out of these labyrinthine subjects, seizing points of rare and subtle importance, with a careless vigor, which proved herself fully equal to the matter in hand, although it might not be altogether the one desired by a girl of sixteen. Imperceptibly she glided away from the dryness of polemics, and Parson Gilman listened with delighted wonder to her graceful and discriminating admiration of Spenser and Milton, for Shakespeare was as yet little known and less approved by the colonists. They looked upon all dramatic representation as little less than wanton exhibition of the cloven hoof of Satan, who, sure of his victims, was at no pains to conceal his designs. But Una, with her snow-white lamb was too far removed from human emotions to create distrust, and she—'in the lap of womanhood'—was meek, as she was fair, and not at all likely to suggest that radical individuality so strongly to be learned from the characters of Shakespeare.[19] Milton, too, with his terrible and majestic Satan, that impersonation of pride against which the pilgrims strove and preached night and day; Milton, the polished courtier yet arrogant republican, the true-hearted man yet earnest puritan;

---

[19] Una, the heroine of Spenser's *The Faerie Queen* Book I, represents the feminine ideals of truth, beauty, and purity.

185

Milton, with his womanly Eve, tender and meek and loving, erring yet always submissive; Milton was the idol of the Puritans, and, had his fame died out at home, had the license and oppression of courts forced him into perpetual exile, he would have found an evergreen fame here, would have been read and treasured and quoted as he is to this day with reverence, which has half mistaken his opinions for the teachings of Holy Writ.

Allegory, mysticism, and speculation were the daily food of men dwelling in the wilderness, with all the memories of stirring thought within them, who, retaining the intellectual ferment which had wrought out a relief from papal bondage as well as relief from royal prerogative, had exiled themselves so far from the influences of each that they had left little wherewithal to satisfy the cravings of that excitement which would not subside, although the occasion was past.

Young and old partook of this tendency to abstruse and introversive thought, which it is most likely did away with much of the urgency of human affection, and much of that sentimental necessity for sympathy, which, while it lends a grace, often not the less weakens the fibre of the mental constitution in a more luxurious state of society.

As yet Lizzie Brewster had naturally read and talked in accordance with the spirit of the times, excepting that a delicacy of perception, and a poetic elevation of view made her often seem to go even beyond them in her pure spirituality; and it was this, which alarmed her clear worldly minded mother into a suspicion that she might not have that practical grasp of life which she considered so essential to the dignity of the family. She never for a moment stopped to ask what might be the individual needs of any one, but what all things considered was for the manifest interest of the individual. For a girl unasked to exhibit any thing like preference for one of the other sex was in her eyes an evidence of monstrous indelicacy, to be treated like some revolting disgrace, which the good sense of a family should hide if possible from the eyes of the world; so that the indifference of Elizabeth to the youth of the period was no matter of surprise to her. She regarded it as the natural result of her careful training, and

FICTION

a proof of her filial submissiveness, while the truth was there was no one with whom she could have any possible sympathy; no one who, had he dared to lift his eyes to Lizzie Brewster, would have found the least return from the proud, intellectual and spiritual-minded girl. The mother was well aware of this, and was not slow to understand how it might be turned to her own purposes. All her ambition, all her love were concentered in her seven sons, and Lizzie with her high breeding, her tenderness, her feminine gentleness, was so enigmatical to her as to be a source of distrust, if not of annoyance. Her beauty even, severely brilliant, seemed out of place in a new country like this, while it would have been so ennobling in a more refined position. But to the imperious, practical and worldly mother, her deep mysterious eyes, her calm, gentle earnestness of manner, and sweet lips expressive of the finest sensibility, were each and all the source of regret and anxiety. In truth poor Lizzie was scarcely sixteen before she had found the subject of establishing her in life one of such vast solicitude that she had determined to leave nothing undone to have her at once placed where she would be safely cared for.

Chapter IV

Thou 'rt like those fine-toned spirits, gentle bird!
Which, from some better land, to this rude life
Seem borne; they struggle, 'mid the common herd
With powers unfitted for the selfish strife!
Happy, at length, some zephyr wafts them back
To their own home of peace, across the world's dull track.

Sargent[20]

At the distance of half a mile from Mr. Brewster's lived Mr. Malcolm, a gentleman of fortune and intelligence, a bachelor with an elderly sister, whose office was nearly a sinecure, involving nothing more than to put brother Malcolm's flannels to the fire, pour out the tea for brother Malcolm, say yes to all that brother Malcolm might utter, yawn in concert with him as dull people, who do not hate each other always will; and ride every Sunday to church where brother Malcolm always sat with his bluish green eyes fixed upon Lizzie Brewster; and go home with him after meeting, when he broke the silence by saying as he did twice every Sunday forenoon and afternoon, 'Lizzie Brewster is a very pretty girl,' at which Miss Sarah always responded, 'so she is, brother,' and no more was said for the day.

Mr. Malcolm was never known to give utterance to more than half a dozen words at any one time in his life; yet he had a way of smiling in just the right place, of lifting up his eyebrows in a mysterious manner, and distorting his parchment cheeks by various expressions of horror or amazement, or interest, whenever any body did in any way different from what every body else did, that people imbibed the impression that Mr. Malcolm was a wonder of propriety, sense and acuteness. True he had never done one single thing in his whole life either good or bad, and his greenish blue eyes had something exceedingly disagreeable about them, yet he was so

---

[20] Epes Sargent, from "Shells and Sea-Weeds, or, Records of a Summer Voyage to Cuba," from *Songs of the Sea* (1847).

FICTION

respectable, so rich, so regular at church, and so proper in every way, that people could give no tangible reason for disliking him, excepting that instinctive one recorded as applicable to Dr. Fell.[21]

Once a week he brought his sister to take tea with the Brewsters, where she sat upon the chintz sofa, and the sound made by her knitting needles as she violently hurried a pair of stockings for brother Malcolm into shape, was the only demonstration she gave of her whereabouts. Mr. Malcolm, on the contrary, listened to the energetic discourse of Madam Brewster, keeping his small full eyes fixed upon Lizzie as she sat with book in hand, or her fair fingers ran over the keys of the spinnet in the corner of the room. Mrs. Brewster, proud as she was, felt not unflattered by the respectful attentions of Mr. Malcolm, who always left her to her own ways of thinking, unlike Parson Gilman, who paid her understanding the compliment of an occasional dissent.

Perhaps no one could well tell how it was, but in the process of time Mr. Malcolm might be seen seated by Elizabeth Brewster, his bald head showing like a withered pippin beside her viny-looking and spring-abundant beauty. It was melancholy to see his parchment cheeks half cracked into sentimental lines, and his pinky eyes devoid of lashes ready to run over with tenderness; how she bore it all it is impossible to tell; but often did she arise with neck proudly curved, and ill-suppressed disgust, and seek in some great thought, or some wild gush of melody, relief from the destiny which she in her gentleness was powerless to escape; then she, the proud worldly mother was at hand to tell her that all this was but maidenly modesty, that all would yet be well. Unaccustomed to sympathy, alone in her dove-like gentleness, pure and timid and self-distrustful, full of deep and earnest thought, and full of emotions unakin to those around her; beset by snares from the cold and the calculating, it is

---

[21] By Oakes Smith's time, satirist Tom Brown's seventeenth-century epigram had become a nursery rhyme:
I do not like thee, Doctor Fell,
The reason why—I cannot tell;
But this I know, and know full well,
I do not like thee, Doctor Fell.

not surprising that the poor girl found herself in a position unsought and undesired, and without the capacity to say how it was forced upon her. Weapons had been forged from the wealth of her own fine nature to be used against herself—her own truthfulness and affectionateness had been turned as instruments to make her the victim for the sacrifice—she was the kid seethed in its mother's milk.[22]

Never was bride so unconsciously led to the altar; with no vanity, with nothing of the coquetries and caprice of her sex, with no affections pleading for tolerance, how could she make others feel that her soul revolted from its destiny! how teach the weakness and conceit of Malcolm to understand it, how awaken the forbearance of her haughty and calculating mother.

Rarely had the simple colonists witnessed splendor and expense equal to that which the wedding of Elizabeth Brewster furnished forth. The day was intensely cold and rain poured in torrents, yet warmth and light and luxury within banished the thought of the gloom without. Old people shook their heads and whispered of the sadness and life-long grief which the storm betokened, but the eyes of Madam Brewster were too keen and too alert to allow currency to these prognostics.

Not one in all that household sought to know the real feelings of Elizabeth. All were intent upon the amusement which the period furnished, and not one asked the meaning of the still pale aspect of the bride. 'Are you ill, Lizzie?' said the mother, bending her eyes sternly upon her child.

'No, Madam,' she answered, but in a voice so low and faltering it would have reached any other heart.

'Then do look up, and not appear so stupid. People will think you have n't any sense, your eyes are so dull.'

Lizzie tried to smile, for she knew her mother's pride, but it would n't come, and so she sat down and put her little hands out towards the fire and was silent.

'I do not see what is the matter of you,' said the lady impatiently; 'this has been none of my seeking; what ails you?'

---

[22] Exodus 23:19.

FICTION

Lizzie looked up again, and her mother's covert falsehood quailed before that mute appeal.

'Do try to look like something, Lizzie, I'm ashamed that a child of mine should have such a pale mawkish face.'

Lizzie placed herself before the large old mirror, and began to roll the curls about her neck, over her fingers. Madam Brewster seeing her thus engaged, left the room to order the maid to assist in dressing her. No sooner did Lizzie find herself alone than she leaned her head against the oaken frame and stood in perfect silence. It would be difficult to describe the feelings which passed over her as she thus stood; but whatever they might have been, they were too deep and too bewildering for external expression. She neither wept nor sighed, a torpor, as of some terrible doom weighed her down to silence and apathy. Rarely might be seen a creature of greater loveliness than she thus presented. Scarcely sixteen, with a form tall for her years, and yet possessing the lightness and grace of a child—one hand grasped the frame, against which she leaned, and the falling laces revealed a rounded arm of marble whiteness, her pale forehead, high, it may be too high for gentleness, gleamed through the clustering brown curls, which swept her cheek and bosom, and nearly hid the melancholy eyes, (those eyes, which had so often provoked the sarcasms of her imperious mother,) and even brushed the round sweet lips, which were parted now, so apathetic were her feelings. As a fresh gust of wind and rain shook the casement a slight shudder passed over her, but she moved not.

Dolly, the maid, gave the last touches to the dress of the fair girl, and then stood apart in wondering delight at her loveliness. There was a quiet dignity about Lizzie, which made it difficult for any one to address her in the language of praise; but Dolly could not now restrain herself.

'You are the most beautifulest creature I ever beheld,' she cried.

Lizzie did not smile, indeed it seemed doubtful if she heard her, so fixed was the expression of her face. Then came Mr. Malcolm to lead her forth to the ceremony, and she put her hand within his like one who is to act a part in some preconcerted scene. Then followed the solemn words to which she gave no response, neither by look

ELIZABETH OAKES SMITH

nor motion—those barren words, which wear so much the aspect of a contract, and so little the language of sentiment—cold words involving maintenance and duty, with no seal affixed thereto, for the Puritans rejected even this time honored and beautiful emblem of unity, the marriage ring. Then followed the sumptuous repast, and the mirth and the jest, in the midst of which Elizabeth moved so hushed and statue-like, that few could have believed all this mockery was to celebrate her nuptials. Then the old carriage of Mr. Malcolm lumbered through the drifts of snow, and wind, and rain, bearing the silent bride, pale, torpid, and like a doomed creature, to her new home.

Chapter V

The garland beneath her had fallen to dust;
The wheels above her were eaten to rust;
The hands, that over the dial swept,
Grew crooked and tarnished, but on they kept,
And still there came that silver tone
From the shriveled lips of the toothless crone,
Let me never forget to my dying day
The tone of the burden of her lay,
'Passing away! passing away!'

Pierpont[23]

We must pass over a period of ten years, which brought about the usual changes of life and its concerns. Madam Brewster was nearly the same. Her handsome boys were busy in the affairs of the colony, which was approaching the great struggle resulting in our independence.[24] Mr. Brewster had an easy leaning to the Whig side, but found himself so strenuously opposed by his wife and sons, that with his constitutional dislike to energetic measures he contented himself

---

[23] John Pierpont, "Passing Away—A Dream," from *Airs of Palestine* (1840).

[24] This rare reference to events occurring outside the narrative dates the marriage of Lizzie Brewster to the 1760s.

FICTION

by simply expressing good will to his hardy neighbors, and an occasional aid in a pecuniary way, while his family by correspondence abroad and active operations at home did all in their power to sustain the cause of royalty. We said Madam Brewster was unchanged. Time had left her handsome features unimpaired, her complexion was still brilliant, her form as well sustained as ever, nothing told of the passage of years except a statelier and more determined bearing, and the silvery threads marking her abundant and still beautiful hair; these she was at no pains to conceal; for indeed Madam Brewster had little of the infirmities of vanity in her temperament, and knew perfectly well the several stages of beauty adapted to each period in life. She was too proud to appear other than what she really was, hence her contempt for all concealment of what might be the approach of age, while her coldness and haughtiness of manners forbid any allusion to the subject in her presence. She was always called the handsome Madam Brewster, and nobody thought to speculate on her probable age, for no one thought upon the subject unless by accident her manly sons gathered about her suggested the idea of her wondrous youthfulness of aspect as being their mother.

And where was Lizzie all this time, the pale, girlish bride sent from the shelter of home upon that night of storm and darkness? Miss Malcolm had ceased to ply the needles in the chimney corner. She had long since ceased to yawn in concert with brother Malcolm or to respond to his few sentences of interest in what passed before him, for a cold and fever had laid her quietly down to her long sleep. Strange as it might seem, Mr. Malcolm nearly disappeared from church and places of pubic resort, and seemed more shy and taciturn than ever. Lizzie too—her existence was well-nigh forgotten. People were absorbed in the stirring events of the time, and the old low house, so silent, so hushed, so solitary from year to year, was rarely the subject of thought. Speculation was sometimes afloat respecting the inmates, but no one presumed to interfere with what seem to be matters so entirely belonging to themselves. Besides Madam Brewster was well known to regard her daughter with a strange severity, and few were willing to face the rebuke of her proud eyes and withering tongue.

For a while Lizzie might be seen in the pew of Mr. Malcolm of a sabbath morning, and then the worshipers, who did not fail to scrutinize her, observed that her figure was more slight than formerly, and a touching waviness approaching a stoop gave a peculiar tenderness to her air; the little fingers which pressed the psalm-book were very fair and slender, and the blue veins of the wrist might all be traced through the transparent skin. As she passed her father's pew she exchanged gentle greetings, rather reserved and timid it was thought with her mother, but Charles Edward she would kiss, and then pass on, nor lift her eyes to the many who longed for a glance from her sweet face.

At length she disappeared altogether, and it was rumored that Lizzie was in effect a prisoner in her own house. A melancholy look had the house indeed. Enormous elms, which should have tossed their long branches forth to the light, had drooped themselves around the roof of the lone dwelling and the common people did not fail to recall the superstition that grief to its inmates is indicated thereby. They remembered that the first blessed day of spring, which should have called gladness about the young bride's home, beheld an owl brooding upon the roof. Then came the swallow to build its nest about the eaves and in the stones of the cold chimney. A sad aspect did the mansion wear with its clustering elms, and singing birds, and all else so hushed. Rarely was the Lady seen about the premises, or if, by chance, a passer-by caught a glimpse of her, amid the abundant shrubbery of the old grounds or through the open casement, her look of intense sadness, her sweet unchanged melancholy beauty affected him like something supernatural. Why did she thus hold herself apart from human sympathy? Surely those round, sweet lips, those deep, loving eyes, and that low-toned gentle voice betokened all that is best and dearest in the affluence of womanhood!

We must add ten years more to the ten already passed, during which Lizzie had scarcely crossed the threshold. No one knew why it was so, although a general dislike existed with regard to Mr. Malcolm. No one believed that a being so ardent, so full of life and

FICTION

thought as Lizzie Brewster had been in her girlhood, would thus voluntarily immure herself in this way from all the genialities of life.

At length, one morning, the old servant of the family hobbled over to the Brewster house, a distance of some miles, requesting the immediate attendance of Madam Brewster.

Did Mr. and Mrs. Malcolm send? No, Mrs. Malcolm doesn't stir from the sofa, and Mr. Malcolm won't speak to nobody. The proud woman's heart sank within her.

On reaching the house, Mr. Malcolm, wasted to a mere shadow, was found seated in a large chair in the centre of the room, with his small pinky blue eyes intently fixed upon the form of Lizzie, which was curled up enveloped in masses of drapery upon one end of the sofa, her head resting upon her arms and her eyes closed.

'Why do you not speak to her?' cried Madam Brewster, shaking his arm violently, and dreading herself to approach her child.

Mr. Malcolm, without moving his eyes, answered mechanically, 'She will not let me.'

'Go to her, speak to her, man, what are you afraid of?' said the stern woman once more.

'I dare not' was the reply, and nothing was left but for the mother to solve the terrible mystery, for indeed she seemed as one dead. Lizzie unclosed her eyes, but they were listless, and she seemed unconscious of all that passed before her. When she was borne away to her chamber, Malcolm followed with his eyes, cold and pale, fixed upon her face. Some simple cordials restored her to a partial degree of vigor, and she became aware of his presence. Raising herself up with an energy to which she seemed a moment before totally unequal, she pointed her thin hand towards him.

'Take that man from my presence, and mother, if you hope for peace in your dying hour, let *me* die, without those hateful eyes upon my face. Oh God, for what have I lived!' she cried, sinking backwards upon the pillow. A few days closed the scene, and Madam Brewster, stung to the heart, stricken with remorse, and her proud intellect humbled that she had so little comprehended a creature whose existence but for her might have been one of love and life-

ELIZABETH OAKES SMITH

imparting happiness, returned to her dwelling to mourn over that which could never be recalled.

At the direction of Elizabeth, she took from beneath an old chest some sheets of paper, upon which she had inscribed some faint records of her sad life, which the mother read, and never from that time was known to smile.

Chapter VI

> I saw a form about my bed,
> That always shrunk from him with dread:
> 'T would come by night, 't would come by day,
> But clearest in the moonbeam show.
> Then always as it nearer drew
> Ere melting from my wistful view,
> With palm reversed it seemed to say,
> If yet with me thou wilt not go;
> Keep him, oh, keep but him away.
>
> *Hoffman*[25]

SUNDAY. Dolly has just brought me some flowers—the first fresh blooms of spring. My heart leaps at their beauty; I feel as if they were tokens from the angels, telling me that such a thing as happiness does exist somewhere, though not for me. I would kiss them, I would weep over them, but I feel that his eyes are upon me somewhere; somewhere peering in with their dead pale glare. I feel that he is somewhere watching my motions, and I would rather he should feel me to be the icy, impassable abstraction, I have schooled myself to appear, than know what my heart tells me I might be.

    *   *   *   *

I felt that he must be near me. I felt it by the dead weighty atmosphere that hung like a bat over me; and there he stood at the door, waiting to catch the sound of my breath, the fall of my foot; would

---

[25] Charles Fenno Hoffman, from "Kachesco: A Legend of the Sources of the Hudson," from *Love's Calendar, Lays of the Hudson and Other Poems* (1847).

FICTION

to God some great thought might awake, no, might find a lodgement in his mind, to crowd out his imbecile tenacity upon a subject which admits of no change; I must write these things, must give form, coherency to my thoughts, or I shall go frantic, and then I must burn all, all, for he will search, search, forever till he finds the record. And yet could I keep these things from year to year, it might, meseems, afford a comfort to read them over, and see how each succeeding one witnessed the triumph of higher thought and purpose, and a nobler surrenderment to God, of what—alas, indeed of what—of what but a poor infirm, outraged heart, which hath never known its idols—never stooped to vain worship, but alone, in silence and secrecy, hath trimmed a barren fane, hath guarded a pure light, against which no wind hath blown; affections which have found nothing akin upon earth, must be wafted heavenward—where, then, is the glory, the triumph? for preachers tell of taking up the cross, that is, of living counter to the impulses of our own natures, distrusting all that affords delight, and in proportion as we recoil from a destiny, so in proportion should we submit thereto, for this is virtue, this is subjecting the inferior to the higher, this is making reason triumph.

*   *   *   *   *   *   Ah! What is life but a succession of sophistries? what is truth to human eyes but the view which each one has of a face over which his own desires have spread dim shadows? and what is truth from God's altar, let me not blaspheme, but the associated views of men, who dole out what they in their littleness deem it safe for men to know.

FRIDAY. My Diary has escaped him, yet I know he hath searched everywhere to find it; yes, even pried up the old cold chimney, where I once hung it beside the swallow's nest; he has searched there again, and here is the poor thing's nest upon the stones, blood too, he has killed the young upon the hearthstone; and that was what all the twittering I heard meant. Well, the evil be upon his own head. They say swallows build about the out-houses, but never visit the eaves of a dwelling where peace is; I do believe it. Last night Dolly chased a bat from my window—poor thing might have staid.

But here is my Diary, which he hath not yet seen. The thought is an exultation. I feel as if winged, so pleasant it is to find a record known only to God and my own heart. Meseems it is a profanation to yield up the sanctuary of the soul to human eyes, or it would be to his. I shall go wild, indeed how often do I test the coherency of my mind, lest I may already have lost a portion of its clearness, so bewildered do I become by this silence, solitude, and *his* pale eyes glaring upon me wherever I am: such eyes, unchanging, wall-like, and moving wherever I move. I will try myself in that art, which I remember good Parson Gilman used sometimes to call 'the down dropped from the wings of angels in the hands of good men, but in the hands of bad men was nought but the pin-feathers of Satan.' It may be an idle art, but I will bless God for the gift since it has been an antidote to grief, without which my soul had clean died out. Meseems after reading the divine Milton, it is presumption and unseemliness to touch a single stop of melody; but since no ear but mine will be jarred at the discord, I will e'en go on.

AIMLESS AND HOPELESS

Oh weary life! It were an easy task
To lay thee down. Thou hast no boon for me,
No beaconing lure save veiled eternity.
Still must I struggle to endure, nor ask
Nor hope for aught, save that which wears the mask
Of joy, to hide the heart's deep agony.
I rise each morn with but the single prayer
For strength life's heavy load of ill to bear
And lay me down at night with all the claims
Of human hearts, called forth in our weak hour,
Each pleading for its own with voice of power.
Ah! wherefore struggle thus debarred from aims
Which fill the soul with their triumphant dower,
And write o'er crushed and weary hearts immortal names.

FICTION

SUNDAY. The rain pours in torrents, and the terrible wind roars through the old house. The sounds, which others often like to hear, fill me with the saddest emotions. I was cast forth from the home roof in such a night. No wonder all people have regarded a stormy bridal as ominous of evil, the fates, even the merciful fates, shrieking as if it were their disapproval. 'A lowery day and lowery bride,' I remember hearing some one quote upon that day so fearful to me. I will reproach no one. It must be a blessed thing for a child to feel itself understood, its nature cared for and loved. I wonder if I am unlike others, or if so, the worse for the unlikeness. Well let it pass, I shall never know. I dare say people get tired of loving each other, even my father and my brothers seem to forget my existence. I will write about it, or I shall weep myself blind.

SUCCORLESS

O thou with grief and pain oppressed,
In thy lone chamber make thy moan,
Nor hope for sympathizing breast,
'T will weary soon.

Love for the gay and careless heart,
But not for thee his blessed boon;
At sight of tears he will depart,
Weary full soon.

Above thy head the gourd may rise
To shield thee from the fervid noon,
But e'er the crimson twilight dies,
'T will wither soon.

'Tis not for thee, thou stricken vine,
To stretch thy tendrils, yearning one,
The prop thy weakness would entwine,
Will weary soon.

Take not the cup, though faint of soul,
Which human ministry doth own,
For all aside the drops will roll,
And mock thee soon.

Seek thou the barren rock for rest,
Pillow thy head upon a stone;
'T were better than a human breast,
Weary so soon.

FRIDAY. How I have lived in illusions! how by the creations of my own soul have I lived in a world by myself. Ah, how the blue sky, the hushed stars have sunk like a great beautiful mystery into my spirit! How the blossoms have been angel-tokens of love to me, and I have placed all that taste could summon in this new country to help out these illusions. How like a nun I have lived! and how little do I know of what is beyond these walls. Dolly says she hears there is war, and great trials and rebellions in the country, yet I know nothing of these things.

Why have I lived? and yet now that I can escape *his* presence I am not unhappy. Yet I am feeble and may die soon, and then, O God! *he* will come, *his* eyes will be upon me, his presence will weigh like a cloud upon me. I shall go mad. No, I will pray to God to spare me this most terrible of all calamities. I will 're-word' the past, that I may be sure that all is right with me.

MONDAY. I have been looking in the glass to see what tricks time has played upon me. Sooth to say he must have been strangely kindly. I am pale but not a line has he traced, and my hair falls like a banner over a marble capitol, truly it is most abundant, thanks to the good Dolly, who devotes herself to all that concerns me. This morning, when the faithful being sat down to dress it, I laid my head against her kind old heart, and wept like a very child. I do not know why I should weep, for I, who have never known happiness, excepting as God has poured it into my soul through thought and truth, surely why should I weep that the scene is drawing to a close. Yet so

FICTION

it is. Poor old Dolly! she did not try to comfort me, she only laid her shriveled hand upon my head, and whispered, 'Bless the dear lamb!' I feel as if I should dissolve in tears: my life has been a blank. Like a child have I lived. Years have passed over me, yet am I still a child. I feel the stirrings of great and beautiful thought within me, but alas! I know not how others in the great world are stirred, and these things may be but the humors of the blood lifting thought into activity, thought which had been as nothing had my life been one of action.

TUESDAY. My nerves must be strangely attenuated. I hear the slightest sound—my sight is so distinct that meseems I see through the lids—and the perfume of the flowers which Dolly brings me affects me to faintness, all but the rose, that loveliest of flowers, which has an odor, so fresh, so like the elements of all other sweet smells that I can bear it always. It is to the senses what beauty is to the soul. I begin to awake to a sense of what I am and what I might have been. Oh God! spare me the sight; I cannot bear it now. Too late, too late, for the material world, for the bonds are wasted to a thread which bind me here. I feel as if buoyed by the wings of angels, as if even now their pure forms were defined in the thin air. I hear pleasant voices in the garden of the soul, and I tremble not to that which says 'where art thou?' Am I not here a child even now? I am glad to see that I have but small space left me, for my thoughts grow too mighty for me, too mighty for this prison house. The great fighting, trafficking, hard world is too terrible a world for me to encounter. I will e'en try to dream again. I will put by the stirrings of this spirit for truly it is not meet for me. I will read that which it prompted me to write last night.

ELIZABETH OAKES SMITH

DESPAIR

There is a Lake whose sullen wave
Reflects no image on its breast;
No flitting bird its wing doth have,
No blossom on its margin rest;
But silence, solemn and profound,
Broods on the solitary shore;
And crumbling ruins strewed around
Tell those who come returned no more.

And thus my bosom hushed to rest,
Shall break no more its death-like sleep.
With dreams perturbed no more oppressed,
I wake no more, to watch and weep.
My perished hopes revive no more,
Hushed and for aye my trembling fears;
Faith points no promise from the shore;
I nothing have to do with tears.

Ah! wherefore o'er this sullen lake
Must I my lightsome banner fling?
Why on its stagnant pulse awake
Where dead knells only round me ring?
My freighted barque goes silent down,
A sealed up mine of wealth is there.
One fitful gleam a moment thrown,
Then sinks in silence and despair.

Alas! it is not well to write in this wise; yet I thank God, who
has given me more strength to endure than things like these might
seem to imply. It must be that when a Poet utters his complaint he
does so because he hath strength beyond, and he permits his heart
to bleed, as it were, because he hath a great strong heart, which is
eased thereby.

*   *   *   *   *

FICTION

There was little more than this, the life-long record, it would appear, having been destroyed, rather than have it desecrated by the action of uncongenial eyes. And thus, unknown, unministered to, in silence and in grief, lived and died one of God's blessed messengers for good, a sweet bird of song, which might have soared to the very gates of heaven; but mewed in the owl's nest, grew fearful at its own voice, and thus expired.

For Further Reading:

Scherman, Timothy H. "Oakes Smith Returns to Maine: 'The Defeated Life,' Katahdin, and the Dangers of Biographical Criticism." Gorman Lecture Series, Yarmouth History Center, North Yarmouth, ME, June 10, 2014. https://neiudc.neiu.edu/cgi/viewcontent.cgi?article=1001&context=eng-pub.

"TWO CHAPTERS ON BEAUTY, VANITY AND MARBLE MANTELS"

On December 13, 1847, Oakes Smith wrote to the prolific and well-known poet Lydia Sigourney, soliciting a poem for *The Mayflower* for 1848. "One of your ungarnered articles" would suit the purpose, Oakes Smith explained, "one that has been printed, if not 'Booked' will answer every purpose."[1] Desperate to bring the volume together in time for Saxton and Kelt to take some advantage of the holiday market, she levels with Sigourney in exasperation:

> The work being New England I am desirous to present our own authors as far as practicable, but the absence of a suitable spirit of enterprise in my Publishers has the effect to keep down the work—it sells well they tell me, and therefore they will not advance upon the expense—content to let well enough alone. This throws a heavier burden upon me and until authors combine in some way, those of us who by necessity must write and must publish, will be held at the mercy of Publishers.[2]

Indeed, Oakes Smith had done somewhat better in her editing effort this year, publishing her own work in only seven of the volume's twenty-eight pieces compared to ten of thirty when she

---

[1] Works printed in journals did not retain copyright in this period and were commonly reprinted both in annuals such as *The Mayflower* and copied in other journals. Poe's "The Raven," read by thousands before it was collected in *The Raven and Other Poems* (New York: Wiley and Putnam, 1845) is a well-known example of the practice, as was Oakes Smith's "The Sinless Child" some years earlier. In Oakes Smith's or Poe's case (if not Sigourney's) such a widely reprinted poem, while bringing no additional royalties itself, might convince a publisher to invest in a collection by the poet (see headnote of "The Sinless Child" above for John Keese's explanation), and hence could lead to some compensation in addition to what was paid for the original publication.

[2] EOS to Lydia Sigourney, December 13, 1847, Lydia Howard Sigourney Papers, Series 1, Watkinson Library Manuscripts Repository, Trinity College.

FICTION

prepared *The Mayflower* in 1846, but she was still obliged to rely on the male pseudonym "Ernest Helfenstein" (if only twice) to make her "editorship" (or ability to provide favor to contributors) appear more genuine. Sigourney did not comply with this request, but she would become a warm correspondent for the next few years until Oakes Smith's public involvement with the woman's rights movement made such a relationship untenable for the more conservative poet.

Along with a companion sonnet entitled "Jealousy," printed earlier in the volume, "Helfenstein's" story "Two Chapters on Beauty, Vanity and Marble Mantels" addresses a perennial theme of female advice columns and conduct books: the need for women to cultivate an independent self-regard, or what Judith Sargent Murray referred to in one of the least punchy titles in the history of essay-writing in 1784,[3] "a degree of self-complacency." Pushing back against puritanic insistence on female "modesty" and self-abnegation, Murray counseled mothers to praise their daughters for every positive attribute, building their self-esteem as a bulwark against the "deep-laid schemes" of designing men:

> Was she, I say, habituated thus to reflect, she would be taught to aspire; she would learn to estimate every accomplishment, according to its proper value; and, when the voice of adulation should assail her ear, as she had early been initiated into its true meaning, and from youth been accustomed to the language of praise; her attention would not be captivated, the Siren's song would not borrow the aid of novelty, her young mind would not be enervated or intoxicated, by a delicious surprise, she would possess her soul in serenity and by that means, rise superior to the deep-laid schemes which, too commonly, encompass the steps of beauty.

---

[3] "Desultory Thoughts upon the Utility of Encouraging a Degree of Self-Complacency, Especially in Female Bosoms," *Gentleman and Lady's Town and Country Magazine* (1784). Like Oakes Smith, Murray's writing career began in an attempt to help her husband John Stevens out of debt.

As Helfenstein, Oakes Smith's attitude is far more cynical, opening with the suggestion that no amount of self-esteem can overcome society's shallow preference for physical beauty—and that those without it should assume those who revere them must be after something other than romantic love, the protestations of literary "twaddlers" notwithstanding. Calling a "truce to sarcasm" at the end of the first chapter, Oakes Smith's narrator does not retract her advice to those without physical charms, but rather reminds her readers of the benefits of true self-regard—the freedom and self-fulfillment made possible by abandoning the habit of measuring ourselves by standards set by polite society or anyone else.

However provocative Oakes Smith's recitation of this common theme may be, what follows in the story's nested narrative is more arresting. Unsatisfied with the female identity of self-possessed and productive "old maid" or maiden aunt, and more determined to live than Lizzie Brewster of "The Defeated Life," Margaret Lincoln is one of Oakes Smith's most radical figures. Jilted by a false lover, she forges an identity sanctioned by no one in her society, taking on not only physical attributes that allow her to "pass" as male, but also the social responsibility and identity of a minister in a church frequented by the narrator's friend. As a physician (invested with the authority to distinguish biological difference), this second narrator guesses the minister's secret and divulges his knowledge to Margaret herself during a confession ritual, but instead of policing the gender boundary publicly, the physician preserves the minister's chosen identity until her death. While it would be too much to ascribe to the story Oakes Smith's defense of transgender identity per se, the story of Margaret Lincoln extends her exploration of the major figures of her novel *Bertha and Lily* (1854) and more personally prefigures Oakes Smith's own life, both in taking on the public female voice Rufus Griswold would call a "hermaphroditish disturber of the peace,"[4] and more obviously her own occupation of the pulpit as

---

[4] For the full development of this point, especially in light of Griswold's own marriage at the time, see Cynthia Patterson, "'Hermaphroditish Disturbers of the

FICTION

minister of a Congregationalist church in Canastota, New York, for a year in 1877.

"TWO CHAPTERS ON BEAUTY, VANITY AND MARBLE MANTELS"[5]

E. Helfenstein

I am very much in doubt whether an ugly woman should ever love. When I say ugly, I use the word in the English sense, applying to the external appearance; not to moral qualities, as the word is now mostly used to signify in New England, where the idioms of Milton still hold the ground. There a person is morally ugly, physically homely; according to the divine bard—

"It is for the *homely* features to keep *home*;
They had their name hence."

My position may sound very oddly in the face of the whole tribe of twaddlers who fill our magazines with stories going to show that mental beauty is the only thing really loveable or loved in this world; which may be a pretty philosophic illusion to the very large class of plain people who go to fill up the common clay of this common world; but the fact is substantially true, that ugly women are not loved. What are such to do then, exclaims ugliness in every possible variety, and in every possible expression of ugliness?

Why, recognise it as a fact, and meet it accordingly.

Peace:' Rufus Griswold, Elizabeth Oakes Smith, and Nineteenth-Century Discourses of Ambiguous Sex," *Women's Studies* (2016): 513–33.

[5] "Beauty, Vanity and Marble Mantels," *The Mayflower for MDCCC-XLVIII* (Boston: Saxton and Kelt, 1848) 172–87, originally published as 'Two Chapters on Beauty, Vanity and Marble Mantels" in *New York Illustrated Monthly* (1847): 5–8.

ELIZABETH OAKES SMITH

I would say still farther, beautiful women are rarely, if ever, vain; ugly women and plain women are always so. Beauty is favorable to self-esteem, plainness to vanity. The beautiful woman may have a very high standard, but she looks about her, and finds she has the advantage of most whom she encounters, and her glass sends back a reflection which, if not faultless, is far, very far from being repugnant to the principles of beauty. She meets her own personal attractions as a fact, to be no more cared for, and the looks of admiration bent upon her, are a natural and every-day occurrence, which in no way affects her.

Not so the plain woman. Her glass gives back a reflection by no means satisfactory to her own standard. She finds herself passed over in social gatherings, and she grows nervous and uncomfortable under a position which she is unwilling to fill. She tries to make amends by particular charms; she will with the frankness, but alas! rarely with the true magnanimity of Madame Roland,[6] be compelled to own that she has "ungloved a fair and slender hand," to do away with the impression of very unattractive features; she will flash out expressive eyes, pout a pretty lip, smile to show even teeth, half violate decorum for the sake of a bust, or with the egregious vanity of Madame de Staël,[7] go with the arms bare, because, as she said, it was

---

[6] Marie-Jeanne "Manon" Roland (1754–1793). Although not an advocate for woman's rights, Roland published reports of revolutionary work in Lyon and later moved to Paris, where her husband became minister of the Interior in 1792 and her salon emerged as a central meeting place for intellectuals, politicians, and revolutionaries. Drawing the suspicion of more radical factions, she was imprisoned for five months before she died by the guillotine in 1793. In her second series of lectures, written in 1852, Oakes Smith's lecture on Roland was grouped with others on Cleopatra and the dignity of labor.

[7] Germaine de Staël (1766–1817). Perhaps more moderate than Mme. Roland, Mme. de Staël was a woman of letters who also engaged in politics as the leader of an important *salon* during the French Revolution. A frequent critic of Napoleon's ambitions, she was forced to spend more than a decade in Switzerland, Germany, and elsewhere in Europe, in exile. Her novel *Corinne, or, Italy* (1807) provided Oakes Smith and some other early American feminists a model of independence, beauty, and talent in its title character, who was assumed to be based on the life of de Staël herself.

FICTION

all the beauty nature had given her, and she would make the most of it.

All this is exceedingly external, appealing to the sense of others, in the weak hope that we may be less ugly in their eyes than we are in our own, which, depend upon it, we never are. This is the action of vanity, a continual reference to others in an estimate of ourselves—a reference which the beautiful woman is protected from making by the existence of unquestionable charms.

Men pay homage to beauty, but there is no doubt their conquests are oftenest made with plain women, for vanity is far more obliging than self-esteem—and the dear creature, who finds her one only charm the subject of admiration, is overwhelmed with love—gratitude!—oh no! with vanity, which answers the same purpose.

The beautiful woman "knows her worthiness," as Shakespeare says, and is unmoved at a whole artillery of the kind; consequently, her emotions are likely to be the more genuine, earnest, and unadulterated. She is less likely to make compromises and mistakes. She is like a queen in her own castle, or like the fabled sleeping beauty, only to be waked when the true and destined knight shall take her by the hand.

What, then, is beauty the great and much to be desired gift? Certainly, if received as a holy gift. It rarely brings happiness to its possessor, but it brings something higher—reverence—constancy. Such, if loved, never cease to be loved. Even in the rude physical age of Homer, the old warriors look with awe upon the frail beauty whom the poet, in this way, has contrived to invest with a mournful and tender dignity. Tasso and Petrarch grew into immortality through their love of such; and Heloise, Mary Stewart, and Josephine, each with their several qualities, have brought the beings of their devotion into the foremost ranks of humanity, to be instinctively approved or condemned. Nobody cares for the learning of Abelard; he is remembered only as the lover of Heloise; Mary—the unqueenly Mary—but the fascinating and beautiful woman, we try to forgive because of her thorough genuineness, a fullness of heart that made her life a long inglorious martyrdom. The loving and unselfish Josephine is too sacred for words. We care little for portraits

209

of women like these. We feel in our hearts they were beautiful, in voice, eye, motion; grace and soul-pervading beauty must have been instinct with them.

Such are the beings who unconsciously challenge love, because they become to the observer impersonations of loveliness. They realize to the nice eye the dreams of the imagination—they are the ideals of grace, of poetry, and they care as little for their own marvellous power as does the statue which chills while it sets the heart astir.

But what are the ugly ones to do? Must they live without love? Certainly, without the poetry of love. They may have esteem, respect, friendship, and many approximations to love, and if they will be rid of vanity, and live content in a great *fact*, in company with the larger part of those about them, they may have what to most of persons is more desirable than the romance of love: they may have every-day content, which is a very respectable and enviable position to be placed in, and with no tendency to flirtiness, which vanity is very apt to produce, they may be thoroughly praiseworthy and respectable, and being the majority they have it in their power to stare down and put down every beautiful woman who may appear like a vision in their path. It is true, by such a course of frowning, they gain nothing from the other sex but a double dose of flattery, which they would not dare to expend upon the really beautiful, and they will find themselves at every moment likely to be deserted of their seeming admirers who flatter them in order to do homage to their more favored sisters.

But a truce to sarcasm. There is certainly enough to do in the world, great human needs enough to occupy every magnanimous mind, without reference to the beauty of the missionary. Once in her life even an ugly woman may be pardoned for yielding to her little romance, her domestic heartbreak; but, after that, let her give her vanity its "quietus with a bare bodkin,"[8] and her life will be little stirring of events, and her real womanhood of ten times the

---

[8] Shakespeare, *Hamlet*, 3.1.75–76.

FICTION

sacredness and value; indeed, she will please, in spite of her plainness, those only whom she should desire to please.

Chapter II

I had a friend once who hated marble mantels; black marble mantels he regarded as the abomination of abominations. He said they had not the frankness and honesty of a mirror, while they revealed quite as much. After much persuasion, he gave the following story as a reason for this dislike.

Passing through one of the by-streets of one of our great cities, said he, as I often had occasion to do in the way of my profession, I observed a small wooden chapel, which, of a Sabbath-day, was thronged with worshippers, and the vestry room through the week was a place of constant resort. Making inquiries, I was told that the young priest who presided there was remarkable for his eloquence, sanctity and benevolence. He was the guide and physician of his people, and had been for nearly five years almost worshipped by them.

Curiosity, one morning, prompted me to attend his ministration. I was struck with the solemnity of the service, which, without being either Catholic or Episcopal, swayed from one to the other. The opening form was confessional, for I observed many of the worshippers placed in a small box, at the entrance, slips of paper, which an old deacon afterward conveyed to the priest. Kneeling before the altar, the priest took each of these, and having read them made a mark upon a slate, and then cast them into a brazier filled with coals, and they were consumed.

He then came forward, and he and all the congregation knelt, while with a voice most earnest and musical, he alluded to the nature of the various offences which had been confessed, and then all responded to his simple, earnest appeals for pity and forgiveness by the cry,

ELIZABETH OAKES SMITH

"Have pity, O God!"[9]

I recollect little of the subsequent ceremonial, unique as it was, for I found myself so impressed with the sublime spirit of worship, that I remembered only that I was a responsible human being, needing the pity and forgiveness of the Most High, who knew the needs of the creature he had made.

At the close, the priest raised his hands with the simple benediction, "The good Father bless ye, my beloved," and he folded his hands meekly and retired. I was so struck with his manner, so truthful and so gentle, so touching the very fibres of the human heart, that I was only aroused by the exclamations of the poor people about, who were saying, "Ay, and ye may well look after him; he is an angel of good." "No preaching for money there; his is for the love of God and poor human souls," and other things of the kind.

Now all these remarks placed the preacher in the masculine gender, and I was convinced I had listened to a woman. The voice, the air, the habits of the preacher; all confirmed me in my opinion. It was in vain I afterward attempted any civilities—with a solemn yet gentle dignity, I felt myself repulsed. All communications passed through the box at the door, and though I did once so far presume as to throw therein a slip containing the word—"I have plucked out the heart of your mystery,"[10] I was so ashamed of the act when he appeared at the confessional that I could have wished for annihilation. When he read the paper, he dropped it into the brazier, but made no mark upon the slate, nor did he lift his eyes, or show, other than by an exceeding paleness, that he was alive to the incident.

I learned the priest occupied some plain rooms in the rear of the chapel, which he had himself built; that he received no pay, in any shape, either for preaching or medicine; that he had an elderly female, who was his only attendant. He never went out; a few flowers, books, and ministering to the poor, filled up his whole life. The dead were brought to the chapel for the service, infants duly received

---

[9] Psalm 51:1–2.
[10] Shakespeare, *Hamlet*, 3.2. 341–42.

FICTION

the sign of the covenant, and the marriage vow was pledged, all in the same area, from which he never strayed.

Many years elapsed, and I had outgrown my unmanly curiosity, when one morning my office was fairly besieged with applications. The priest had fallen ill. I went immediately, but was refused entrance; the old woman telling me with tears in her eyes, that he was certainly near dying, out of his head, yet raving with all the sweetness of an angel. With professional freedom I pushed her withered hand aside from the lock and entered the sick room, closing the door against all obtrusive curiosity.

The poor old woman rushed forward and threw herself at the side of the bed in an agony of grief. There were the fair hands, the long locks, and the expression of patient suffering which only woman wears. She was delirious, and in a high fever. I left a prescription, and administered a palliative myself upon the spot.

Ill as she was, her delirium was suspended partially, a moment, and she fixed her eyes upon me sternly, saying:

"God deal gently with thee according as thou dost respect my secret."

I bowed reverently, and left the house. I was not allowed a second entrance, although she must have hovered for weeks upon the verge of the grave, and when she next made her appearance in the chapel she was a white shadow, nothing more, and the house was filled with tears and sobs, in the midst of which arose her clear sweet voice like a chord of music. I noticed one petition which I knew was designed for me.

"May the good in any heart, though rejected here, be a sacred deposite in the bosom of God, to be hereafter brought forth and receive its reward!" I found myself weeping like a little child, while listening to her words.

She lived in this way many years, and at length expired in the midst of the morning confessional, surrounded by the prayers and blessings of the poor.

Hitherto I have said nothing as to her personal appearance. The long priestly garments she had assumed were favorable to disguise, and her amber colored hair, parted upon the top of her head, gave her an exceedingly apostolic interest. As a priest, she was earnest, true, beautiful; but as a woman exceedingly plain. The only handsome feature she had was her nose, and nothing can be made of that even by the most consummately vain. It is a fixture which can never be tortured into anything like availableness. But the soul speaks in the voice, and hers had all the depth of intonation, and all the flexibleness of a spirit like hers, always conversant with what is highest and best. I never heard her laugh, but her smile was just, not mortal.

And now for her story, which may be told in a few words. I had it from the old nurse after her death, who gave me the only record she had left behind her—a short poem, which she would seem to have written at the time of her grief, and to have preserved with a convulsive and monkish feeling of penance. And now for the reason why my friend so hated marble mantels—black marble mantels.

THE STORY

Margaret Lincoln had always been a very plain girl; but having a mind of clearness and order, she put the subject of personal attractions aside as a thing from which she was entirely set apart, and found herself content with the many resources of a virtuous and elegant life. She was high bred and amiable, and had a fortune at her own disposal, so that life might have seemed to promise well for her in spite of her plain face and slight twist of the shoulders.

Unfortunately she accepted an invitation to visit a cousin of hers, a handsome but giddy woman, whose house was the resort of the wealthy and the fashionable. Here the delicate assiduities of Mr. ——, a man of intellect and refinement, won, not only upon the esteem but the affections of Margaret; and she who had never felt a pulse thrill at the language of either flattery or love, found herself entirely absorbed in one who seemed to love her for the beauty of her soul, the fine issues of a fresh and earnest and loving spirit.

They were engaged for a length of time, waiting some business arrangements, and Margaret found the whole world like a scene of enchantment. One feeling of distrust had never crossed her innocent

FICTION

mind. She thought so little of her own personal appearance, that she never questioned whether it weighed in the mind of her lover.

One day she was sitting by a table, writing a note, when, accidentally raising her eyes toward the black marble mantel, she found herself powerless to move them from the images therein reflected. She raised her eyes to herself in the opposite mirror and then glanced at the marble mantel, where she beheld her own beautiful lover, her own beautiful cousin. It was enough—they were both false, disloyal.

Again she glanced at her own reflection. In the agony of the moment, she grew hideous to herself. She even found herself making faces, distorting herself with instinctive disgust.

"Haven't you finished that note yet, Maggie?" It was the musical tone of her lover. Poor girl! she tried to leave the room, but she fell down convulsed.

The false pair rushed toward her, and everything kind and gentle was uttered. She did not tell the cause of her emotion, and they always supposed it the prelude to a fever which followed. Margaret, in her weakness and lovingness, tried to forgive—to forget. It was a trifle—the way of the world. But her heart told her it was an evil way, and she, in the depth and singleness of her love, felt she could not abide the test. She could do better without love than with jealousy, and in the strength of her own womanly truth, she at length was able to withdraw herself entirely from the evil influence. Subsequent developments proved the justice of the course she adopted. Hence sprang her pious seclusion, and her entire devotion to the needs and the sufferings of humanity, and hence sprang the invariable axiom of my friend, an ugly woman should never love, or should avoid black marble mantels.

The following is the poem, the only record of Margaret Lincoln:

LOVE DEAD.

The lady sent him an image of Cupid, one wing veiling his face. He was pleased thereat, thinking it to be Love sleeping, and betokened the tenderness of the sentiment. He looked again, and saw it was Love dead, and laid upon his bier.

MS.

This morn with trembling I awoke,
Just as the dawn my slumber broke:
Flapping came a heavy wing sounding pinions o'er my head,
Beating down the blessed air with a weight of chilling
    dread—
Felt I then the presence of a doom
That an Evil occupied the room—
And I dared not round the bower,
Chilly in the grayish dawning,[11]
Dared not face the evil power,
With its voice of inward warning.

Vain with weakness we may palter—
Vainly may the fond heart falter,
Came there then upon my soul, dropping down like leaden
    weight,
Burning pang or freezing pang, which I know not 'twas so
    great;
Life hath its moments black unnumbered,
I knew it not if mine eyes had slumbered,
Yet I little thought such pain
Ever to have known again—
Love dies, too, when Faith is dead,
Yesternight Faith perished.

---

[11] Oakes Smith's copy of *The Mayflower* for 1848 deletes "dawning," inserting "morn."

FICTION

I knew that Love could never change—
That Love should die seems yet more strange—
Lifting up the downy veil, screening Love within my heart,
Beating there as beat my pulse, moving like myself a part—
I had kept him cherished there so deep,
Heart-rocked kept him in his balmy sleep,
That till now I never knew
How his fibres round me grew—
Could not know how deep the sorrow
Where Hope bringeth no to-morrow.

I struggled, knowing we must part,
I grieved to lift him from my heart,
Grieving much and struggling much, forth I brought him sor-
    rowing—
Drooping hung his fainting head—all adown his dainty wing,
Shrieked I with a wild and dark surprise—
For I saw the marble in Love's eyes—
Yet I hoped his soul would wait
As he oft had waited there—
Hovering, though at Heaven's gate—
Could he leave me to despair?

Unfolded they the crystal door,
Where Love shall languish never more—
Weeping Love thy days are o'er. Lo! I lay thee on thy bier,
Wiping thus from thy dead cheek every vestige of a tear—
Love has perished—hist, hist how they tell,
Beating pulse of mine, his funeral knell—
Love is dead, aye dead and gone;
Why should I be living on?
Why be in this chamber sitting,
With but phantoms round me flitting?

For Further Reading:

Patterson, Cynthia Lee. "'Hermaphroditish Disturbers of the Peace:' Rufus Griswold, Elizabeth Oakes Smith, and Nineteenth-Century Discourses of Ambiguous Sex." *Women's Studies* (2016): 513–33.

Schiff, Karen L. "Objects of Speculation: Early Manuscripts on Women and Education by Judith Sargent (Stevens) Murray." *Legacy* 17/2 (2000): 213–28.

MEMOIR

A PILGRIMAGE TO KATAHDIN

Of all the events Oakes Smith left out of the manuscript autobiography she called "A Human Life," her ascent of Mt. Katahdin in the summer of 1849 is probably the most egregious.[1] Achieved at the peak of her literary celebrity, the feat was widely noted by newspapers, but what she wrote privately about the achievement to friends marks her perception of this moment as nothing less than the turning point of her career—a turn from her professional success as a "poetess" and writer of sentimental fiction to a new self-awareness and self-confidence, leading her to something "beyond" belletristic work. Between August 5 and August 13, 1849, Oakes Smith and her friend Nancy Mosman, Mosman's husband, and their guide, James Haines,[2] covered more than fifty miles of dense wilderness. Six weeks later, she tried to describe her feelings to Lydia Sigourney:

> It has done me good, not physically merely, but in my very soul. For weeks after my return I was conscious of a

---

[1] Oakes Smith's narrative reflecting on her experience appeared in four letters to *The Portland Daily Advertiser*, September 12, 15, 26, and October 8, 1849. In her work, Kirkland notes the significant omission of Oakes Smith's several months' service as minister of the Independent Church in Canastota, New York, in 1877, in an instance of "fiction" (her novel *Bertha and Lily*) "foreshadowing life" (7).

[2] Haines was a companion of Marcus Keep, who is credited for blazing the trails used by the earliest recreational adventurers on Katahdin in the later 1840s and notably served as Henry David Thoreau's guide to the mountain in 1846. This early period of the shift from scientific and economic activity on the mountain to more modern recreational uses is ably documented by Neff in *Katahdin, An Historical Journey*. It is remarkable that Oakes Smith and Thoreau met, walked, and conversed in Concord in December 1851 when Oakes Smith was booked to lecture before the Concord Lyceum (by Thoreau himself, as secretary) without either of them recording any conversation about their adventures on the mountain. When Haines guided Thoreau on his attempt to summit the mountain in late August 1846, the party met with suddenly inclement conditions common to the area and were forced to return on September 8 before achieving the summit.

sublime tranquility, a heavenly repose such as I had never known before. My enthusiasm hitherto has evolved tears, poetry, or a wild yearning for sympathy—against which my pride, my taste, my principle rebelled, and then I flew to prayer with groanings that cannot be uttered; for nothing of what I have felt, nothing of my real self, my whole self, has appeared in my writings. But now (I trust God it will last) a cheerful calm, a holy repose seem to raise me above the pettiness, the discomforts, and the ambitions of the world. I take all as it comes unmoved. This is not favorable to poetry, not to that of the fugitive kind, but if this state, so deep, so earnest, and clear should continue, I feel as if some poem or tragedy beyond what I have done hitherto must grow out of it.[3]

Odd it seems that Oakes Smith's revelation was shared with a woman of a generation for whom the move beyond literary fame would have seemed unnecessary, if not blasphemous to womankind,[4] but at the moment, Oakes Smith herself seems only to suggest (at least to Sigourney) a move from poetry "of the fugitive kind" to, well, poetry of some more significant kind. To be fair, positions of influence or social action for middle-class American women "beyond" the kind of success Oakes Smith and Sigourney enjoyed in the 1840s had not come into being by 1849—or at least their contours were hardly clear. But if "nothing of her real self" had been seen in her writing to this point, what would happen

---

[3] EOS to Sigourney, October 3, 1849, Lydia Howard Sigourney Papers, Series 1, Watkinson Library Manuscripts Repository, Trinity College.

[4] On June 4, 1851, perhaps in response to the news that Oakes Smith was planning to launch her public lecture career that evening at Hope Chapel, Sigourney remonstrated, "Now, let us do all the good we can in the world, by all means, for how soon we shall be out of it. Let us strengthen the foundation of good things and stand against innovations. The loud clamor for woman's rights, what does it signify? If we were...in the places of men, it would not help us—or them—or the world at large—for in our own sweet sphere—well-filled—is our happiness and beauty and true influence." Lydia Sigourney to Elizabeth Oakes Smith, Box 2, Papers of Elizabeth Oakes Prince Smith, Accession #38–707, Special Collections, University of Virginia Library, Charlottesville, VA.

MEMOIR

when the "real" Elizabeth Oakes Smith emerged out of this experience? She was hardly the only woman poised to reveal something of her full capacities in American social, economic, and political life. The first woman's rights convention at Seneca Falls, New York, had taken place a little over a year before, and Oakes Smith's steps up Mt. Katahdin were the first she'd take toward joining the movement in earnest in 1850.

What is most remarkable about Oakes Smith's journey and its self-documented effect on her sense of self can easily be missed in the spandexed twenty-first century, when Kate Brown's casual free-climb of Fisher Towers in Moab, Utah, may or may not have drawn eyes to an advertisement for a Citibank credit card in 2009. Indeed, while it remains a national embarrassment that women in the United States have yet to climb in equal numbers to those places of social and political power still reserved for a male elite, the literal meaning of the subtitle of Brown's book of that year, *Girl on the Rocks: A Woman's Guide to Climbing with Strength, Grace and Courage*, seems downright needless in light of the fact that there is already a large market for such books in the US and around the world today. In a culture replete with strong, graceful, and courageous women (who, incidentally, write books, too), we easily forget that in 1849, mountain climbing wasn't yet a thing in the United States—at least in the modern sense of individual "sport"; that is, a physical challenge taken on as a personal test of mental or physical fortitude, a method of awakening a person to a true sense of their capacities, or as a welcomed relief from the visual, mental, and physical boredom and pressures of life under capitalism. White men in the modern world may suffer from very real economic disadvantages under capitalism and psychologically from various inferiority complexes, but since Oakes Smith's time, at least, the dominant ideology has made "proving" their position beside the point. It need not be questioned that women have *always* demonstrated "Strength, Grace and Courage" in human history, but the assumptions of the history of patriarchy has forced them to *prove* these characteristics, and thus it actually makes perfect sense that a woman might be one of the first to treat a mountain this way—or at least the first to write about this challenge and its overcoming.[5]

It might be assumed that the ascent of Mt. Katahdin was a common occurrence for the Native American tribes in the area before European contact, but evidence of Abenaki mythology and oral histories seem to argue against it.[6] Not until the late eighteenth century would the mountain find itself in the path of European explorers establishing boundaries of their conquered territory. Mention of the mountain is made by John Chadwick in his expedition of 1764, at the request of the governor of the Massachusetts Bay Colony, who wanted to locate a land route for a highway between Fort Pownal and Quebec, but anyone who has been to Katahdin (then or now) knows no sensible overland route could get (or would get) near its peak. As historian Jeff Neff has argued, while "it is reasonable to assume there were other surveyors, as well as explorers, traders, adventurers, missionaries, soldiers, or sojourners who came to the 'lofty pyramid' to explore its treasures" before the nineteenth century, all we can say is that early exploration of the region had "at last opened

---

[5] Accounts of women's mountain-climbing before the twentieth century are rare, though Elizabeth C. Wright's *Lichen Tufts: From the Alleghanies* (1860) draws on her vigorous hiking and camping experience along the Allegany River to achieve the earliest identified feminist theory of the environment. Wright attended the first truly coeducational university in the United States, Alfred University, where on July 3, 1854, she likely attended Oakes Smith's lecture before the Ladies' Literary Lyceum on Mme. Roland.

[6] Stopping at Penobscot Indian Island Reservation near Old Town, Maine, in 2018, the editor was lucky to speak to several Penobscot who knew of Oakes Smith's writing on her climb and that of Thoreau and others. To Oakes Smith's claim that native people had avoided the mountain—especially the summit—they suggested the legend may have been circulated to keep white people away more than anything else. They also agreed that apart from a meagre wild cranberry crop each summer, their ancestors had little reason to venture any higher than the tree line. As for the physical feat involved, the Penobscot have nothing to prove to anyone.

MEMOIR

the West Branch [of the Penobscot River] to non-Native American travelers."[7]

Once the land around Mt. Katahdin was surveyed and militarily and politically secure, more travelers entered the region, but science and commerce were their principal purposes. In September 1837, Charles Thomas Jackson, Maine's first state geologist, led a "major scientific expedition" through all of Maine's public lands, including an ascent of Katahdin in a "whirling" snowstorm. Only five months earlier, in mid-April, Jackson had been in Portland, lecturing to an audience that included Elizabeth Oakes Smith and her two elder sons on the geological processes that form mountain ranges.[8]

Guided by James M. Haines and accompanied by her childhood friend Nancy Mosman and Mosman's husband, Oakes Smith arrived at William Hunt's farm on the way to Katahdin on Monday, August 5, 1849. By Wednesday, they had reached Katahdin Lake, and by Friday, made a camp at Avalanche Brook, where they used birch bark as "stationery" to write friends at home and to address a note to future climbers regarding their ascent. The weather turned cold and stormy on Saturday August 11, and thus while they did somewhat better than Thoreau on his climb recorded in *The Maine Woods*, the party seems only to have achieved the lowest summit before descending the mountain the way they came. According to Rev. Marcus Keep and another guide, who found Mosman's and Oakes Smith's "note" waiting for them the following week on Keep's own quest to bring his wife, then fiancée, up Katahdin as the first woman to succeed, the women in Haines's party were first, but not highest. If it was a race, nobody won.

Hardly a defender of woman's capacities or rights himself (indeed, his wife is given no voice whatsoever in his narrative), Keep

---

[7] John W. Neff, Katahdin: An Historical Journey—Legends, Explorations and Preservation of Maine's Highest Peak (Boston: Appalachian Mountain Club Books, 2006) 21.

[8] See Oakes Smith's letter dated April 20, 1837, on pages 42–43 in this volume.

225

ELIZABETH OAKES SMITH

repeatedly emphasized his belief that only those who "had been to the academy a quarter or had been to Massachusetts once" would be shocked at the "indelicacy" of women climbing a mountain—"as if they had lost their knowledge of a hayrake or the feet that could once splash round the farmyard." More important than any competition between men and women on this venture, which would seem to lead back to the autobiography's regretful and at times resentful tone, is Oakes Smith's ebullient, celebratory, emancipated tone in her writing of this experience. The pace of her writing on her Katahdin trip is itself invigorating, providing a clear sense of the writer's joy and experience of a challenge far from the delicacies of the literary salons, whose attendance counted, back in New York, as an "achievement." "It was a merry sight," Oakes Smith writes, on the way up Avalanche Brook,

> to see us leaping from rock to rock, springing over these surging and roaring cataracts for three long miles; and truth to say, it grew to be no holiday task, for ancles will be ancles, in spite of resolution and careful "findings;" but when our spirits flagged, a look upward at the sportful Nymph above, or below where she disported amid the shadows and with frolicsome grace sang onward in a torrent of melody, so invigorated our hearts and sent new beauty into our souls, that we clapped our hands and sang, and called to the mountain echoes, as if we had become a part of this exulting jubilant Oh! one hour of life like this, is worth an eternity amid the dust and dullness of cities.

Before she left Bangor on her return to New York, Oakes Smith took the opportunity to advertise the writing she'd done on her experience, stopping at the offices of the *Bangor Whig and Daily Courier* to entertain the editors with the story of her adventure. The brief article appearing there on August 29 was the first public notice of not only this but also Oakes Smith's earlier excursions to Mount Kineo:

> Mrs. E. Oakes Smith, one of the most accomplished female poets of America, has been spending some time with

MEMOIR

her friends in this city, and has recently, in company with one of the accomplished women of our city, made an excursion to, and spent a night upon, the top of Katahdin mountain! Mrs. Smith has great fondness for exploring mountains. She was the first white woman who visited Mount Kinneo at Moose Head Lake, four years since; and she is the first white woman who has ever visited the top of Mount Katahdin. The visit to Katahdin was attended with great exertion and no little peril; and verbal account which Mrs. S gives of the ascent, of the magnificent scenery, after reaching the top of the mountain, of the terrors of a stormy night there, and of the varied incidents of a week in the woods, fording streams, and walking fifty miles on foot, is so animated and unique as to make us exceedingly anxious to see her written description, which is soon to appear.

This promotion of her prose account was accompanied by her poem "Strength from the Hills," the last lines of which reveal the effect of the experience and the new energy and self-conception Oakes Smith would begin to draw upon in the political phase of her career. Having arrived for rest in rural home quarters, she returns motivated to celebrate a life of work that demanded she depart from the "safety" of her secure position as a celebrity to the "gladness of unrest"—something larger, and something requiring much more bravery and strength, than writing for the magazines.

> Come up unto the hills! The shattered oak
> Here clings unto the rock
> With arms outstretched as 'twould the storm invoke,
> And dare again the shock
> Come where no fear is known—the sea bird the nest
> On the old hemlock swings,
> Here thou shalt feel the gladness of unrest
> And mount upon thy wings.

Correspondence of the *Advertiser*.
Bangor, August 1849[9]

Journey to Katahdin – Log Houses – Crossbills – Wild flowers – Camping out – Cry of the Moose

Mount Katahdin, the highest summit of Maine had been from childhood associated with all my dreams of wild and magnificent scenery. Throned in the north amid frost and snows, amid old primeval forests, the haunt only of huge animals, who spurned the luxury of the level country and bide themselves amid its savage recesses, I had often brooded over the intense solitude and wished that some grand old legend of love or strife were mingled with its name; now I rejoice that Katahdin stand unassociated with the puny pulsations of human hearts, a solitary Wendigo, or Stone Giant, heavy with age and seamed with the scars of ages. I even half regret that a woman's foot has touched its height, and wish it had remained inaccessible even to me—for now the spell is broken and Katahdin will be the resort of idleness and gossip,[10] and no longer the remote king of the north.

Our party consisted of Mr. and Mrs. M.[11] and myself, and a guide who met us about ninety miles from Bangor. Leaving the above-named city, the road was upland through thrifty villages, of which I may speak hereafter, and over a road so picturesque, and withal so good in every point of view, that one constantly wished to be on horseback to enjoy it in full. Much of the way it runs parallel with the east branch of the Penobscot, which though now shrunken

---

[9] *Portland Daily Advertiser*, September 12, 1849.

[10] It is not known if Oakes Smith and Marcus Keep ever met, or if their only correspondence involved Oakes Smith's archly worded message left in a bottle on the mountain to mark her achievement, but this brief allusion to "gossip" directly anticipates what would be Marcus Keep's criticism of her adventure, which he seems to have read not as a woman's effort to heal herself, challenge herself, or change the expectations of others, but rather a mere publicity stunt.

[11] Mrs. N. C. Mosman, of Bangor, Maine, is listed in the annual report of the Female Medical Education Society of 1853.

MEMOIR

by the long continued drought is still a broad beautiful stream, dotted with islands of rare loveliness, which are covered with the finest forest trees I had ever seen. The river is filled at present with logs, greatly to the detriment of people in this region whose wealth depends upon the lumber brought down by the many streams of the country; and when, as now, the season is too dry to float down the logs great inconvenience and stagnation of business ensues.

The islands to which I referred above belong entirely to the Indians of the Penobscot tribe and I was interested to observe many very good framed houses amongst them and some thrifty looking farms. The land is a steady rise from Bangor to Conway, so that as you look back from the top of the hills you have climbed, the scenery is grand beyond description. Rivers, lakes and mountains are spread out before you, all reposing amid the solemn and unbroken forces, which seems without stint or limit, and above all Katahdin looms into the sky with its bald top and yellow scars where the avalanches have ploughed their way. I counted nine of these distinctly upon one side visible from the road. Mars Hill, over which runs the demarcation line between us and Great Britain, is seen like a faint cloud in the horizon. Conway, or number two as it is called, is a Catholic township, in whose history I became much interested, and the priest, Mr. Moran, was found not only communicative, but intelligent and devoted to his people.

With gentlemanly courtesy he took his own horse and carried a part of our company to the point of the road, where we must turn our backs on civilized life. Here taking our guide, and bidding adieu to the good priest we commenced the real hardships of the adventure to Katahdin. The road turns sharply to the left, and is simply a passage between the stumps of trees; where a marsh intervenes logs are laid transversely, making what is called a "gridiron road," or "corduroy turnpike," or whatever a whimsical fancy may suggest but one of the most abominable modes of jostling and shaking human bodies you can conceive of. Mrs. M. and myself made ourselves not a little merry as our wagon in some cases jolted a quarter of a mile over these logs, throwing us into attitudes unconceived of by the Graces, and we certainly did rejoice when this mode of shaking was exchanged for the variety of a plunge over boulders, stumps, and the immense roots of trees which shot across our path. But overhead the scene was magnificent—immense primeval trees shot up into the sky which was blue and serene; the singing of birds, the busy chatterings of the squirrels, and the shy movements of partridges darting across the road wrought a soothing and harmonious influence upon our spirits. Katahdin was before us, the wicked noisy world cast behind our backs, and nature seemed to spread forth her arms lovingly to receive us.

We passed one or two log houses, but by no means wearing the aspect of poverty. There were the hardy pioneers of the wilderness, who sought here independence for themselves and children, and the "clearings" gave evidence of their hardihood and perseverance. After traveling about six miles over the worst road I had then ever seen, we came to a thrifty clearing, where an intelligent looking man shouldered his axe to assist us in crossing a stream, for the fires were raging in the woods through which our course lay, and the bridge had been burned. There was a melancholy dignity in the air of this man which could not fail to interest. He was accompanied by a little boy of perhaps five years, whose delicate beauty attracted my attention. My remarks touched the heart of the father and then he told me the story of his rare and beautiful child, which had sickened and died a few months before. It was the story so often told by our early settlers, of wild-wood solitude, of patient endurance, and bereaved affection. I could see that the loneliness of nature had failed to soothe; but rather that she laid her hand heavily upon the stricken head in times like these and thence grief was protracted beyond its just dues.

Reaching the current whose babblings had been for some time audible, we found the ground all about blazing and scorching beneath our feet, while the heat and smoke were nearly suffocating. With much difficulty we were able to get the horse and wagon across, while my lady companion and I prided ourselves much on the skill with which we forded the stream. Our guide facetiously remarked that "our courage was good, for we went through fire and water at the first start." Subsequently when we were compelled to

MEMOIR

ford rivers, we laughed heartily at our little glorification in fording this brook. But this was our day of small things.

Four miles more brought us to "Hunt's" the last house on the road. Hunt's is the "Johnny Grouts" of this region. What "old Crawford" used to be to the White Hills, Hunt is to Katahdin. He has a fine thrifty farm with corn fields up into the side of a mountain, the east branch of the Penobscot flows by his door, with a green slope, "green to the very threshold" down to the river brim. It is a wild picturesque spot, and beautiful withal—the river sweeps by in graceful course, the mountains rise from the opposite side, and it is just that broken, Swiss kind of view so delightful to the eye of an Artist. Added to this the table was excellent, with hot cakes, salmon and other comforts to a traveler—the beds coarse but cleanly, the family obliging, and the reader will see that "Hunt's" is by no means an undesirable place.[12]

We noticed innumerable Crossbills flying about with an appearance of great zeal and preoccupation; it was cherry time, reminding one of prim gossiping little quakers with a touch of fancy about their drab coats, and a smart holding of high crowned caps. The sun was warm, the air bland, and altogether Hunt's farm wore an air of exceeding comfort.

A bateau propelled by Mr. M and our guide, carried us up the Penobscot a few miles into the Wisatticook, a deep, rapid stream with water as clear and cold as crystal. We sang songs, and poured out libations to the mountain nymph, and the Genii Loci,[13] as cheerful a party as ever passed this wild region—peculiar indeed we

---

[12] William Hunt, from Carthage, Maine, had established his farm on the east side of the east branch of the Penobscot around 1834, originally to provide food and supplies for men and horses involved in the logging industry in the area. While Hunt's Farm continued its role as an industrial supplier well into the nineteenth century (Hunt himself continuing only until 1848), it quickly became the "wilderness gateway to the Wassataquoik Stream" and the last refuge of "civilized" accommodation for tourists and naturalists before they began the arduous hike to Katahdin. A detailed history is available at the Patten Lumberman's Museum website (https://www.explorekwwnm.com/hunt-farm).

[13] In Roman religion, "spirits of the place."

Hunt's Farm photographed by F. E. Hardy, 1873.
Courtesy Patten Lumberman's Museum

View across the crater (right) from Pamola Peak to Baxter Peak, Mt. Katahdin, Piscataquis County, Maine.

Courtesy Timothy H. Scherman

were, for women had never before penetrated thus far into this wilderness. Leaving the boat and certain articles superfluous in a savage life, we struck at once into the woods. It was a magnificent primeval growth of hard wood, which is of little value in this part of the country and has therefore been left intact; there is but little undergrowth and the scene wears the appearance of a superb park, the trees nearly excluding the sky. We passed ferns the most beautiful to be conceived, often five and six feet high. The botany was throughout interesting—berries of the richest hue clustered about our feet; the Indian pipe, like a pearl moulded into blossom, gathered itself into lovely clusters, and the Dragon's tongue, and Solomon's Seal showed that sentiment might here find abundance of language, while the Pitcher Plant, filled with its pure liquid, told how lovingly and providently the good Father spreads a table in the wilderness.

Presently the trees swaying back and forth with a great noise, and the fitful moanings of the wind told of a gathering storm. The rain began to fall like shot upon the branches of the trees, and we realized to the full the comfort of our well-wadded woodland dress. The tent was pitched for the night—an immense fire kindled in front—and green branches spread for our bed. A camp in the deep woods is suggestive of a thousand whimsical associations, and jest, story and song came as freely as the free airs that surrounded us. How eloquent we grew in those rude encampments! How readily and daintily pleasant thoughts careened about us; and language sprang spontaneously even to reserved lips.

Our guide, Mr. Haines, was perfect in all woodland expedients—hung a crane in Indian style, and made excellent tea in the tea-kettle; constructed pretty spoons from alder bark, and by no means contemptible platters and plates from the integuments of larger trees. Then he manufactured nice napkins from the inner fold of the birch tree, and even in an idle and luxurious hour prepared us no mean quantity of birch bark stationery, cards and note paper, upon which we wrote letters to our friends and prepared visiting cards, dated Mount Katahdin. He sang too, a good song, and was altogether the very prince of guides. He had been much in this part

MEMOIR

of the century exploring, for he is a man well-to-do in the world, and had camped out for months together.

But I am anticipating. Gradually the awe of our position grew upon us, and all were silent. I looked out into the black night and saw the sparks ascending into the vault of this vast and sublime cathedral; arch beyond arch, up, into the overhanging heavens and saw how puny were the buildings made with human hands, compared with this framed by the handy-work of the Eternal.

The pattering of the rain—the surgings of the forest and our own isolation, and littleness, filled me with a sense of the most intense and helpless solitude, such as language would fail to express. I gathered the fold of our tent drapery about me and strove to shut out the images that were growing too wild and oppressive.

I must have slept, for I was startled by a cry so distinct and near, with the crashing of the limbs of trees, that we all started in our feet and the gentlemen seized their firearms for defence. I, I am ashamed to say, with a most unfeminine instinct, unsheathed a dirk, which I had at my side, and grasped it in a very determined manner. The cry continued to recede, and presently all was still. The men laid down their arms, and I closed my dirk with hand, shame on my courage, trembling in a manner that set my femininity quite at rest.

The voice was that of a Moose, more than one having undoubtedly passed very near our night lodging. The cry was something between the low of an ox, and the quick winding of a horn; and to me, in that dense solitary woods, was one of the most startling yet melancholy sounds I ever heard; it was majestic, too, as if the lordly denizens of the place questioned why we intruded upon their province.

My letter is growing too long, and I must defer Katahdin for another number.

A PILGRIM

ELIZABETH OAKES SMITH

Correspondence of the *Advertiser*.
Bangor, Aug. 1849[14]

*Roads to Katahdin – Marshes – The office of mosses—Solitary Lake –
Fording Sandy Brook – Roach Lake – Katahdin ten miles from the
Mountain*

With our night of slumber, all sense of fatigue had passed away. I
am convinced people do not take cold from exposures of this kind,
unless laboring from some organic disease, in which case they
should never hazard the experiment, but content themselves with
the sickly air of warm rooms and flannels, and leave the luxury of
hemlock boughs and free mountain firs for those whose better descent or better training has given courageous nerves, and elastic
limbs, such as blessed the pair in paradise, who started from sleep

> Light and airy, from pure digestion bred
> And temperate vapors bland.[15]

Our way led through the same interminable forest, constantly
rising—for we had more than one mountain to surmount before we
should reach Katahdin. A rough path had been marked out by explorers and designated by a cleft from the bark of trees, right and
left, at intervals, called the "spots" or "blazes." We each grew expert
in tracing our path by these marks and followed on, mile and mile
on foot, (for horses were dispensed with from the time we reached
Hunt's) now climbing over windfalls, where the trees were prostrate
at every conceivable inclination, and no small skill and activity were

---

[14] *Portland Daily Advertiser*, September 15, 1849.
[15] Oakes Smith quotes Milton's *Paradise Lost* imperfectly—evidently from
memory:
When Adam waked, so customed, for his sleep
Was airy light, from pure digestion bred
And temperate vapors bland, which the only sound
Of leaves and fuming rills, Aurora's fan,
Lightly dispersed.

MEMOIR

requisite in surmounting them; anon a dip of the hill would lead us in to a ravine, stagnant with water, in which we could trace the tracks of wild animals which had passed a few moments before. These marshes were black uncanny looking places, threaded with roots of trees, and fallen trunks, slippery to the tread, and yet if we except the clumps of coarse grass, affording the only foot hold for miles together. We moved on by a sort of hop-skip and jump, sometimes coming up short in a very uncomely black pool, from which we emerged merrily.

How we overcame our womanly horror of snakes I know not, but so it was; and we would travel on as demurely in this rough untidy road as if we had never known the luxury of the green earth or the comfort of cleanly sidewalks. The truth is, and the truth must be told, we were not blest with the sight of a single huge or terrible animal, did not come up to the dignity even of a snake; and in this dearth of adventure we made much ado when an owl flitted through the trees; but, when an eagle, that kingly suggestor of Freedom, grandeur and daring, sailed over our heads, dotting with his shadow some still, mountain cinctured lake, and soaring away over rock and fell and forest, disappeared amid the mist and shadows of Katahdin, I felt my blood stirred and a lofty exultation mingled with his stately image. Then two squirrels would now and then come out, and sit upon an old stump and chatter to us defiantly—turn about to the limb of a tree, and then suddenly whisk round and chatter again, as if taken with a new thought. Pretty lizards crept amongst the mosses, and now and then a bird poured out its soulful life in song. But this was rare and gave an impression of deeper loneliness. The singing of a bird was oppressive, while the quivering cry of the loon, across the lake, and the sharp stream of birds of prey were in harmony with the savageness of nature.

I remember we took our dinner one day beside a small lake surrounded with birches. Now the blue shade of the larch is gloomy of itself, and the stiff angular branches have a forbidding, unpitying look; the Lake had a small outlet just visible where a flock of ducks made their escape in a streak of sunshine behind the branches. We were in a small amphitheatre where these somber trees had stepped

235

down the hillside into the dip of the water; the leaves of the beautiful "pond lily" (nympha alba) were lying thickly upon the surface, but alas! not a blossom was left, nothing but the yellow beaver plant, which always grows beside the lily, an old duenna guarding its loneliness. Dragonflies with their gossamer wings darted about and the rough voice of the locust broke harshly upon the ear. The sky was one blue, changeless and hushed. I could scarcely eat, so melancholy were the images presented. It seemed a little Acheron, and we were miserable spirits lowering about its ghostly shores.[16]

Indeed, constantly as we advanced into the wilderness we were impressed with the intense and unbroken stillness of nature. The animals in this vast solitude are huge solitary creatures, delighting in the ragged cliff and seeking the forest only when in need of food or shelter. The traces of them were upon every side of us, and at night their wild startling cry was audible, but day after day we traveled without encountering a living creature. The woods were all primeval excepting now and then an interval through which fires had passed, and through these, we found it difficult to make our way owing to the dense growth and lowness of the branches, while the primeval woods were stately monarchs towering into the sky and leaving a free passage beneath. To add to the silence of the forest, the mosses of this region are exceedingly beautiful and abundant, and everything is draped over with them. Huge boulders rising to the height of twenty or thirty feet, have their threatening aspects softened by this luxuriant growth—while those of smaller size are bound captive to the soil by the cable roots of immense trees, over all which the silent mosses have spread their covering. Hoary old trees and growth and decay of centuries lie prostrate and draped for the burial, by their pitying and unpretending love, as if the whole sentiment of nature were to veil the ravages of death, and hide what is unseemly even from its own eyes.

---

[16] In Greek mythology, Acheron is the "river of woe" over which the souls of the dead must be carried by Charon to cross over into the Underworld. Throughout her narrative, Oakes Smith maintains a balance between a sense of nature's familiar and benign "embrace" and its formidable strangeness and menace.

MEMOIR

As we walked for hours nearly in silence through those immense solitudes, how lovely, how refreshing were the gleams of mountain torrents, and how ennobling the aspect of Katahdin as he rose monarch-like in the distance; occasionally we would come to an old camp, where travelers had passed before us, and a sympathizing tenderness grew upon us as we looked upon these fading vestiges of our kind—a piece of decaying flannel, the foot of a stocking, homely relics indeed, were they, but we had been camping out night after night, unchecked with any faces but our own active group, and these things we quietly compared to the foot-prints of Robinson Crusoe, and whimsically created the history of their adventures.

Our path for many miles lay along the course of the Wisatticook, one of the coldest, clearest, and loveliest of rivers; indeed for bathing, nothing can be more luxurious than the rivers of Katahdin; as limpid as the air itself, and affording nooks and dells which a Grecian fancy would people with dainty Nymphs and piping Satyrs. Slips of white sand, like a scroll, unrolled from the verge of the forest to the water's brim, tempt the foot to disport therein and make the morning toilet where Titania herself might have been enchanted, and which Dian might seek for the sake of seclusion. Often in moving silently through the hushed wilderness, these beautiful myths would crowd upon the fancy, making one desire belief therein. And indeed, I yielded full credence to Pan, who has found an asylum from his desecrated shrine amid the savage grandeur of Katahdin.[17] Often did I behold his melancholy face peering from behind some huge and moss-grown rock, and I caught a gleam of his hurrying hoofs at some lonely fountain, and saw the branches close and quiver behind him; while off on the hill-side where the sunlight glinted amid the leaves, and lighted the boles of ancient oaks and beechen trees, the sad cadence of his pipes mingled with the many voices that come to the internal ear, "Alas! I had heard Pan!"

---

[17] Greek god of the wild, Pan was associated with fertility, springtime, and sexuality, often depicted as half-man and half-goat, in company with the nymphs of Arcadia, a mythical region of unspoiled wilderness.

ELIZABETH OAKES SMITH

Fording the Wisatticook, which here runs a rapid stream of more than a hundred feet in width, our way grew more solitary, and the traveling exceedingly laborious. We averaged from five to eight miles a day, which ought to be a trifle to a healthful woman, properly dressed for the occasion;[18] but this distance notwithstanding all our comfortable preparations, left us nearly exhausted, and never was sleep more ready or more refreshing than we found it at night on our hemlock boughs. As we grew further into this mountainous region, frequent rains and hurried showers kept us wet half the time, while the black flies were a perpetual annoyance; to counteract the rain, we fitted ourselves shoulder pieces of birch bark; and to escape the flies and mosquitoes, wore a napkin loosely over the head, which we wet in the many streams we were obliged to cross—our traveling caps in the meanwhile being suspended upon the arm. This wet covering for the head had a two-fold advantage—the moisture was repugnant to the midges and black flies, and as our feet were half the time wet, it preserved the balance of circulation.

We grew very courageous in fording streams, and learned to balance over slippery logs and decaying trees quite to the admiration of our guide, who seeing me take a pole and walk the trees, a single trunk in width, which constituted the only bridge over Sandy Brook,

---

[18] We do not know what Oakes Smith wore on the climb, but we might guess from her description of what women might wear, with attention to both modesty and comfort, in her pamphlet *Hints on Dress and Beauty* (Fowler and Wells, 1852, 56), included in Volume II of *Elizabeth Oakes Smith: Selected Writings*: "Let us have a simple Grecian jacket, or sack reaching below the knee, with pockets upon each side, buttoning from the throat downward. Trowsers, of the same material for the street, the Turkish form seems most approved, but is less convenient I apprehend, and less becoming than the simple plain trowsers form. A small snug covering for the head, perhaps a gipsy hat; and boots such as are worn by ladies of rank in Russia, which can be put on without the trouble of lacing." Given her particular needs on this journey, the following passage is also relevant: "If the dress be adapted to the occasion, it is of no consequence what it may be.... For instance, in a rain or snow-storm, a woman may appear in sack or trowsers, and be received with approval" (19–20). However, if one was not in this situation, then "the robe gather[s] with gems upon the shoulder, and bound to the waist by a girdle, is so beautiful and classical, that every woman covets to wear it" (11–12).

MEMOIR

declared I was "nearly as good at it as a river driver," a praise which I liked right well, as helplessness and nervousness form no part of my feminine creed. Now Sandy Brook,[19] which we crossed several times, is deeper, broader, and more rapid than the Saco in any place where it has to be crossed on the route to Mount Washington, and a trip to the mountains of New Hampshire is a summer-day excursion, a baby play compared to Katahdin.[20]

We had been so long buried in the heart of the forest that when we emerged upon Lake Katahdin, ten miles from the mountain,[21] the sensation was delightful beyond expression. The Lake was a lovely sheet of water embowered in woods, the curves and inlets exceedingly graceful and picturesque, and the expanse sleeping under a saffron and rose tinged atmosphere, with here and there a dimple where a fish darted to the light. In front of us rose Katahdin, without a cloud, resting against the sky like the battlements of the Eternal, while hill and mountain flanked his throne far as the eye could reach. Katahdin is not a range, one of a group, but a solitary peak, the highest in the State, and casting the lesser points quite beneath his feet.

It is this singleness of position that imparts so much of interest and grandeur to this northern height. There is one ravine upon the rim[22] which at a distance looks like the crater of a volcano. Mr. M.

---

[19] Possible former name of what is now Katahdin Brook, which enters Rocky Pond, then Katahdin Lake, from the east, or Oakes Smith has confused the stream on her route before Katahdin Lake with one after it. She would have crossed Sandy Stream on her way along what is now Katahdin Lake trail to the Avalanche Field (fairly unstable in her time) and Avalanche Brook, which she follows until the group begins ascending the avalanche itself to Pamola.

[20] New Hampshire's Mount Washington (6,288 feet) is taller than Mount Katahdin (5,268 feet), each being the tallest mountains in their states. In modern times, Washington has become more of a tourist attraction than Katahdin, with the Mount Washington Cog Railway providing visitors who do not hike the means of traveling to the summit.

[21] The distance to Pamola from Katahdin Lake is roughly six miles.

[22] Oakes Smith would have looked down on this crater-like ravine from Pamola, the lowest peak. To gain the highest peak, Marcus Keep's group, including

ELIZABETH OAKES SMITH

found some fossils and a substance marvelously resembling lava, but I am not geologist enough to pronounce upon these matters.

Mrs. M. and myself amused ourselves by "luring the scaly tribe," while the gentlemen prepared the tent, fires and supper; we wrapped our fish in pocket-handkerchiefs to still their struggles, and flinched not a little as we took the poor things from the hook, the sport is a cruel one despite our enthusiasm for Isaak Walton, and my own individual penchant that way. While busied in this way the twilight shadows deepened, and the mountains seemed to approximate like stony ramparts shutting us out from the world. Suddenly a heavy plunge as of some immense body into the water, and I am afraid likewise, two very decided and emphatic screams broke the stillness of the night and caused the very stars to wind with mortification. We hurried to our tents, and kept up a reserved and disguised aspect to counteract this slight lapsing of womanly courage. All night at intervals the call of the moose, the prolonged cry of the loon, and the screaming of the owl gave us a gloomy cast to the hours, while in the morning the Lake wore again its cheerful aspect—if cheerful it can be in the midst of creatures which seek remoteness and solitude. The eagle and the hawk sailed away into the humid air, and ducks and geese dived at our approach. Old Katahdin showed but a meagre view, for he was enveloped in clouds, which curled about his hoary head, and rose up in endless shapes white and beautiful, and moving in the distance like an army of Ossian's shadowy ghosts, ancient, and silent warriors hastening to their vapory hells.[23] A rain cloud after giving us a morning salutation, swept down to the low country, trailing a rainbow behind it, festooning

---

his wife and several other women, had to navigate Knife Edge Trail, 1.1 miles in length, notorious for steep drop-offs of more than 2,000 feet on both sides.

[23] Ossian is the mythic narrator of an epic poem cycle set in the dark ages of Scotland narrating the exploits of Fingal, a Scottish warrior. Ossian's poems were purported to be "translated" by James Macpherson during the 1760s, though later discovered to have been created by Macpherson himself.

MEMOIR

lake and forest with rare loveliness, as if the beautiful Isis would lure us from this savage region.[24]

A PILGRIM

Correspondence of the *Advertiser*[25]
Bangor, Sept. 1849.
Avalanche Brook – The Indian Camp – A night upon Katahdin – Rain – Intense Cold – Difficulty of procuring a Fire.

Our way led us aside from the Lake again through the forest. The ascent began to be more precipitous and rocky, and the whole route seemed little else than innumerable pathways for the deer and moose, traces of whom were as palpable as those of cattle about a farmhouse. The trees were gnawed by their teeth, and semi-circles in the bushes showed where they were in the habit of grouping together. The trees growing stinted, with wide horizontal branches impeding the way, and but for these paths, worn hard by wild animals, would have been utterly impassable. At length the roaring of waters that had been increasing on the ear, warned us of the proximity of Avalanche Brook. I dare not describe a creature so wildly beautiful as this mountain Undine.[26] Imagine a rocky chasm as if a seam had been opened into the side of the mountain, laying bare rocks of vast size, and crowded together in every conceivable way; now, two or three pressed into a narrow space, with the green boughs clasping above, and leaving a perpendicular descent of many

---

[24] Isis was one of the major goddesses in ancient Egyptian mythology, commonly known as the goddess of the moon and rebirth, who protected women and children. She became one of the most important goddesses in all of Egypt as she became crucial to many of their religious beliefs, one of which was her connection to rites of death.

[25] *Portland Daily Advertiser*, September 26, 1849.

[26] The name the Renaissance alchemist Paracelsus gave to the elemental spirit of water, "Undine," was also a fictional character from Fredrich de la Motte Fouqué's book of the same name (1811), which tells the story of a water spirit who marries a knight and attempts to gain a human soul. She is referenced in many other EOS works, including *The Salamander* (1848).

feet below; then spreading away with twenty of these chasms side by side, arched, sloping or precipitous, as if some playful giant were preparing the prettiest possible bed for a torrent; working in wild wantonness three miles together; carving, and dipping, and climbing up a steep so sharp that bodies will "stay put" and only so. Then imagine the riotous waters of the mountain to leap from their concealment, roaring and dashing, boiling and foaming their downward way—plunging over steeps, reveling in eddies, and laughing from rock to rock; and you have Avalanche Brook.

And now our way led, not by the side of this torrent, but directly up its bed. The trees were so thick and low upon each side, and the ground so irregular, and cumbered with fragments from the mountain, that ascent was impossible in any other way.[27] It was a merry sight to see us leaping from rock to rock, springing over these surging and roaring cataracts for three long miles; and truth to say, it grew to be no holiday task, for ancles will be ancles, in spite of resolution and careful "findings;" but when our spirits flagged, a look upward at the sportful Nymph above, or below where she disported amid the shadows and with frolicsome grace sang onward in a torrent of melody, so invigorated our hearts and sent new beauty into our souls, that we clapped our hands and sang, and called to the mountain echoes, as if we had become a part of this exulting jubilant Oh! one hour of life like this, is worth an eternity amid the dust and dullness of cities.

At length the brook diverged,[28] and we clambered the bank in search of a foothold for the night which was no easy matter to find, owing to the precipitous nature of the ground. In doing this, we came upon an old Indian camp, and a winter camp, judging from

---

[27] Hikers approaching the mountain from this direction agree on this strategy to this day.

[28] From a climber's vantage arriving from the east, Avalanche Brook splits into several tributaries that descend the mountain about a mile and a half hike from Pamola. Turning northwest, the group began to climb in earnest up the avalanche itself, which had destroyed the thick growth as far as it descended. In blazing his early trail, Keep chose this path precisely for the clearing the avalanche had provided.

MEMOIR

the height of the stumps which they had cut for wood. The trees here are birch, small and stinted, making a wretched material for fire, yet these were cut five and six feet from the ground, indicating a heavy mass of snow at the time they were felled. The occupants must have suffered terribly in wintering in a place like this, for we in August found the damp air set in motion by the strong winds of this region exceedingly cold and uncomfortable; and what motive could have induced a human being to brave it in December, it would be hard to divine. Sad, affecting images of sickness, peril and human suffering in their many shapes, suggested themselves to the mind, but the truth is garnered away in that great book wherein are recorded the destinies of those who are accounted worthy to suffer.

At length an area, a sort of shelf in the side of the mountain was selected for our night's encampment; a rude broken spot it was, within the roar of the cataract, and disjointed rocks and stinted trees; where we were more than once startled by the cry of Moose and the ominous voice of the owl. It was difficult to feed the fire, and the night was cold, so that the masculines must have had a most uncomfortable night of it. Morning at length dawned, cold and rainy; Mrs. M. and myself remained in camp while Mr. M. accompanied the guide in quest of adventure. No fruit was to be found excepting cranberries, so that we could not expect much in that line. However, wrapped well up we passed our time most agreeably—I, with the aforementioned dirk, and a loaded pistol by my side, which I wisely determined not to use unless some wild beast should give us more than a friendly stare. We amused ourselves in filling out cards of bark, dated Mount Katahdin, and writing letters upon birch bark to our friends five or six thousand feet below us, on the earth's surface, whatever might be their elevation in other respects. Then we wrote a letter to be left upon the top of the mountain and enclosed it with our cards in a bottle for the next visitors, desiring them to do the same, and thus establish a literature and Post Office upon Katahdin. In this letter we modestly asserted our right to the distinction of being the first women, who had ever set foot upon the mountain, and in a manner pledged that our memories shall not be unworthy of its lofty associations.

While buried in this way a tremendous cracking and crashing of branches below our tent caused me to lay my hand gently upon the pistol, and if ever eyes did good service ours were wide awake at this moment. But the sounds died away and I resumed my pen with a slight tremor of the nerves not favorable to elegance of chirography. Our companions had started a bear of large size further up, and he probably made a sweep to the bed of the stream to avoid our tent. The guide presented me a little paw of a rabbit which had probably served as a tidbit for the monster.

The weather having cleared up at noon we continued our escort a portion of the way through this stinted shrubbery which never disappeared and we climbed the bold side of the mountain with only here and there an old root scattered by the tempest, and small cranberries threading themselves like emeralds and rubies along the velvet mosses. We were obliged to climb a long distance up the dry bed of an avalanche, than which I can conceive of nothing more fatiguing, or more savage in aspect. The soil was so loose that our feet slipped backward in the sand, and the huge rocks seemed every moment ready to topple down and crush us beneath them. Indeed a misstep would have been perilous if not fatal, for often these rocks shook and swayed at the touch,[29] and a circuit must be made to avoid their fall. The ascent is so steep that the hands are in constant requisition, and how these loose mosses keep their position at all, looked a mystery till one saw how the whole was wedged and jammed together, and routed to some huge foundation of the "everlasting hills."

Right glad we were to reach to the top of the avalanche and climb by the surer sides of the mountain, although all vegetation except mosses had disappeared, and the cold winds swept by like a hurricane threatening to throw us from our hazardous position. Never was such a wind; so ferociously penetrating, and clipping one about with sudden whirls, as if some malicious mountain imp were

---

[29] Although the avalanche is more stable now, in 1849 the area may still have been classified as "scree," or unstable rock, still settling into position as it froze and thawed.

MEMOIR

bent upon casting us down headlong. Our guide declared that these winds "had blown the granite rocks to pieces," which we could readily conceive; and these rocks do wear a singular appearance, being often in heaps so shattered and worn, that their disintegration resembles a sort of "head cheese" badly formed, (we hope the reader appreciates the elegance of the comparison,) which a child could pick to pieces with his fingers.

It was now nearly sunset, and we had climbed thus late in the hope of seeing the sun rise and set from the summit. The masses of clouds which had more than once scattered pearls from their retiring skirts upon our heads, were disporting capriciously with old Katahdin, now veiling his bald head, and now leaving his rough honest face open to the lesser hills, and yet threatening to cover him for the night, with their many folds. We turned and looked backward to the country below. There was one grand moment of exultation, of wild sympathy with this savage inhospitable height—this eternal rock, vast and Promethean with its unpitying blasts, and enduring cold. Human feelings were merged in the magnificence of this overwhelming solitude, where the voice of man is a feeble reed, shorn and echoless and only mountain calling to its brother disturbs the death-like repose.

> "Jura from his misty shroud
> Calls to the listening Alps, that cry to him aloud."[30]

---

[30] This quotation appears in EOS's later submission to *Baldwin's Monthly* 11 (July 1875), where she wrote,
"I thought of Byron's—
—'And Jura, from her misty shroud,
Calls to the listening Alps, that cry to her aloud.'"
The passage is from Lord Byron's *Child Harolde's Pilgrimage* XCII. In Oakes Smith's time, readers had already begun to associate Byron with other male poets with "too much sleeve," but her reference to *Child Harolde* seems especially significant in light of Byron's semiautobiographical hero's "pilgrimage" and the displeasure with past pursuits that inspires him. While Oakes Smith's signature "A Pilgrim" may signify the religious significance of her destination, as John Neff has recently suggested, her reference to Byron's work reminds us how the American

ELIZABETH OAKES SMITH

It was but a moment, and then I looked where the clouds were settling like an immense banner down upon our heads, and how lovely looked the vale below; how yearningly the heart pleaded for its lowliness, its homely comfort. There we were at this cold elevation with not one ray of sun-light and the tempest gathering and sweeping about us, while below, beautiful lakes, green slopes, undulating forests, and far, far off a cultivated opening, were all bathed in the genial sunshine, sleeping in tranquil beauty, below the tempest, and the still biting frost. It was a sad, symbolic view, too obvious to be mistaken—it is thus greatness is achieved by patient toil upward, and such is its isolation.

The view from the summit of Katahdin is indeed sublime—and though we had but a momentary and imperfect gleam, it is one to live and grow upon the memory. Mountains spread in the distance, Moosehead Lake fifty miles to the west shows its rare beauty, and Chesuncook, with its hundred isles; the Twin Lakes, whose Indian cognomen I have forgotten, and Katahdin Lake ten miles in the distance, which looked as if one might toss a pebble into it. These lakes and rivers, including the east and west branches of the Penobscot, are beautiful indeed, but solitary images, with not a vestige of civilization, and the prevailing impression from Mt. Katahdin is one of immense and desolate grandeur. The unbroken sweep of forest lies low, and the irregularities so hidden in space, that the idea of trees is lost and looks like a smooth lawn with varied and striking shades of greenness.

We were witness to one beautiful atmospheric to be a gigantic rock, with perpendicular sides adown which streamed trailings of the wild vine, and from the top arose a crown of lofty trees. Gradually the light changed and we found this to be a gem-like lake, the waters of which had looked like a white granite surface, and its fringe of trees had made the vines. These little lakes are often exceedingly beautiful. Sometimes we passed them in the shape of pools not more than eighteen feet across, perfectly limpid and

---

Pilgrims were also departing *from* an environment of persecution and alienation to a place of freedom.

MEMOIR

embowered in trees, the most lovely and tempting basins for a bath imaginable.

The clouds that had been hovering over us gradually shut us in as it were, descending like a marked line, and the sheet of light in the country below narrowed imperceptibly like the girdle of the White Lady of Avenal, till it wasted away, and we were left, not to a dim twilight, but almost total blackness. I could hardly have conceived a change so sudden and entire—the wind continued to increase, and the rain fell fitfully, now it was a dense mist so penetrating that nothing could resist it, and now it poured in great drops, yet unheard for the wind howled through the fissures of the rocks and the moss was nearly a foot in height, ready to muffle any sound even if the winds should chance to be silent. And now with much difficulty the tent was held to the ground by huge stones, leaving us room only to breathe, for not a stick could be found in the vicinity, and we were in danger of being swept off by the wind. After hours of severe toil and difficulty our companions were able to collect from the sides of the mountain below, a few withered roots of trees in the hopes of building us a fire, a need which we should have escaped in ordinary weather, so well we were provided with blankets for the occasion, but now the intense cold and heavy rain promised to be more than we could endure. I said internally, "it is one of those ugly Friday nights, which never bode good to anybody." Friday is and ought to be banned by every good Christian, and I made a new vow to regard it as such in all times to come, and never hope good therefrom. Cowards have been known to shake when not able to run from the battle-field—orators shake in their shoes, and poets behind their maiden blushes—Caesar shook with the ague, Byron from swimming the Hellespont,—Belshazzar's knees smote together—but these and all imaginable shakings cannot compare with ours upon Katahdin.[31] I had been recently ill from a fever and my teeth loosened thereby, were hardly firm in my head. Surely said I, not a tooth will be left, and yet they kept such a chattering as indicated a

---

[31] In a series of ironic comments, Oakes Smith finds overblown literary, historical, and biblical references to dramatize her shivering in the cold and rain.

tolerable hold. We tried to be cheerful but our looks must have been ghostly enough. The blood retired from our heads and feet and cramps began to assail us. These were terrible, and for awhile I solemnly thought I should never survive till morning; a stiff faint feeling made me dull and the sounds that syllable men's names, crept along the mountain, then my mind grew into fearful activity, and lent a new vigor to my blood. I remember some one has said, "as a man dies, so the world thinks of him," a death upon Katahdin! The everlasting hills for a Mausoleum! But what was the motive that impelled to this height? The good of science? The journeying of a great mission to carry light and truth and love to benighted human minds? Alas! Alas! Will a single heart be lifted to aspiration by the toil I have encountered? shall I breathe into these records a single thought of a nobleness and beauty that shall become a watchword or incitement to another? God knows,—and with him let it rest. I was not to perish upon Katahdin, a destiny like that is the award of singleness of aim, and abnegation of self, and my thoughts clung too tenaciously to life and its many hopes, and loves, and claims, to desert me now.

Oh what is life, when but one *hope* remains!
The sea-borne wretch in icy regions bound
Lights first the quivering flame with anxious pains,
Spreads wide his wasted hands to shield it round—
Gathers the stinted shrub to feed the spark—
Fans with his breath, and trembling stirs it o'er
And thus puts out with over care—the dark,
Cold vapor shuts him in, and he awakes no more. [32]

---

[32] Oakes Smith published a similar poem in *Graham's* 26 (1845):
"One lingering hope, one source of life to me remains–
The sea-borne wretch in icy regions bound,
With but one quivering flame, guards it with ceaseless pains:
Spreads wide his wasted hands to shield it round:

Gathers the stinted shrub to feed the precious spark;
Fans with his breath, and trembling stirs it o'er—

MEMOIR

It was thus I felt as we watched Mr. M. and the guide in their efforts to light a fire. The matches had become damp by the mountain mist, and although they had resorted to the Yankee expedient of whittling some splinters from the old roots, which they had collected, yet the pouring rain and gusty winds afforded but a poor prospect. Added to this the hands of the men shook like an ague, (no shame to their manhood,) from the cold, and though I have since laughed at the unsuccessful efforts of the two, in bringing their hands to a juxtaposition, at the time I never was conscious of a more intense and terrible anxiety, as match after match flickered and expired. At length I bethought me of some writing paper and slips of thin birch bark, which I had in my pocket, and with these after many efforts a flame was kindled. The wind whirled the smoke and sparks into our faces, but we were too grateful for the warmth to murmur. With the first beam of light, we deposited the bottle containing our letter in a cleft of a rock,[33] and hastened our departure in a torrent

---

And thus puts out the flame with over care: the dark
Cole vapor shuts him in, and he awakes no more."

[33] Marcus R. Keep, who found the bottle on his own excursion to the summits some days later, included Oakes Smith's and Mosman's letter in his article "Katahdin—Again" in the *Bangor Democrat* of October 23, 1849, which read as follows:

Top of Mt. Katahdin
Aug. 11*th*, 1849.

O thou, whosoever thou art that shall next penetrate to this grand and solitary region, we give thee kindly greeting in the name of the Good Father, our Maker and Preserver, for surely Katahdin is worthy to be the footstool of the Eternal, and here should the heart be lifted up: and as touching this our mission we desire to say a few words with that modesty that beseemeth our sex.

Whereas, some achieve greatness and some have greatness thrust upon them, and it is the privilege of man to carve out his own career, whether in the council hall, the battle field, or the varied walks of literature and art; while women are doomed for the most part to regard these as Pisgah heights overlooking to her an interdicted land; what wonder, then, that having achieved even an ordinary greatness she should be tenacious of its honors; what wonder if by the exercise of courage and endurance beyond her sex she has been able to reach a point never before attained by any of her kind, she should desire to secure the glory thereof, to magnify her office as it were.

ELIZABETH OAKES SMITH

of wind and rain. The descent of the mountain, though nothing as laborious as the ascent, is still not without its perils owing to the loose nature of the soil, rocks and sand giving way and following the retreating foot.[34]

We remained in our camp till noon, too much exhausted to move. The rain poured incessantly, and the roar of the Avalanche

---

Know then that we the undersigned did, on the day above specified, reach to the highest point of Mount Katahdin; the *first* women who were ever here; the first and only women who have achieved the perilous and toilsome ascent. And lest it should be thought we arrogate too much to ourselves, we must acknowledge our indebtedness to the manly aid of David Mosman, Esq., and the most efficient and careful pioneering of our guide, Mr. James H. Haines, who certainly bore unwonted hardship in providing for our comfort as the unconscionable packs of each fully testified, and the aching shoulders therefrom we fear may bear painful witness. So much to the chance pilgrim. And now a word in particular. On our way hither it was more than once told us of a rash and boastful vow made by the Rev. Mr. Keep, that his wife should be the first woman that set foot upon Katahdin. Inconsiderate man, thou shouldest have called to mind the excellent Scripture from which we doubt not thou hast often edified thy hearers, which runneth in this wise: "Let not him that girdeth on his armor boast like him that layeth it aside." We doubt not the daintiness of the foot nor the pretty ambition of its owner, but ours (of which we say nothing) is there before it, and while we sympathise with her disappointment we beg her to reap consolation from the thought we hope to bear our honors meekly, and never in all time leave any memories unworthy the lofty and hallowed associations of Katahdin. And now God bless you, and farewell!

E. Oaks Smith, New York.

N. C. Mosman, Bangor

[34] In his account of his own party's climb the week after Oakes Smith's ("Mount Katahdin—Again" 1849), Marcus Keep describes his discovery of her letter in terms that question whether her party reached even the lowest peak: "Two of our party came down before us to the Horse-Back, 1000 feet below the first and lowest peak, for the purpose of picking cranberries. While thus engaged, before we reached [them], they found where a camping fire had been previously built, and evident signs that a tent had been spread for the night. Near by was a bottle containing the cards of Mrs. E. Oaks Smith and her party and also a letter" (21). Typescript owned by Maine Historical Society Library.

Given the storm described in Oakes Smith's account and the lack of even ground on Pamola, it is possible that the paragraph break after Oakes Smith's description of her brief view from the first summit indicates the party's rapid descent before finding ground to camp.

MEMOIR

Brook increased in volume. We were still far up the mountain in the midst of stinted birches, which afforded but little comparative warmth. The rain which had continued to pour down all night, had by this time so swollen Avalanche Brook, that we began to entertain fears that the other streams would be impassible. So at mid-day we again took up our uncomfortable march, abandoning all hope of being screened from the rain, we only sought by rapid movements to counteract its ill effect. Accordingly, we walked boldly down Avalanche Brook, now a deep rapid current, so strong as often to nearly lift our feet from beneath us. We leaped chasms and forded shallows and crawled down falls, for three long laborious miles, and then struck across the country for the west branch of Sandy Brook. Here we found a nice log camp, and our guide, who had preceded us, had prepared the canvas covering, and a good fire was glowing amid the trees. Never was anything more cheering, the rain had fallen without intermission, and we had traveled an unwonted distance, so that fresh garments and a bed in this wilderness, though comprised of boughs dried with much labor over the fire, were most welcome to us. It was now late Saturday night, and here we determined to pass the Sabbath and recover from fatigue.

A PILGRIM

Correspondence of the *Advertiser*[35]
Bangor, Sept. 1849

Katahdin Letters – Aboriginal superstition in regard to Katahdin – Idea of a Prometheus – Sabbath in the wilderness – Attachment to our wooden lodge – Return to Hunt's.

It was late Saturday night when we stopped and made our camp on the banks of Sandy Brook, now swollen and turbid from the rain which continued to fall without intermission. We were thoroughly wet, tired and most of us hungry, our provisions nearly exhausted

---

[35] *Portland Daily Advertiser*, October 8, 1849.

251

and no prospect of fair weather. Fortunately for myself, I was too much fatigued to eat, and needed nothing but the great restorative, sleep, which evaded me for many hours in consequence of a severe headache. I shrank from the uproar of the elements, faint and oppressed. Nature was too mighty for my womanly nerves, and I felt ashamed of a growing imbecility, and wondered after all if I really had the true spirit by which dangers and hardships are confronted as if they were not much. Sleep gradually stole over me before I came to any reconciliation with myself, leaving me to climb innumerable mountains and encounter myriads of woodland monsters, in sleepland.

At midnight I awoke refreshed and joyful. The party was asleep—our camp fire burning brightly and the dancing sparks upheaving into the midst of the rain drops. The wind swept in mighty gusts through the forest, wrestling with the huge branches, and dying away in shrieks and moans, till another and another, giant voiced, drowned the wailings of its compeer. Rocks forced from the bed of the stream above, came booming down the falls of the Brook, with a sound resembling the rambling of thunder, or the distant roar of artillery, laying the ear to the ground as we did on our bed of green branches, all these sounds were magnified, and yet entirely unlike those on the top of the mountain.

There we heard whisperings, gurglings, low rumbling sounds as if the place were alive with mysterious agents, who came and went talking to their fellows. It required no stretch of fancy to imagine the mountain full of beings who took council together—and I did not wonder that the poor Indian believed it to be the great resort of Evil Spirits—the home of Nachinito, whose power was counteracted only by the perpetual vigilance of the Master of Life.[36] Indeed the Aborigines tremble with dread even at the name of Katahdin, are unwilling to talk of the word or its signification, and the boldest among them are silent and awe-struck as they approach the vicinity. Their eyes dilate, they become rigid, taciturn, and apparently absorbed in secret incantations by which the evil spirits are to be

---

[36] See note 6 above.

MEMOIR

appeased. They have a tradition that two hostile tribes met by accident in one of the many lakes of Katahdin, and a battle in canoes ensued, which left scarcely a man to tell of the disasters of the fight. To this day they pass these lakes in total silence, for the dead are sleeping beneath, and the mountain is filled with the hovering ghosts of men, who were never gathered dust to dust—for the Indian, like the ancient Greek, believes in the need of burial to ensure the repose of the soul, and stories, beautiful as the devotion of Antigone, might be told of these children of the woods. Katahdin is indeed the place for these awful associations; a solitary peak such as one would conceive worthy to be the prison house of the mighty Titan; and the top fit for the chained Prometheus,[37] above whose untold agonies beat the unpitying elements, and roared, and screamed the moody vultures of the wilderness. Were I an Artist I would copy the rock as it is—fancy can lend it no aid—paint it hoary with the seers of ages, savage—lone,—landscape beneath dwindled to a smooth surface with a faint tinge of warm sunshine upon the lake, to contrast with the smoky vapors drives about the mountain, with the dim outline of a vulture amid the folds; and then bring the whole imagination to frame a fitting attitude for the daring yet benign creature of mystery, who shadows forth an inconceivable good,—an attitude that shall leave him, less subject to the vengeance of the Gods, than of a terrible fate; the chain made powerless by the sublime endurance of the sufferer. Prometheus would be a world-wide myth, and Katahdin be upon canvas what it is on the face of nature. Cole has left us a Prometheus, but his imagination, though beautiful and faithful to nature, was not sublime—his craig is

---

[37] Shifting from what she has heard of the Native American to its cognate in Western culture, Oakes Smith's competing word-painting stands to show how the romantic artist's rendering has fallen short of the view from experience in nature. In his article "'I commend you to Alleghany underbrush': the Subversive Place-made Self in Elizabeth C. Wright's Treatise on Nature, *Lichen Tufts*," Daniel Patterson notes how, similarly, Elizabeth Wright "satirically condemns her 'sentimental' and 'croaking neighbors' who 'professed to love poetry, and to appreciate the enthusiasm of the poet-lovers of Nature'" but who refused to experience the reality of the natural world first hand" (35).

unworthy of the subject and his chained giant looks like a contorted pigmy.[38]

At early dawn our guide left us, while he returned to Wisatti-cook river for provisions which we had left there for our homeward journey. It still rained though less violently, and partly caused by fatigue, and partly the absence of food we were dull and inclined to sleep. Towards noon the rain cleared up, the blue sky showed itself through the trees, and clouds white and floating hurried in crowded battalions to the stormy top of Katahdin, from where we could hear the distant peaks of the thunder storm. It was indeed a lovely Sabbath day quiet, which now settled around us. No church-going bell urged the summons to prayer; no cathedral hymn pealed through the fretted miles of a house made with hands; but that heart must have been dull indeed not to feel the holier and higher promptings that steal into it amid the solitudes of the desert and incite to worship. It was in scenes like these, that the earlier devotees for the truth went up their trembling aspirations, seeking the purer worship in God's own temple; living in the wilderness, scattered and exiled, rather than debase the soul with the grosser forms of their persecutors, and those who live nearest to the truth need least the friction of other minds to evoke their highest emotions.

It was just four in the afternoon when our guide returned with provisions and the addition of a string of partridges to add a zest to our woodland feast. To say we had grown hungry by this time would be a tame expression of our needs. It was more than twenty four hours since I had broken fast, and now, rested and exhilarated by the enthusiasm engendered by the wilderness and beauty of our scenery. I waited only for a dinner to make me as good as new. Of

---

[38] Thomas Cole was born in England but was considered an American artist and founder of the Hudson River School, whose works featured Romantic representations of nature. His *Prometheus Bound* was completed in 1847, more recently described in a review of an exhibition of his work as "a lumpy sunbather on holiday in the Alps checking his tan." Cole died the year before Oakes Smith's climb, in 1848. Oakes Smith likely saw the painting at the New York Gallery of Fine Arts in 1848, where the painting was exhibited after its failure to gain attention in a London competition.

MEMOIR

that dinner partaken with each relish it would be unbecoming to speak—if Apicius would have caviled at the mode, he could never have eaten with our delicious sauce of a good appetite.[39] After dinner we walked, bathed and dressed with a whimsical reference to the day—sang, recited and told tales of adventure till the clear beautiful light faded into the gentle tints of twilight.

In the morning we resumed our line of march. In leaving our pretty camp I felt an indescribable sadness. I could not bear to leave even a bit of bark astray. A strip of hemlock which hung dilapidated from the roof, I adjusted with care, and was most anxious that our lodge in the wilderness should be left in seemly wise. I felt even a homesick tenderness in turning away for I should see the spot no more in this world, and an unconscious attachment had endeared this place of resting to me. Others would come and go, and find shelter and repose there, but I never more. There was something in the place to touch the fancy. It was a sloping camp built of logs, pealed, so separated that reptiles would not harbor in it. Across the front ran what lumbermen whimsically call a "deacon's seat," and when the whole was covered with hemlock bark, and the interior spread with green boughs, it looked a gem of neatness and comfort. I found on our route back as we reached the various places where we had encamped on our way to the mountain, I hailed them with delight. They were endeared to me—pleasant associations clustered about them, and I left them with a feeling of more pain than I was willing to confess.

We reached Hunt's after "camping out" eight nights and having walked more than fifty miles—yet in good health and unabated spirits—indeed we made our last toilet in the Wisatticook with great care and crowned our heads with green chaplets, so that when our bateau grated upon the sand we were hailed by the Hunt family with delighted surprise at our spirited appearance. Here an excellent table tempted our wild wood appetites, and tidy beds invited to repose;

---

[39] Marcus Gavius Apicius, a notorious gourmand who lived during the reign of Emperor Tiberius, was a lover of luxury and only the best of foods. Sources have traced his reputation to the first Roman cookbook, *Apicius.*

but, we could scarcely sleep with doors and windows wide open. I thought I should suffocate—and would have made any sacrifice to be restored to our open camp and hemlock boughs

A PILGRIM.

For Further Reading:

Abbs, Annabel. *Windswept: Walking in the footsteps of remarkable women*. London: Two Roads, 2021.

Geller, William W., "The Mount Katahdin Peaks: the First 12 Women Climbers, 1849–1855" (2016). Maine History Documents. 118. https://digitalcommons.library.umaine.edu/maine-history/118

Keep, Marcus. "Katahdin Again." *Bangor Democrat*. October 1849. Typescript copy owned by Maine Historical Society, Portland, ME.

Neff, John W.. *Katahdin: An Historic Journey - Legends, Exploration, and Preservation of Maine's Highest Peak*. Appalachian Mountain Club Books, 2006.

Patterson, Daniel. "'I commend you to Allegany underbrush': The Subversive Place-made Self in Elizabeth C. Wright's Treatise on Nature, *Lichen Tufts*." *Legacy* 17/1 (2000): 31–47.

Thoreau, Henry David. *The Maine Woods: A Fully Annotated Edition*. Edited by Jeffrey S. Cramer. New Haven: Yale University Press, 2009.

Van Dette, Emily E. "Profile: Elizabeth C. Wright." *Legacy* (forthcoming, 2022).

Wright, Elizabeth C. *Lichen Tufts: From the Alleghanies*. Edited and introduced by Emily Van Dette. Albany: State University of New York Press, 2022.

BIBLIOGRAPHY

Abbs, Annabel. *Windswept: Walking in the footsteps of remarkable women*. London: Two Roads, 2021.

Barry, William D. "John Neal: The Man Who Knew Everything Else." *Portland Monthly Magazine* (July/August 1994): 9–17.

Beam, Dorri. "Fuller, Feminism, Pantheism." In *Margaret Fuller and Her Circles*. Edited by Brigitte Bailey, Katheryn P. Viens, and Conrad Edick Wright. Durham: University of New Hampshire Press, 2013: 52–76.

Carey Jr., David. "Comunidad Escondida: Latin American Influences in Nineteenth- and Twentieth-Century Portland." In *Creating Portland: History and Place in Northern New England*. Edited by Joseph A. Conforti. Hanover, NH: University Press of New England, 2005: 92–94.

Charlotte Perkins Gilman's "The Yellow Wall-paper" and the History of Its Publication and Reception: A Critical Edition and Documentary Casebook. Edited and compiled by Julie Bates Dock. University Park, PA: Penn State University Press, 1998.

Charvat, William. *The Profession of Authorship in America, 1800–1870*. Edited by Matthew Bruccoli. Columbus: Ohio State University Press, 1968.

Colesworthy, D. C. *School Is Out*. Boston: Barry and Colesworthy, 1876.

Creating Portland: History and Place in Northern New England. Edited by Joseph A. Conforti. Hanover, NH: University Press of New England, 2005: 90–100.

Geller, William W. "The Mount Katahdin Peaks: the First 12 Women Climbers, 1849–1855" (2016). Maine History Documents. 118. https://digitalcommons.library.umaine.edu/maine-history/118.

Ginsberg, Leslie. "Minority/Majority: Childhood Studies and Antebellum American Literature." *The Children's Table: Childhood Studies and the Humanities*. Athens: University of Georgia Press, 2013: 105–23.

Gosse, Van. *The First Reconstruction: Black Politics in America from the Revolution to the Civil War*. Chapel Hill: University of North Carolina Press, 2021: 200–217.

Jaroff, Rebecca. "'To Understand the Hidden Things': Uncovering the Gothic, Recovering the Aesthetic, in Elizabeth Oakes Smith's 'The Sinless Child.'" Unpublished paper delivered at the American Literature Association conference, San Francisco, CA (May 2018).

Kanes, Candace. "Slavery's Defenders and Foes." Maine History Online. Maine Historical Society. https://www.maine-memory.net/sitebuilder/site/777/page/1186/display?use_mmn=1.

———. "Uncomfortable History." Maine History Online. Maine Historical Society. https://www.maine-memory.net/sitebuilder/site/1418/page/2082/display.

Kete, Mary Louise. "Gender Valences of Transcendentalism: The Pursuit of Idealism in Elizabeth Oakes-Smith's 'The Sinless Child.'" In *Separate Spheres No More*. Edited by Monika Elbert. Tuscaloosa: University of Alabama Press, 2000.

Kirkland, Leigh. "A Human Life: Being the Autobiography of Elizabeth Oakes Smith—A Critical Edition and Introduction." PhD dissertation, Georgia State University, 1994.

Larson, Kerry. "The Passion for Poetry in Lydia Sigourney and Elizabeth Oakes Smith." *A History of Nineteenth-Century American Women's Poetry*. Edited by Jennifer Putzl and Alexandria Socarides. New York: Cambridge University Press, 2017: 53–67.

The Letters of Edgar Allan Poe, 2 vols. Edited by John Ward Ostrom. New York: Gordian Press, 1966.

Neff, John W. *Katahdin: An Historic Journey—Legends, Exploration, and Preservation of Maine's Highest Peak*. Appalachian Mountain Club Books, 2006.

Oakes Smith, Elizabeth. *The Bald Eagle, or The Last of the Ramapaughs: A Romance of Revolutionary Times*. New York: Beadle and Adams, 1867.

———. *Bertha and Lily, or The Parsonage of Beech Glen: A Romance*. New York: J. C. Derby; Boston, Phillips, Sampson & Co., 1854.

———. *Hints on Dress and Beauty*. New York: Fowler and Wells, 1852.

BIBLIOGRAPHY

———. "A Human Life: Being the Autobiography of Elizabeth Oakes Smith." Series 2: Writings, Elizabeth Oakes Smith Papers, Manuscripts and Archives Division, New York Public Library.

———. *The Mayflower* for MDCCC XLVII. Edited by Elizabeth Oakes Smith. Boston: Saxton and Kelt, 1847.

———. *The Mayflower* for MDCCC XLVIII. Edited by Elizabeth Oakes Smith. Boston: Saxton and Kelt, 1848.

———. *The Poetical Writings of Elizabeth Oakes Smith*. New York: J. S. Redfield, 1845.

———. *Riches Without Wings or, The Cleveland Family*. Boston: G. W. Light, 1838.

———. *The Salamander: A Legend for Christmas, found amongst the papers of the late Ernest Helfenstein, edited by E. Oakes Smith.* New York: G. P. Putnam, 1848.

———. *Shadowland, or, The Seer.* New York: Fowler and Wells, 1851.

———. *The Sinless Child and Other Poems*. Boston: W. D. Ticknor, 1843.

———. *Woman and Her Needs*. New York: Fowler and Wells, 1851.

Patterson, Cynthia Lee. "'Hermaphroditish Disturbers of the Peace:' Rufus Griswold, Elizabeth Oakes Smith, and Nineteenth-Century Discourses of Ambiguous Sex." *Women's Studies* (2016): 513–33.

———. "'Illustration of a Picture': Nineteenth-Century Writers and the Philadelphia Pictorials." *American Periodicals* 19/2 (2009): 136–64.

Patterson, Daniel. "'I commend you to Allegany underbrush': The Subversive Place-made Self in Elizabeth C. Wright's Treatise on Nature, Lichen Tufts." *Legacy* 17/1 (2000): 31–47.

Prins, Yopie. *Victorian Sappho*. Princeton, NJ: Princeton University Press, 1999.

Prins, Yopie and Virginia Jackson. "Lyrical Studies." *Victorian Literature and Culture* 27/2 (1999): 521–30.

Reed, Ashley. *Heaven's Interpreters: Women Writers and Religious Agency in Nineteenth-Century America*. Ithaca, NY: Cornell University Press, 2020.

Richards, Eliza. "Elizabeth Oakes Smith's Unspeakable Eloquence." In *Gender and the Poetics of Reception in Poe's Circle*. Cambridge University Press, 2004.

Ruby, Reuben. "To the Public." *The Eastern Argus* (15 September 1826).

Rucker, Walter C. *The River Flows On: Black Resistance, Culture, and Identity Formation in Early America*. Baton Rouge: Louisiana State University Press, 2006: 85–86.

Scherman, Timothy H. "Oakes Smith Returns to Maine: 'The Defeated Life.'" Gorman Lecture Series, Yarmouth History Center, North Yarmouth, ME, June 10, 2014. https://static1.squarespace.com/static/5422a3cee4b0ef23d87b531 0/t/5803fde5b8a79b9e80092198/1476656648235/Scherman+Re-turns+to+Maine+10-2016.pdf

Schiff, Karen L. "Objects of Speculation: Early Manuscripts on Women and Education by Judith Sargent (Stevens) Murray." *Legacy* 17/2 (2000): 213–28. http://www.jstor.org/sta-ble/25679339.

Schroeder, John H. "Major Jack Downing and American Expansion: Seba Smith's Political Satire, 1847–56." *The New England Quarterly* 50/2 (June 1977): 214–33.

Tomc, Sandra. "Cheap Poe and Other Bargains: Unpaid Work and Energy in Early Nineteenth-Century US Publishing." *ELH* 86/1 (Spring 2019): 189–222.

Tuchinsky, Adam. "'Woman and Her Needs': Elizabeth Oakes Smith and the Divorce Question." *Journal of Women's History* 28/1 (Spring 2016): 40.

Van Dette, Emily E. "Profile: Elizabeth C. Wright." *Legacy* (forthcoming, 2022).

Walker, Cheryl. *American Women Poets of the Nineteenth Century: An Anthology*. New Brunswick, NJ: Rutgers University Press, 1992.

———. *The Nightingale's Burden: Women Poets and American Culture before 1900*. Bloomington: Indiana University Press, 1982.

Watts, Emily Stipes. "1800–1850: Sigourney, Smith and Osgood." In *The Poetry of American Women from 1632 to 1945*. Austin: University of Texas Press, 1977: 83–120.

BIBLIOGRAPHY

Wayne, Tiffany. "A Woman's Life and Work: Self-Culture, Vocation, and the Female Intellectual." In *Woman Thinking*. Lanham, MD: Lexington Books, 2005: 79–106.

The Western Captive and Other Indian Stories by Elizabeth Oakes Smith. Edited by Caroline Woidat. Toronto: Broadview Press, 2015.

Wiltenberg, Joy. "Excerpts from the Diary of Elizabeth Oakes Smith." *Signs: Journal of Women in Culture and Society* 9/3 (1984): 534–48.

Wright, Elizabeth C. *Lichen Tufts: From the Alleghanies*. Edited and introduced by Emily Van Dette. Albany: State University of New York Press, 2022.

Wyman, Mary Alice. *Selections from the Autobiography of Elizabeth Oakes Smith*. Lewiston, ME: Lewiston Journal Company, 1924.

Wynn, Mary Alice. *Two American Pioneers: Seba Smith and Elizabeth Oakes Smith*. New York: Columbia University Press, 1927.

Zellinger, Elissa. "Elizabeth Oakes Smith's Lyrical Activism." In *Lyrical Strains: Liberalism and Women's Poetry in Nineteenth-Century America*. Chapel Hill: University of North Carolina Press, 2020: 62–97.

INDEX

Abbs, Annabel, 256
Abyssinian Society of Portland, 125
Apicius, Marcus Gavius, 255, 255n
Bangor *Democrat*, 249n
Bangor *Whig and Daily Courier*, 226
Barry, William, 126n, 134
Baym, Nina xx, 58
Beam, Dorri, 121, 153
Benjamin, Park xiv, xxxin
Blanchard, Hepzibah Drinkwater, 172
Blanchard, Sophia, 172
Bloomer, Amelia (costume) xxv
Bogart, Elizabeth, xxxviii, xxxviiin
Bouchard, Kelly, 125n
Brooks, Erastus 28, 28n
Brown, Kate, 223
Brown, Tom 189n
Bryant, William Cullen, xv
Byron, George Gordon (Lord), 245, 245n-246n
Carey, Matthew 13, 13n
Carey Jr., David, 126n
Charvat, William xxiiin
Child, Francis James, 138n
The Christian Annual, A Miscellany for 1846, 144n
Clay, Henry, 12n, 12-14
Cole, Thomas, 253, 254n
Colman, Samuel xxx, xxxn, 7,7n, 23
Colesworthy, D.C. xiiin
Conforti, John, 134

Cutter, Hepzibah (Prince), 172
Cutter, Richard Loring, 172
Davis, Charles (printer at Portland *Courier*), 5n, 10, 10n, 30n, 30-31, 34
Davis, Charles Augustus (NY editor), 10n, 12n, 21, 21n, 29n
Dock, Julia Bates xxxvi, xxxvin
Eastern Argus xxix, 126n, 125-127
Elliotsville (Maine), 41n
Emerson, Ralph Waldo, 57, 57n
Emerson's United States Magazine xxxviin
Everett, Edward, 20n, 20-21
Fern, Fanny (Sara Willis Payson Parton), 135-136, 136n
Fuller, Margaret xxi, 56-58, 58n, 155, 155n
Gawo, Rebecca, 59n
Geller, William W., 256
Giftbooks, 170n
Gilman, Charlotte Perkins xxxv-xxxvi, xxxvin, 170, 173
Gilman, Caroline, 15n
Gilman, Samuel 15, 15n-16n
Gilman, Tristram, 177, 177n
Ginsberg, Leslie, 57n
Godey, Louis A., xxx, 156
Godey's Lady's Book, xiv, xxx-xxxi, 156n
Goldsmith, Oliver, 7, 7n
Gorham, Benjamin, 13, 13n
Gosse, Van, 126n, 134
Graham, George, 135
Graham's Magazine xxxii-xxxiii, 135, 144n, 157n, 248n
Gray, Ira, 126, 129

ELIZABETH OAKES SMITH

Greeley, Horace, xv
Greenleaf, Simon 17, 17n
Greenleaf, P.H., 30, 30n
Griswold, Rufus, xiv, xxxi-xxxviii,
  xxxin-xxxiiin, 54-55, 55n,
  135, 136n, 206, 207n
Haines, James, xv, 221, 221n,
  225, 231-233, 249, 250n
Hale, Sarah Josepha, xxxvii
Halleck, Fitz-Greene, 179, 179n
Harris-Culver, Abigail, 127n,
  127-29
Hoffman, Charles Fenno, xxxi,
  xxxvin, xxxvi-xxxvii, 196,
  196n
Homestead, Melissa, xxiiin
Howells, William Dean xxxv-
  xxxvi, xxxvin
Hunt, William, 231n
Hunt's Farm, ix, 225, 231n, 256
Jackson, Andrew 13n, 35
Jackson, Charles Thomas, 40,
  40n, 42, 225
Jackson, Virginia, 122
Jaroff, Rebecca, 59, 59n
Johnston, David Claypoole, 6n,
  6-7, 11, 14, 19, 21, 25
Jonson, Caleb, 125
Jordan, William, 127n
Kanes, Candace, 134
Mt. Katahdin (Maine), ix,
  xxxviii-xxxix, 221-257
Keep, Marcus, 225-226, 228n,
  239n-240n, 249n, 250n, 256
Keese, John, 53, 53n, 55, 204n
Kete, Mary Louise, xxin, 56n,
  122
Mt. Kineo, 226-227
Kirkland, Caroline, 135, 135n
Kirkland, Leigh, 145-46, 146n,
  221n
Kirkland, William, 135n

Larrabee, Ann, 18, 18n, 41
Larson, Kerry, 122
Lossing, Benson, 135
Macpherson, James ("Ossian"),
  240n
Manuel, Christopher, 126, 129
May, Caroline, xxxvi
The Mayflower xiv, 170
McMurtrie, Dr. Henry, 30, 30n
Mellen, Grenville, 7, 7n, 18
Mellen, Frederick, 7
Mellen, Prentice, 7n
Mosman, Nancy, xv, 221, 225,
  228, 228n, 229, 240, 243,
  250n
Mosman, David, xv, 221, 225,
  228, 231, 240, 243, 249, 250n
de la Motte Fouqué, Fredrich,
  241n
Mount Desert (Maine), 42n-43n
Mowatt, Anna Cora, xv
Murray, Judith Sargent, 205,
  205n
*Neal's Saturday Gazette and Lady's
  Literary Museum*, xv, xxxvii
Neal, John, xxxv, 25, 25n, 36,
  53n, 55, 58n, 126
Neal, Rachael, xiii, 37
Neff, John, 224-225, 225n, 256
New England Galaxy, xxx
The New World xiv, xxv, xxxi
The Boston *Notion*, 54
Oaksmith, Alvin, xiii, xxix, 9n,
  12, 25, 31, 33, 37-38, 42-45,
  48
Oaksmith, Appleton, xiii, xxix, 9,
  9n, 37, 38, 41, 44, 125
Oaksmith, Benjamin xiii, xxix, 3
Oaksmith, Edward xiii, xxix, 35,
  38n, 38-40, 48
Oaksmith, Rolvin xiii, xxix, 3, 9n,
  20, 20n

INDEX

Oaksmith, Sidney xiii, xxix, 9, 9n, 38, 41, 44

Panic of 1837, xiv, xxviii, xxixn, 35, 40-47

Page, Thomas Nelson, 127

Patterson, Cynthia, 169, 206n-207n, 218

Patterson, Daniel, 253n, 256

Percy, Bishop Thomas, 138n

Pierpont, John, 15, 15n, 192, 192n

Pinkney, Edward Coote, 184, 184n

Portland Daily Advertiser, xxviii, 43, 127, 221n, 228, 234, 241, 241n, 252

Portland Daily Courier and Family Reader, xiii, xxviii, 5-34, 125, 127, 131n

Poe, Edgar Allan, xxi-xxii, xxin-xxiin, xxxi, xxxv, 54, 73, 136, 170, 204n

Prince, David Cushing, xiii

Prince, Hebzibah D. Cutter, 45n

Prins, Yopie, 122

Read, Thomas Buchanan, xxxvii

Reed, Ashley, 129n-130n, 134, 153

New Berne *Republic Courier*, 125n

Richards, Eliza, 58, 58n, 122

Roland, Marie-Jeanne (Madame), 208, 208n

The Rover, xiv, 144n

Ruby, Reuben, 125, 127, 129, 134

Rucker, Walter C., 134

Sargent, Epes, 188, 188n

Sawyer, Lemuel, xiii, 18, 18n

Scherman Timothy H., 203

Schiff, Karen L., 218

Schoolcraft, Jane Johnston (Bamewawagezhikaquay), xxxi

Siggs, John, 125

Sigourney, Lydia, xxxvii-xxxix, xxxviiin, xxxvixn, 204, 204n, 221, 222n, 222

SMITH, ELIZABETH OAKES (Prince)

as editor, 3, 10, 17, 20-21, 23, 25-31, 170, 204-205; "Ernest Helfenstein" (pseudonym), xv, 156, 206-207; on gender identification, (see "Beauty, Vanity and Mantels" 204-218); on Native American culture, xxxi, xxxin, 46, 224n, 224-25, 229, 243, 253; on spiritualism xxxiv, 129n-130n; resistance to gender expectations, 30, 30n, 42-43, 135, 221-223; Correspondence with Seba Smith, 1833, 3-34; Letters to Seba Smith at "No. 8" 1836-37, 35-49

Works by:

The Bald Eagle xv, xxxi, xxxviin; *Bertha and Lily*, 129n, 156, 206, 221n; "The Black Fortune-Teller" xxviii, xxxiv, 125-134; "Coming to Get Married," 154-169; *The Complete Poetical Writings of Elizabeth Oakes Smith* xiv, 59; "The Defeated Life" xxiv, xxvi, xxxv, 4, 170-203; *Destiny*, 130n; "The Destiny," 130n; "The Dignity of Labor" xxiiin-xxivn; "Dress: Its Social and Aesthetic Relations," xxv; "The Drowned Mariner" xxn;

265

Hints on Dress and Beauty,
130n, 238n; "Hints to Parents" xxix; "How to Tell a
Story," 135-143; "A Human
Life" ix, ixn, xxxvi-xxxvii,
xxxviin, 130n, 170-172, 221;
*The Intercepted Messenger of
Ramapo Pass,* xxxviin; "Jealousy," 205; "The Lover's Talisman, or The Spirit Bride,"
130n; *The Mayflower* (editor,
1846-1847), 144n, 175n, 204-205; "The Ministry of Childhood," 56n; "The New England Meeting House," 171n,
173; "The Old Meeting
House below the ledge" viii,
171, 175, 175n; *Old New
York; or, Democracy in 1689,*
xv; *The Remapo Pass: A Story
of the Revolution,* xv, xxxviin;
Riches Without Wings, xiv, xxx,
42n; *The Roman Tribute; or,
Attila the Hun,* xv; *The Sagamore of Saco,* xxxin; *The Salamander,* xv, 156, 241n; *Shadowland, or The Seer,* 144,
144n; "The Sinless Child,"
xiv, xxvi, 53-121, 204n; *The
Sinless Child and Other Poems*
xiv, 53n, 54n, 59; "Strength
from the Hills," 227; "Two
Chapters on Beauty, Vanity
and Marble Mantels," 204-218; *The True Child, The Moss
Cup, and The Dandelion,* xiv;
The Western Captive (*The New*
World) xiv, xxv, xxxi-xxxv,
xxxin, xxxiiin, 118n; *The
Western Captive* (Broadview
edition) xx, xxxin; "The
White Man's Party," 125n;

"The Witch of Endor" xxiv-xxv, 129, 144-153; *Woman
and Her Needs,* xxiiin, 130n,
173n

Smith, Abiel, 45
Smith, Leonard 14, 14n, 16, 18
Smith, Manly, 16, 16n, 25
Smith, Seba xiii, 5-34, 125,
125n-126n, 128; *The Life and
Writings of Major Jack Downing* xiii, 3, 5n, 5-34; *Dew
Drops of the Nineteenth Century,* (editor), 144n
Snowden's Ladies' Companion xiv,
xxxi
Southern Literary Messenger xiv,
54, 59
Spenser, Edmund, 186n
Springer, John S., 43, 43n
De Staël, Germaine, 208, 208n
Stephens, Ann, 7n
Stowe, Harriet Beecher, 56
Thatcher, Benjamin Bussey 6, 6n;
27
Thomson, Clement, 125
Thoreau, Henry David, 221n,
225, 256
Tomc, Sandra, xxiiin
Tompkins, Jane, 55
Tuchinsky, Adam, xxn, 169
Tuckerman, Henry xxxv, xxxvn,
53n, 54, 54n
Uncle Tom's Cabin, 55-56
Undine, 241, 241n
Van Dette, Emily, 256
Ware, Asher (Judge), 37, 40, 40n
Walker, Cheryl, xxn, 58n-59n,
122
Mt. Washington, 239, 239n
Watts, Emily Stipes, 122
Wayne, Tiffany xxin, 155n

INDEX

Wentworth, Job L., 125
White, Thomas, 54
Willis, Nathaniel Parker, 17
Wiltenburg, Joy, xxin
Wright, Elizabeth C., 224n,
    253n, 257
Wyman, Mary Alice, 5
Zellinger, Elissa, 58n, 73n, 122